D1262818

PANZERS IN WINTER

The Stackpole Military History Series

THE AMERICAN CIVIL WAR

Cavalry Raids of the Civil War
Ghost, Thunderbolt, and Wizard
Pickett's Charge
Witness to Gettysburg

WORLD WAR II

Armor Battles of the Waffen-SS, 1943–45
Army of the West
Australian Commandos
The B-24 in China
Backwater War
The Battle of Sicily
Beyond the Beachhead
The Brandenburger Commandos
The Brigade
Bringing the Thunder
Coast Watching in World War II
Colossal Cracks
D-Day to Berlin
Dive Bomber!
Eagles of the Third Reich
Exit Rommel
Fist from the Sky
Flying American Combat Aircraft of
*   World War II*
Forging the Thunderbolt
Fortress France
The German Defeat in the East, 1944–45
German Order of Battle, Vol. 1
German Order of Battle, Vol. 2
German Order of Battle, Vol. 3
Germany's Panzer Arm in World War II
GI Ingenuity
Grenadiers
Infantry Aces
Iron Arm
Iron Knights
Kampfgruppe Peiper at the Battle
*   of the Bulge*
Luftwaffe Aces
Massacre at Tobruk

Messerschmitts over Sicily
Michael Wittmann, Vol. 1
Michael Wittmann, Vol. 2
Mountain Warriors
The Nazi Rocketeers
On the Canal
Packs On!
Panzer Aces
Panzer Aces II
The Panzer Legions
Panzers in Winter
The Path to Blitzkrieg
Retreat to the Reich
Rommel's Desert War
The Savage Sky
A Soldier in the Cockpit
Soviet Blitzkrieg
Stalin's Keys to Victory
Surviving Bataan and Beyond
T-34 in Action
Tigers in the Mud
The 12th SS, Vol. 1
The 12th SS, Vol. 2
The War against Rommel's Supply Lines

THE COLD WAR / VIETNAM

Flying American Combat Aircraft:
*   The Cold War*
Here There Are Tigers
Land with No Sun
Street without Joy

WARS OF THE MIDDLE EAST

Never-Ending Conflict

GENERAL MILITARY HISTORY

Carriers in Combat
Desert Battles

PANZERS IN WINTER

Hitler's Army and the Battle of the Bulge

Samuel W. Mitcham, Jr.

STACKPOLE
BOOKS

Published in paperback in 2008 by
STACKPOLE BOOKS
5067 Ritter Road
Mechanicsburg, PA 17055
www.stackpolebooks.com

PANZERS IN WINTER: HITLER'S ARMY AND THE BATTLE OF THE BULGE,
by Samuel W. Mitcham, Jr., was originally published in hard cover by Praeger, an
imprint of Greenwood Publishing Group, Inc., Westport, CT. Copyright © 2006 by
Samuel W. Mitcham, Jr. Paperback edition by arrangement with Greenwood Publishing Group, Inc. All rights reserved.

Cover design by Tracy Patterson

Printed in the United States of America

10 9 8 7 6 5 4 3 2 1

ISBN 0-8117-3456-0 (Stackpole paperback)
ISBN 978-0-8117-3456-1 (Stackpole paperback)

The Library of Congress has cataloged the hardcover edition as follows:

Mitcham, Samuel W.
    Panzers in winter : Hitler's army and the Battle of the Bulge / Samuel W.
    Mitcham, Jr.
        p. cm.
    Includes bibliographical references and index.
    ISBN 0-275-97115-5 (alk. paper)
    1. Ardennes, Battle of the, 1944–1945. 2. Germany. Heer—History—World War,
    1939–1945. I. Title
    D756.5.A7M57 2006
    940.54'219348—dc22   2006009795

Contents

Photo essay follows page 94.

Tables and Figures

Preface

The Battle of the Bulge was the "last hurrah" for the German Army on the Western Front. The purpose of this book is to describe this battle from the German point of view.

The greatest military disaster the United States suffered in the European Theater of Operations in World War II took place in the Ardennes Offensive, when most of the U.S. 106th Infantry Division was destroyed in the Schnee Eifel (Snow Mountains). This disastrous defeat was not inflicted by the vaulted panzer troops, the elite paratroopers, the hardened SS (*Schutzstaffel*) men or Skorzeny's commandos. It was administered by a mediocre and unheralded unit—the 18th Volksgrenadier Division. Most of its men had been industrial workers or in the Luftwaffe or navy the year before. This book covers the Battle of the Schnee Eifel from the German point of view in greater depth than any other book has ever done, using unpublished German after-action reports and manuscripts—especially those of Lieutenant Colonel Dietrich Moll, the chief of operations of the 18th Volksgrenadier. Elsewhere, the manuscript also refers to similar unpublished German manuscripts, as well as the unpublished papers of Theodor-Friedrich von Stauffenberg, to produce a unique account of the Battle of the Bulge, again, mostly from the German point of view.

This book is also organized differently than other books. The first two chapters set the stage for the offensive. Chapter III deals with the first day of the offensive. From then on, the battle is covered by sector, from north (Chapters IV and V) to center (VI and VII) to south (VIII and IX). The last two chapters cover the clearing of the bulge and the subsequent lives and careers of the major participants. I believe that this organization will help the general reader to understand the battle more clearly than if a strictly chronological approach was adopted. Experienced and highly knowledgeable World War II readers will find most of the "new" material in Chapter VI, although I hope they learn something new in each chapter.

I wish to thank my long-suffering wife Donna for her support in this effort. In addition to being the perfect wife and mother, she is also an outstanding proofreader. Special thanks also go to my editor, Heather Staines, who "hung in there" when the pressures of a new business forced me to miss deadlines. Heartfelt appreciation is also extended to Professor Melinda Matthews, the incredibly efficient head of the Interlibrary Loan Department at the University of Louisiana at Monroe, who managed to obtain unpublished manuscripts for me via interlibrary loan, and thus spared me the necessity of traveling thousands of miles to various archives, as I have done in the past.

I alone assume responsibility for any mistakes, errors, or omissions that may appear in this book. I hope you enjoy *Panzers in Winter*.

CHAPTER 1

Setting the Stage

The beginning of World War I in August 1914 began a cycle of violence in central Europe which lasted—with brief periods of interruption—until 1945. After four years of war, the Second *Reich* (empire) of Kaiser Wilhelm II ended with the collapse of Imperial Germany in November 1918. It was replaced by the Weimar Republic, which signed the Treaty of Versailles on June 28, 1919. It was a very harsh, punitive peace and bore little resemblance to U.S. President Woodrow Wilson's Fourteen Points, upon which the German people had been led to believe that the peace would be based.

The treaty was 70,000 words long (the average book is about 60,000 words long) and the German delegation was not permitted to take part in the negotiations. Among other things, the treaty ceded the territories of Alsace and Lorraine to France without a plebiscite, in spite of the fact that many of the people of these provinces were German. German territory west of the Rhine River, which was currently under Allied occupation (the Rhineland)—including the cities of Cologne, Koblenz, and Mainz—was to be occupied by Allied troops for at least 15 years. The right bank of the Rhine was to be permanently demilitarized for a distance of 30 miles and the Saar basin—a clearly German area that possessed some of the richest coal deposits in Europe—was to be administered by a League of Nations commission for 15 years, during which time the French would be in charge of the mines. The largely German districts of Moresnet, Eupen, and Malmedy were turned over to Belgium. Upper Silesia, Posen, and West Prussia were handed over to Poland, as was a corridor across East Prussia (the Polish Corridor), to give Warsaw access to the Baltic Sea. The Prussian port city of Danzig was placed under the administration of the League of Nations, in spite of the fact that its population was 95 percent German. The Prussian city of Memel was turned over to Lithuania. In all,

Germany lost one-eighth of its national territory, as well as all of its colonies.

Germany was also reduced to a state of military impotence. It was allowed an armed forces (the *Reichswehr*), which included the army (*Reichsheer*) and navy (*Reichsmarine*). The army was limited to 100,000 men, of which only 4,000 could be officers. The General Staff was abolished, as was the elite cadet school of Gross Lichterfeld. Germany was denied the four great innovations of World War I—tanks, airplanes, submarines, and poisonous gas.

The commercial clauses were as bad as the others. Germany's merchant fleet was reduced to one-tenth of its prewar size, German products were effectively barred from most foreign markets, and German shipyards would have to construct 200,000 tons of shipping per year and hand it over to the Allies, free of charge. Germany also had to agree to pay whatever reparations the Allies demanded, although this amount was yet to be determined. Germany was, in effect, required to sign a blank check.

The terms of the treaty were so bad that French Marshal Ferdinand Foch, who certainly had no love for the Germans, declared, "This is not a peace treaty. It is a 20 years' truce." Even President Wilson said that, if he were a German, he would not sign it. But Germany, which was on the verge of civil war, had no choice.

The Treaty of Versailles dealt the Weimar Republic a blow from which it never fully recovered. The German people had been led to believe that only a democracy could extract advantageous terms from the Allies. Now their last illusions were shattered and their faith in democracy was permanently undermined.

Meanwhile, Germany was in the throes of a civil war. Communist and other leftist organizations seized power in several German cities and established "Red Republics." They were put down by the *Freikorps*—right wing paramilitary forces led by former German officers with the clandestine support of the government. Many future Nazis were members of the Freikorps, but so were many future generals, including Baron Hasso von Manteuffel, who commanded the 5th Panzer Army in the Ardennes. "The war after the war," as the Germans called it, lasted until late 1923.

Because of the Treaty of Versailles and the French Army's seizure of the Ruhr (Germany's main industrial region) on a thin pretext, the Weimar Republic was unable to control Germany's inflation.

It traditionally takes four German marks to equal one U.S. dollar. By the end of World War I, it took 7.45 marks to buy a dollar. By the summer of 1919, the marks-to-dollar ratio stood at 15.5 to 1, when the mark began another free-fall. By July 1920, however, it was rather stable at 60 marks per U.S. dollar. Then the Weimar Republic announced a Policy of Fulfillment vis-á-vis the reparations clauses of the Treaty of Versailles. The mark began to fall again. By November 1921, the exchange rate stood at more than 200 marks per dollar, and by mid-July 1922, the purchasing power of the mark was less than 20 percent of what it had been 14 months before.

The depletion of the Reich's gold reserves, her unpaid war debt, her reparations burden, the flight of private capital from Germany to avoid attachment as reparations, and the government's deficit spending policies all contributed to the ultimate collapse of the mark, but the French seizure of the Ruhr coal mines and the assassination of Germany's highly respected foreign minister, Walter Rathenau, by right-wing reactionaries were the final blows. (The murder of Rathenau shook what little faith remained in international financial circles concerning the possibility of a viable future for Germany.) As a result, the mark per dollar ratio fell from 272 to 1 on June 24, 1922 (the day Rathenau died) to 4,500 to 1 by the end of October 1922.

When the French seized the Ruhr on January 11, 1923, Germany lost 73 percent of her coal and 83 percent of her iron and steel. Now, the currency collapsed altogether. By the end of July 1923, it took more than 1 million marks to buy a dollar. Then the bottom fell out of the mark. Inflation became so bad that the government only printed bills on one side to save time. Bank clerks used the back of them as scratch paper, because the bills were literally worth less than the paper upon which they were printed. People who were previously paid monthly were now paid twice a day. They rushed out to spend their money before 1 p.m., when the New York Stock Exchange issued its currency figures. People eating at that time literally saw the price of their meals double while they were eating them. The inflation became so bad that the same amount of money that would buy a full dinner one evening would barely buy a cup of coffee the next day. An egg that cost 25 pfennings (one-forth of a mark) in 1918 cost 80 billion (80,000,000,000) marks in 1923. Old people who had worked hard all of their lives saw their lifetime savings wiped out overnight. Fixed pensions became absolutely valueless. There were many joint suicides–grandmothers and grandfathers taking the only way out left to them, except starvation. Malnutrition was widespread, and the desperate daughters of respectable families turned to prostitution, just to feed themselves.

Before the inflation ended, one U.S. dollar was worth 4,210,500,000,000 marks (four trillion, 210 billion, 500 million marks) and the German currency was virtually worthless. German democracy took another blow from which it never fully recovered.

Among the people who sought to take advantage of this situation was a former corporal named Adolf Hitler. By 1923, he was the head of the National Socialist German Workers' Party (*Nationalsozialistische Deutsche Arbeitpartei*, called the NSDAP or Nazi Party). On November 8, 1923, he launched the Beer Hall Putsch in Munich. He captured the Bavarian government in a beer hall, but the putsch collapsed the next day, crushed by the army and the provincial police. Hitler himself went to prison for several months. When he was released, he vowed that he would take power by legal means—which is exactly what he did.

The brilliant head of the Reichsbank and national currency commissioner, Dr. Hjalmar Horace Greeley Schacht, ended the inflation by abandoning the old currency on November 15, 1923.[1] When Hitler left prison, the NSDAP was only a minor political force. It remained a minor party until 1929, when the Great Depression hit Germany. Unemployment reached 25 percent and many desperate middleclass Germans had to resort to soup lines, just to feed their families. The government of the Weimar Republic proved to be totally incapable of dealing with the situation. Near anarchy broke out in the German cities as street thugs from the Nazi, Communist, and other parties clashed in the streets. Economic conditions were so poor that the German people resembled a drowning man. A drowning man will take anybody's rope. Hitler offered them hope, so they took his rope, and the cycle of violence entered a new phase–the domestic terrorism phase, with the government the primary agent of terror.

After winning a number of legal elections, Hitler became chancellor of Germany on January 30, 1933. By the next year, all possible opposition to Nazism had been eliminated from German life—except the army. Even this source of potential overt opposition was eliminated in early February 1938, when the war minister, Field Marshal Werner von Blomberg, was forced to retire when it was discovered that his second wife was a former prostitute, and Hitler forced the commander-in-chief of the army, Colonel General Baron Werner von Fritsch, into retirement on trumped-up charges of homosexuality.[2] The Fuehrer then abolished the war ministry and established the High Command of the Armed Forces (*Oberkommando der Wehrmacht* or OKW), with his yes-man, Colonel General Wilhelm Keitel, as head.[3] Hitler also established the High Command of the Army (*Oberkommando des Heeres* or OKH) to direct army ground operations, with himself as supreme commander. Executive authority at OKH rested with the chief of the General Staff.

Inside the German Army, territorial responsibility for training, replacements, mobilization, base and maneuver area establishment and maintenance, and a host of other duties fell to the military districts or *Wehrkreise*. These districts (which had existed for decades before World War II) were placed under the control of the Replacement or Home Army in Berlin in August 1939, but they continued to be of the utmost importance throughout the war.

From 1933 to 1939, Hitler restored the German economy, built the autobahns, established the German Air Force (*Luftwaffe*), renounced the Treaty of Versailles (on March 16, 1935), began the persecution of the Jews, and rebuilt the military. He also reannexed the Rhineland and the Saar, seized

Austria by political means, took over the Sudetenland by diplomatic means, and annexed Czechoslovakia. Meanwhile, by the fall of 1939, the German Army had more than 2.5 million men under arms.

The Third Reich invaded Poland with 1.5 million men and hundreds of tanks on September 1, 1939. By October 6, it was all over. Contrary to Hitler's expectations, however, Great Britain and France declared war on Nazi Germany on September 3. World War II had begun.

The military technique Germany used was called *blitzkrieg* or "lightning warfare." It featured quick and powerful strikes, spearheaded by the vaunted *panzer* (tank) divisions, supported by motorized formations and the Luftwaffe with its dive bombers. Most of the German divisions, however, were and remained "marching" infantry, which featured horse-drawn artillery and wagons. They had very few motorized vehicles. Typically, the only fully motorized unit in a German infantry division was the ambulance company.

Hitler's conquests reached their peak in 1940, when he overran Denmark, Norway, the Netherlands, Belgium, Luxembourg, and France. Although checked in the Battle of Britain, he conquered Yugoslavia and Greece in 1941 and committed the Afrika Korps to help his Italian ally in Libya and later Egypt. On June 22, 1941, however, he made a fatal mistake when he invaded the Soviet Union.

The German *Wehrmacht* invaded Russia with 148 divisions (19 of them panzer and 15 motorized): 2.5 million men, 3,350 tanks, 7,184 guns, 2,770 airplanes, 600,000 motorized vehicles, and 625,000 horses. This represented about 75 percent of its total strength. Stalin's generals met the offensive with 170 divisions or about 3 million men at or near the frontier. The Red Army supported them with 24,000 tanks, 17,745 mostly inferior aircraft, and 67,335 guns or heavy mortars. German military intelligence had, as usual, failed miserably and had vastly underestimated the strength of the Soviet forces.

Operation "Barbarossa," as the invasion was codenamed, was the height of the blitzkrieg. Bialystok and Minsk were encircled by June 29. They yielded 324,000 prisoners, along with 3,332 tanks and 1,809 guns captured or destroyed. Army Group Center encircled Smolensk in July and, by the time the pocket was liquidated on August 5, an additional 310,000 prisoners had been captured, and 3,205 tanks and 3,120 guns were captured or destroyed. Another smaller Red Army was surrounded at Roslavl on August 8. This pocket yielded 38,000 prisoners, as well as 258 tanks and 359 guns destroyed or captured. On the southern flank, Gerd von Rundstedt's Army Group South took another 103,000 prisoners at Uman during the first week of August, and 317 tanks and 1,100 guns were captured or destroyed. The greatest battle of encirclement of all history took place when Kiev was surrounded on September 16. The pocket eventually yielded 667,000 prisoners, as well as 884 armored vehicles and

Figure 1.1
Battles on the Eastern Front, 1941

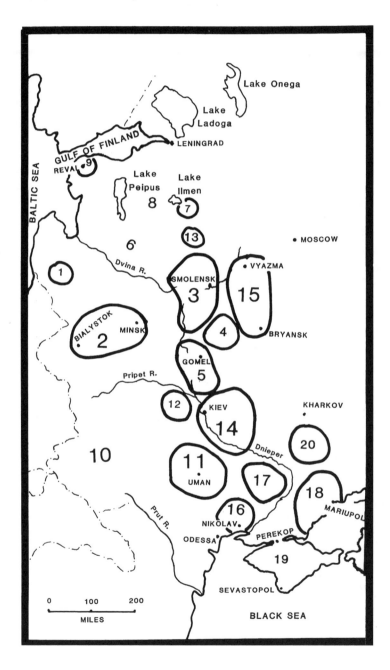

3,718 guns. Rundstedt's men then drove south, pinning two Soviet armies against the Sea of Azov. This trap netted more than 100,000 captives, as well as 212 tanks and 672 guns captured or destroyed. Army Group Center, meanwhile, fought the battle of the Vyazma-Bryansk Pocket (September 30 to October 17) It took 663,000 more prisoners, and destroyed or captured 1,242 tanks and 5,412 guns. Figure 1.1 shows the major battles on the Eastern Front in 1941. Although these victories were very impressive, they did not tell the whole story. Much more quickly than Hitler, Stalin put his entire nation on a total war footing. By July 1, 1941, he had already mobilized 5.3 million men. By December 1, despite extremely heavy losses, he had 279 divisions and 93 independent brigades. He managed to stop the Wehrmacht within 15 miles of Moscow.

Stalin launched a massive winter offensive on December 6, 1941. The mean temperature that month was minus 19.3 degrees Fahrenheit (minus 28.6 degrees Centigrade). Hitler's armies were thrown back an average of more than 100 miles in heavy fighting. Although he had taken millions of prisoners, Hitler's own armies suffered almost 1 million casualties, and

---

THE BATTLES OF ENCIRCLEMENT ON THE EASTERN FRONT, 1941

1. **Rossizny:** 200 tanks
2. **Bialystock-Minsk:** 290,000 captured, 3,332 tanks, 1,809 guns
3. **Smolensk:** 310,000 men, 3,205 tanks, 3,120 guns
4. **Roslavl:** 38,000 men, 250 tanks, 359 guns
5. **Gomel:** 84,000 men, 144 tanks, 848 guns
6. **Dvina:** 35,000 men, 355 tanks, 655 guns
7. **Staraya Russa:** 53,000 men, 320 tanks, 695 guns
8. **Luga:** 250,000 men, 1,170 tanks, 3,075 guns
9. **Reval:** 12,000 men, 91 tanks, 293 guns
10. **Galacia:** 150,000 men, 1,970 tanks, 2,190 guns
11. **Uman:** 103,000 men, 317 tanks, 1,100 guns
12. **Zhitomir:** 18,000 men, 142 tanks, 123 guns
13. **Valdai Hills:** 30,000 men, 400 guns
14. **Kiev:** 667,00 men, 884 tanks, 3,718 guns
15. **Vyazma-Bryansk:** 663,000 men, 1,242 tanks, 5,412 guns
16. **Nikolav:** 60,000 men, 84 tanks, 1,100 guns
17. **Dnieper Bend:** 84,000 men, 199 tanks, 465 guns
18. **Mariupol (Sea of Azov):** 106,000 men, 212 tanks, 672 guns
19. **Crimea:** 100,000 men, 160 tanks, 700 guns
20. **The Donetz:** 14,000 men, 45 tanks, 69 guns

NOTE: Soviet losses in men refers to those captured only; losses in tanks and guns refer to those captured or destroyed.

the German Army was never the same. The war in the east now assumed the characteristics of a war of attrition. Germany had a population of about 90 million people, including ethnic Germans (*Volksdeutsche*). The Soviet Union's population was about 200 million, and they were backed by the enormous industrial might of the United States, upon whom Hitler had foolishly declared war on December 9. After December 1941, Germany's chances of winning the war were very poor.

In 1941, the German Army in the east launched its invasion in all three sectors: those of Army Group North, Center, and South. In 1942, it could only attack on one sector and even then only after stripping the panzer divisions on the other sectors of many of their tanks. Even so, the southern offensive ended in disaster at Stalingrad, where Friedrich Paulus's 6th Army was surrounded on November 23, 1942, with 240,000 men. When its last remnants surrendered on February 2, 1943, only 90,000 of its soldiers were left alive.

Field Marshal Erich von Manstein assumed command of the southern sector after Paulus's army was encircled in Stalingrad.[4] He could not save the 6th Army; however, by a series of brilliant maneuvers and counterattacks, culminating in the Battle of Kharkov, he was able to stabilize the southern sector. At Kharkov alone, Manstein captured or destroyed 615 tanks, 354 guns, and a large quantity of other equipment.

After Kharkov, a lull descended on the Eastern Front. During this time, Hitler's generals on the southern sector mustered their strength for another offensive. In 1941, they advanced on all three sectors; in 1942, they advanced on one sector; in 1943, they attacked on only part of one sector. This advance resulted in the Battle of Kursk (July 5–17), the largest tank battle of all time, and it was a disaster for Germany, which lost hundreds of panzers. After that, all roads in the east led back to the Third Reich.

Meanwhile, under pressure from the Anglo-Saxon air forces and navies, the German supply lines to North Africa collapsed. This led to the loss of Army Group Afrika (the 5th Panzer and 1st Italian-German Panzer Armies) and another 230,000 Axis soldiers in May 1943. The German civilians called this disaster *Tunisgrad*.

The Axis surrender in North Africa was followed by the Allied invasion of Sicily, the fall of the Mussolini government in Rome, and the invasion of Italy in September 1943. By the spring of 1944, however, both the Italian and Eastern Fronts were more or less stabilized. Nazi Germany then faced its greatest challenge and its greatest remaining opportunity. Everyone knew that the Western Allies under the command of U.S. General Dwight D. Eisenhower were about to launch their invasion of western Europe. If the Germans—led by the OB West, Field Marshal Rundstedt—could repulse the invasion, the Anglo-Americans would not be able to try again for another year.[5] Panzer and motorized divisions could then be transferred to the Eastern Front, where they could be used to (hopefully) turn back Stalin's armies. Meanwhile, German scientists would be given another year or more to complete Hitler's "miracle weapons": V-1 and V-2 rockets, super submarines, jet airplanes, and possibly even an atomic bomb.

OB West (*Oberbefehlshaber West*) was the commander-in-chief of the West, or his headquarters. Rundstedt, however, was too old to command effectively and preferred to remain in his luxurious headquarters in Paris. He left the details of command to his two senior commanders, Field Marshal Erwin "the Desert Fox" Rommel (Army Group B) in the Low Countries and northern France and Colonel General Johannes Blaskowitz, the commander-in-chief of Army Group G in southern France.[6]

By now, Hitler had largely lost confidence in not only his army generals, but the army as well. Since 1941, he had been increasingly allowing his Reichsfuehrer-SS, Heinrich Himmler, to create *Waffen-SS* (armed SS) divisions. By 1944, they were consuming much of Germany's tank, truck, self-propelled artillery, and armored personnel carrier production. By 1945, 40 SS combat divisions had been created. Most of them had been formed since 1942. They would play a major role in almost every major battle on the Eastern and Western Fronts for the rest of the war.

The Allies landed in France on D-Day, June 6, 1944. Field Marshal Rommel was able to halt, but not to repulse, the Great Invasion. Now he had no choice but to hold the Allies in check in Normandy. If they broke out, Rommel said, then "there is little hope for us."

Break out they did. After extremely heavy fighting in the *bocage* (hedgerow) country of Normandy in June and July, the Allies launched Operation Cobra on July 25. That morning, more than 2,200 Allied heavy and medium bombers dropped more than 60,000 bombs on a 3.5- by 1.5-mile rectangle, which was defended by the battered and greatly understrength Panzer Lehr Division, which had already lost 11,000 of its original 16,000 men. The Allies dropped 12 bombs for every German in the rectangle. Panzer Lehr suffered 70 percent casualties and, when the Allies attacked the next day with two armored divisions and one motorized division, it was unable to hold. Army Group B had no significant reserves remaining and was unable to plug the gap in their lines. The Allies had their breakthrough.

Meanwhile, Hitler had sacked Field Marshal Rundstedt and replaced him with Field Marshal Guenther Hans von Kluge on July 2, 1944.[7] Rommel was seriously wounded by an Allied fighter-bomber on July 17, and Kluge assumed command of Army Group B as well. Three days later, Colonel Claus von Stauffenberg, the chief of staff of the Replacement Army, entered Fuehrer Headquarters at Rastenburg, East Prussia (now Ketrzyn, Poland) with a bomb in his briefcase. At 12:25 p.m., he primed the bomb for detonation, pushed it under Hitler's table a few minutes later, and left the room. At approximately 12:35 p.m., it exploded. Hitler was painfully wounded but not killed by the blast.[8]

Thinking Hitler was dead, the Replacement Army, the military governor of France, and certain generals and officers of the General Staff launched a military coup that afternoon. Most of the leaders of the coup were Christians, like Stauffenberg and General Ludwig Beck, the former chief of the General Staff, who was slated to replace Hitler as head of state.[9] They managed to seize control of Paris and part of Berlin before Hitler, Field Marshal Keitel, and their supporters were able to crush it. Stauffenberg and Beck were both executed about midnight.

That night, in a broadcast to the German people, Hitler promised to ruthlessly exterminate the conspirators of July 20. That was one promise he kept.

As Hitler soon found out from the Gestapo, Hans von Kluge, the OB West, knew about, and was sympathetic to, the anti-Hitler conspiracy. He sacked Kluge on August 16, replaced him with Field Marshal Walter Model, and ordered Kluge to report to Berlin. Knowing what that meant, Kluge committed suicide at Metz on August 19. Meanwhile, the 5th Panzer and 7th Armies of Army Group B were encircled in the Falaise Pocket on August 18. When the battle ended on August 22, about 10,000 of the 100,000 men trapped in the encirclement had been killed and another 40,000 to 50,000 were captured or missing. Fewer than 50,000 escaped, and most of these were service and supply troops. In material terms, Army Group B was wrecked. It lost 220 tanks, 160 assault guns or self-propelled artillery pieces, 700 towed artillery pieces, 130 anti-aircraft guns, 130 half-tracks, 5,000 motorized vehicles, 2,000 wagons, and some 10,000 horses. It had lost 1,300 tanks and assault guns since D-Day. The seven panzer and SS panzer divisions that were encircled and broke out of Falaise had escaped with only 62 tanks and 26 guns combined. The Panzer Lehr, 9th Panzer, and 10th SS Panzer Divisions did not have a single "runner" (operative tank).[10]

Although Hitler, Himmler, and others did not realize it, Normandy was also, to a large degree, the graveyard of the Waffen-SS as an elite fighting force. SS Oberfuehrer Kurt "Panzer" Meyer, the commander of the 12th SS Panzer Division "Hitler Jugend," had spent years in the Leibstandarte Adolf Hitler (Hitler's SS bodyguard unit, now the 1st SS Panzer Division). He visited his old outfit on August 20, and barely recognized it, so few of the "old hands" were left. When he heard who was missing or dead, he could not stop the tears from pouring down his cheeks. The Waffen-SS was never the same after Normandy and the retreat to the Reich. A partial list of the key SS men lost in Normandy is shown below:

- SS Captain Wilhelm Beck, commander of the 2nd Company, 1st SS Panzer Regiment, and winner of the Knight's Cross on the Eastern Front, killed near Caen on June 10;

- Reserve Captain Otto Toll, company commander in the 12th SS Panzer Engineer Battalion and winner of the Knight's Cross as a platoon leader in the Afrika Korps, an officer on loan from the army, killed on June 10;
- SS Major General Fritz Witt, holder of the Knight's Cross with Oak Leaves and commander of the 12th SS Panzer Division, killed on June 12;
- SS Master Sergeant Alfred Guenther, Knight's Cross holder from the Eastern Front and platoon leader in the 1st SS Assault Gun Battalion, killed in action in June;
- SS Sergeant Emil Duerr, gun commander in the 4th (Heavy) Company, 26th SS Panzer Grenadier Regiment of the Hitler Youth Division, killed in action at St. Mauvieu (near Caen) on June 27, and awarded the Knight's Cross posthumously;
- SS Major Georg Heinrich Karl Karck, commander of the II Battalion/2nd SS Panzer Grenadier Regiment of the 1st SS Panzer Division Leibstandarte Adolf Hitler, killed in action in July;
- SS Captain Karl Keck, commander of the 15th (Engineer) Company of the 21st SS Panzer Grenadier Regiment, 10th SS Panzer Division "Frundsberg," killed at Avenay, Normandy, and awarded the Knight's Cross posthumously;
- SS Lieutenant Colonel Christian Tychsen, the scarfaced commander of the 2nd SS Panzer Division "Das Reich" and holder of the Oak Leaves, killed in action, July 28;
- SS Master Sergeant Adolf Rued, a member of the staff of the 3rd SS Panzer Grenadier Regiment "Deutschland" of the 2nd SS Panzer Division, killed in action on August 2 and awarded the Knight's Cross posthumously;
- SS Private First Class Hermann Alber of the 20th SS Panzer Grenadier Regiment, 9th SS Panzer Division "Hohenstaufen," killed in the Battle of Hill 176, August 2, and awarded the Knight's Cross posthumously;
- SS Major Ludwig Kepplinger, commander of the 17th SS Panzer Battalion, 17th SS Panzer Grenadier Division, killed by Maquis seven miles southeast of Laval in August;
- SS Lieutenant Helmut Wendorff, platoon leader in the 13th (Heavy) Company of the 1st SS Panzer Regiment LAH, who had knocked out 30 Soviet tanks on the Eastern Front, killed in action southeast of Caen, August 6;
- SS Lieutenant Michael Wittmann of the 501st SS Heavy Panzer Battalion, considered by many to be the greatest tank ace of all time and a holder of the Knight's Cross with Oak Leaves and Swords, killed south of Caen, August 8, and posthumously promoted to SS captain;
- SS Captain Karl Bastian, commander of the II Battalion, 21st SS Panzer Regiment, 10th SS Panzer Division "Frundsberg," killed in the Argentan-Falaise zone, August 10, and posthumously awarded the Knight's Cross;

- SS Major Karl-Heinz Prinz, commander, II Battalion, 12th SS Panzer Regiment, killed in action, August 14;
- SS Sergeant Hans Reiter, member of the staff company of the 21st SS Panzer Grenadier Regiment, 10th SS Panzer Division, killed in action at St. Clair and posthumously awarded the Knight's Cross;
- SS Major Hans Becker, Knight of the Iron Cross and commander of I Battalion, 2nd SS Panzer Grenadier Regiment in the Leibstandarte Adolf Hitler, killed in action, August 20;
- SS Major General Theodor Wisch, commander of the 1st SS Panzer Division, seriously wounded in both legs, August 20;
- SS Reserve Technical Sergeant Josef Holte, platoon leader in the 9th SS Panzer Regiment, killed near Livarot, August 20, and posthumously awarded the Knight's Cross;
- SS Major Heinrich Heimann of the 1st SS Assault Gun Battalion, 1st SS Panzer Division Leibstandarte Adolf Hitler, killed in action west of Chambois, August 20;
- SS Lieutenant Josef Amberger, commander of the 8th Company, 1st SS Panzer Regiment, killed in action, August 21, and posthumously awarded the Knight's Cross;
- SS Colonel Max Wuensche, commander of the 12th SS Panzer Regiment and holder of the Knight's Cross with Oak Leaves, severely wounded in the Falaise Pocket and captured on August 24;
- SS Lieutenant Colonel Otto Meyer, commander of the 9th SS Panzer Regiment, 9th SS Panzer Division "Hohenstaufen," killed in action northeast of Amiens, August 28, and posthumously awarded the Oak Leaves to the Knight's Cross;
- SS Major Erich Olboeter, commander of the 26th Panzer Grenadier Regiment of the 12th SS Panzer Division "Hitler Youth," had both legs blown off on September 2, when his vehicle ran over a mine laid by a Belgian partisan, and died that night;
- SS Oberfuehrer Kurt "Panzer" Meyer, commander of the 12th SS Panzer Division, captured by Belgian partisans on the night of September 5/6, who handed him over to the Americans; and
- SS Lieutenant Colonel Hans Waldmueller, another Knight of the Iron Cross and commander of the I Battalion, 25th SS Panzer Grenadier Regiment, 12th SS Panzer Division "Hitler Youth," died of wounds on September 8.[11]

Since D-Day, the 5th Panzer and 7th Armies had lost at least 50,000 men who were killed and more than 200,000 who were captured.[12] With his main two armies smashed, several vital questions remained: could Field Marshal Model hold the Allies on the Seine and stabilize the Western Front? Could he stabilize the Western Front at all? And, if not, could he save the remnants of Army Group B and prevent the Allies from pushing into Germany, overrunning the Ruhr Industrial Area, and ending the war? Or was the Third Reich already doomed?

Otto Moritz Walter Model was born in Genthin, near Magdeburg, on January 24, 1891. His father Otto was a music teacher at a girls' school–and not a very prosperous one. Model grew up in relative poverty, but his Prussian family saw to it that he reached an excellent education at the liberal arts gymnasium in Erfurt. His climb to the top of the military ladder was based almost entirely upon ability; he owed very little to family connections. As a youngster, he developed many of the virtues of a typical Prussian: physical and mental toughness, a superior work ethic, great efficiency, and an attention to detail. His energy level was not typically Prussian: it was higher than anybody's, regardless of nationality. On the Eastern Front, it became legendary. He also developed the major Prussian vice: an unquestioning obedience to authority. There was also a dichotomy—indeed, a contradiction—in his personality. He was a religious man who served Adolf Hitler. Although this was a source of great inner conflict, he suppressed it and did his duty as he saw it. In the end, he served Hitler and Nazi Germany, not Christ. This would be his undoing.

Model was somewhat shorter than average in height but was also somewhat thickset. He sported a close-cut "whitewall" haircut and a monocle, which he wore constantly. He joined the Imperial Army as a *Fahnenjunker* (officer-cadet) on February 27, 1909. He attended the War School at Neisse, where the training was harsh. He had a difficult time adjusting to military life and considered dropping out of officer training. In the end, however, he stuck it out and was commissioned second lieutenant in the 52nd Infantry (6th Brandenburger) Regiment on August 22, 1910. He soon earned a reputation as a tremendously energetic and highly competent, though very uncomfortable, subordinate who had no friends and spoke his mind on all occasions. This reputation followed him throughout his career.

Model spent most of World War I on the Western Front. He served as a battalion adjutant in the 52nd Infantry (1913–December 1914) and later as adjutant of the regiment itself (December 24, 1914–April 11, 1916). He was seriously wounded in the shoulder near Sedan in May 1915 and was awarded the Iron Cross, 1st Class, for bravery. After he recovered, he also fought at Verdun (where he was wounded again) and was a company commander from April until the end of September 1916. He then served as a brigade adjutant (1916–17), before again commanding a company (May 18–June 5, 1917), and briefly served as a deputy battalion commander (June 1917). In the meantime, he was nominated for the abbreviated General Staff course at Sedan by Prince Oskar of Prussia. Model had no trouble with the three-month General Staff course and returned to the front at the end of 1917 as a General Staff officer and a newly promoted captain (effective December 18, 1917). He was given the first of several staff assignments, including one to the Greater General Staff in Berlin. He ended the war as a captain and a General Staff officer to a reserve division.[13]

During "the war after the war," Captain Model commanded security troops and helped put down Communist rebellions in the Ruhr. At one point in 1919, he was quartered in the Huyssen home in Wuppertal, in the Ruhr district, where he fell in love with Herta, the daughter of the house. They were married the following year. She gave him three children: daughters Hella and Christa (born in 1923 and 1929, respectively), and one son, Hans Georg (born March 1, 1927), who followed in his father's footsteps and became a General Staff officer and later a general in the West German Army.[14] Model, however, hated war stories and would not discuss war or politics at home. Interestingly, his children were baptized into the Lutheran church by his good friend, Pastor Martin Niemoeller, a former U-boat commander who later became a leader in the Christian resistance to Adolf Hitler.[15]

Although certainly not an aristocrat, young Model was selected for the Reichsheer in 1920 and was assigned to the 2nd Infantry Regiment at Allenstein, East Prussia. "During the inter-war years he gained notoriety for his ruthless performance of duty," Carlo D'Este wrote later. "Utterly lacking tact, Model rode roughshod over his subordinates and was outspoken in openly criticizing his superiors . . . he not only lacked the social sophistication of the Prussian aristocracy but was equally far removed from the peasant and working-class backgrounds of Hitler [and the Nazis] . . . Model's attempt to offset his crudeness by behaving like a *junker* was typical of his zeal to attain success."[16]

Model commanded the 9th Company, 8th Infantry Regiment for three years (1925–28), and then spent one year on the staff of the 3rd Infantry Division in Berlin (1928–29). He first made a name for himself in 1929 when, as a young officer, he wrote a monograph about Field Marshal August Neithardt Gneisenau (1760–1831). He progressed slowly in the Reichsheer (which is typical for a small army) but, on November 1, 1932, he was promoted to lieutenant colonel. Two months later, Hitler came to power.

After being assigned to the Defense Ministry in 1929, Model made a reputation for himself as an expert on the technical details of rearmament. He assumed command of the II Battalion/2nd Infantry Regiment (abbreviated II/2nd Infantry) in 1933 and of the regiment itself in 1934, when he was promoted to full colonel. The following year, he became the chief of the Technical and Doctrinal Department of the Army. In this post, which he held for more than three years (1935–38), he became an early advocate of motorized and armored warfare, despite his infantry background. He also became a fervent supporter of the Nazi Party. He impressed Dr. Joseph Goebbels, the minister of propaganda, who introduced him to

Hitler, who was also impressed. Model's army superiors also admired and respected him. He was earmarked to be chief of staff of an army during the invasion of Czechoslovakia in 1938, but the triumph of appeasement at Munich rendered that war unnecessary. Model, meanwhile, was promoted to major general in 1938.

During the invasion of Poland in 1939, he was chief of staff of the IV Corps. He became chief of staff of Ernst Busch's 16th Army on October 25, 1939, and served in this post during the French campaign of 1940.[17] He was promoted to lieutenant general on April 1, 1940, and on November 3, 1940, he was named commander of the 3rd Panzer Division. He led this division into Russia when Operation "Barbarossa" began on June 22, 1941.

From the moment he assumed command, General Model demonstrated single-mindedness of purpose, great physical courage, incredible energy, and an excellent grasp of tactical situations. Up at 5 A.M. every morning and always at or near the front, his troops loved him. He was, however, overly harsh on his officers, many of whom disliked or even detested him.

Model led the 3rd Panzer Division across the Bug, then the Berezina, and the Dnieper. He captured Bobruysk and took part in the battles of encirclement at Bialystok, Minsk, and Smolensk. He spearheaded Colonel General Heinz Guderian's 2nd Panzer Group at Kiev in September 1941. When he linked up with the 9th Panzer Division of Colonel General Ewald von Kleist's 1st Panzer Group, he completed the largest encirclement in the history of warfare. When the pocket was cleared, Germany took 667,000 prisoners. He was rewarded with an advancement to the command of the XXXXI Panzer Corps. A promotion to general of panzer troops quickly followed.

On January 12, 1942, not far from Moscow, the 9th Army on the northern wing of Army Group Center was facing encirclement and its commander, Colonel General Adolf Strauss, was on the verge of physical and mental collapse.[18] To everyone's surprise, Model was named his replacement.

"It was a strange thing," Paul Carell wrote, "but the moment Model assumed command of the Army the regiments seemed to gain strength. It was not only the crisp precision of the new C-in-C's orders—but he also turned up everywhere in person. . . . He would suddenly jump out of his command jeep outside a battalion headquarters, or appear on horseback through the deep snow in the foremost line, encouraging, commending, criticizing and occasionally even charging against the enemy penetrations at the head of a battalion, pistol in hand. The live-wire general was everywhere. And even where he was not his presence was felt."[19]

From the standpoint of morale, Model was to the German Army what George S. Patton became to the American army later on. When he took over, 9th Army was all but surrounded and seemed doomed. Its XXIII Corps was already completely surrounded southeast of Lake Volga, west of Rzhev. Model launched a counterattack on January 22, 1942, broke through, and rescued it. He then cut off and encircled the Soviet 39th Army, which had broken through to the south. Stalin hurled five armies against Model's forces. They came at him in fanatical human wave frontal assaults but with little tactical skill, and he beat each off in turn.

During this battle, Model had his first run-in with Hitler—and he won it. On January 20, Model flew to Fuehrer Headquarters and asked for a new corps to reinforce his struggling army. Hitler agreed but wanted to commit the fresh troops in the vicinity of Gzhatsk, northeast of Vyazma. Model wanted it committed near Rzhev, nearly 100 miles further north. After what Major General Friedrich Wilhelm von Mellenthin called an "acrimonious argument," Model silenced his supreme commander with a cold stare. "Who commands the 9th Army, my Fuehrer—you or I?" Without waiting for an answer, he frostily informed the startled and open-mouthed dictator that he knew the situation at the front far better than Hitler and his entourage, who had only maps. For once, Hitler gave way. A few days later, the Russians attacked exactly were Model said they would and were slaughtered by his fresh reinforcements.[20]

"Did you see that eye?" Hitler asked one of his cronies after his argument with Model. "I trust that man to do it. But I wouldn't want to serve under him."

Neither did many other people. He had a fierce temper and pushed his officers hard—to the point that some of them contemplated suicide. In Russia his Ia, Colonel Gunther Reichhelm, often had to follow behind Model and visit frontline commanders to smooth over disputes and calm upset feelings.

Meanwhile, fighting in waist-deep snow and in temperatures 30 degrees below zero Fahrenheit, Model destroyed the Soviet 39th Army. Of its 32,000 men, only 5,000 surrendered. The rest were killed in desperate fighting, which ended on February 24. Six Red Army divisions were wiped out, another four nearly so, and dozens of others were badly shot up. The Communist efforts to cut the Moscow Highway all failed. Stalin's winter offensive had met a decisive and completely unexpected defeat at Rzhev. Model had saved Army Group Center. For his amazing victory, Model was promoted to colonel general (his fourth promotion in three years) and Hitler personally decorated him with the Oak Leaves to his Knight's Cross.

Absolutely furious, Stalin determined to destroy 9th Army in the Rzhev salient, which was only 112 miles from Moscow and pointed at the Soviet capital like a dagger. He launched major offensives against it in March, April, and late July through mid-October 1942. Model defeated them all. During the process, he was severely wounded and received the Wounded Badge in Gold on May 25, 1942, for the fifth wound in his career. Then,

Figure 1.2
Operation "Buffalo"

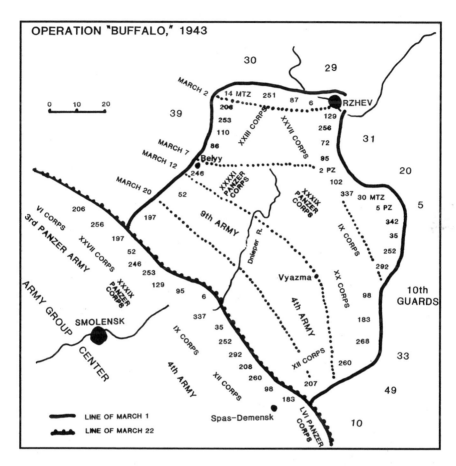

after the fall of Stalingrad, he pulled 21 divisions back 100 miles, reducing his front from 330 to 125 miles, and thus freed an entire army for Hitler's next offensive in the east (see Figure 1.2). The Soviets tired to disrupt this brilliant retrograde, only to meet a series of bloody defeats. German casualties were minimal.

Following the Rzhev withdrawal, 9th Army was transferred to the southern wing of Army Group Center. Here it was charged with directing the northern pincher of the German effort to cut off the Kursk salient at his base. Kursk (or Operation Citadelle) was largely Model's battle, and he must be given the lion's share of the responsibility for losing it. It was he who persuaded Hitler (in stages) to delay the start of the offensive from May 15, 1943, to July 5, so that he would receive major shipments of the new Ferdinand tanks and so he could ensure that absolutely everything was ready. The Ferdinands were major disappointments and the series of delays benefited the Soviets much more than they did the Germans. Model was stopped less than 12 miles from his starting line.

Hitler's faith in Model does not seem to have been shaken by his defeat at Kursk, for he later called Model "my best field marshal." He even allowed Model to conduct an elastic defense in the east. As he retreated, Model instituted a "scorched earth" policy, laying to waste anything he could. He was undeniably harsh in his dealings with Russian civilians. He also cooperated with the SS murder squads and their Jewish "resettlement" policies.

Model increased his reputation as a superb defensive fighter in the second half of 1943. This led to his elevation to army group command in early 1944. He soon earned the nickname "the Fuehrer's fireman" because he was only sent to the most critical sectors, and he was only given the most difficult and dangerous missions. He successively commanded Army Group North, Army Group South, Army Group North Ukraine, and Army Group Center in one desperate situation after another. After he launched a sharp counterattack near Warsaw, which finally checked Stalin's summer offensive of 1944, Hitler was openly referring to him as "the savior of the Eastern Front."[21] The Western Front, meanwhile, had also reached a point of near collapse. On August 16, 1944, the Fuehrer again called upon his fireman. He decorated Model (a field marshal since March 1) with the Knight's Cross with Oak Leaves, Swords, and Diamonds, and named him OB West—supreme commander of the Western Front.

Model turned up unannounced at Army Group B Headquarters on August 17, relieved Kluge of his command, and immediately ordered an evacuation of the Falaise Pocket—an order his predecessor had never been able to get out of Fuehrer Headquarters. He thus saved half of the 5th Panzer and 7th Armies, but he immediately faced three more crises: (1) The U.S. 6th Army Group (Lieutenant General Jacob L. Devers) had landed on the French Mediterranean coast on August 15, was rapidly destroying Kurt von der Chevallerie's 1st Army in the south of France, and was threatening to cut off Georg von Sodenstern's 19th Army in southwestern France;[22] (2) U.S. Lieutenant General Patton's 3rd Army was south of Paris and was sweeping eastward into the German rear area against minimal opposition; and (3) Model still had to get his battered forces behind the Seine, in spite of the rapid pursuit of the victorious British and American armies.

It should be noted here that the German Army went from being one of the most mobile armies in the world in 1939 to one of the least mobile in 1944. This was because Germany reached its maximum potential in terms of motorized warfare in 1940 and had done little to improve its position, other than adopt new tank and assault gun designs. The U.S. Army, on the other hand, had been ranked 16th among the world's armies on September 1, 1939—just behind Portugal. America had, however, awakened to the Nazi and Japanese threats and had taken the appropriate measures, including the institution of a draft. It had also harnessed its industrial potential for its war effort, motorizing not only its own army but (to a large extent) those of Great Britain and the Soviet Union as well. (For years after World War II, the word "Studabaker" was a synonym for "truck" in Russia.) Because of its lack of mobility in relation to the Anglo-Americans, many German "marching infantry" formations were simply swamped by the on-rushing Allies.

The fact that Paris was in revolt did not seem to bother Model at all, because he knew that he could not hold it anyway. When Hitler ordered him to defend it, Model tartly signaled back that 20,000 security troops could not keep a lid on a city of 3.5 million.[23] Hitler then maliciously ordered that the city commandant, General of Infantry Dietrich von Choltitz, destroy the city, but he did not. Instead, he surrendered it on August 25, 1944. Model then filed court-martial charges against the captured general.[24]

Meanwhile, Model got the remnants of Army Group B behind the Seine—but only barely. SS Colonel General Sepp Dietrich later remarked that, from the point of view of equipment lost, "the Seine crossing was almost as great a disaster as the Falaise Pocket."[25] According to General of Infantry Guenther Blumentritt, the chief of staff of OB West, only 100 to 120 of the 2,300 tanks and assault guns committed to the Battle of Normandy ever made it back to the east bank of the Seine. The panzer units were now down to a strength of less than 10 tanks per division. The Wehrmacht lost at least 15,000 other vehicles in this battle.[26]

The contradiction of Hitler's "strategy" in France was now clear to see. He had used his panzer divisions in Normandy (ideal terrain for infantry fighting), while the Desert Fox begged for infantry. Now that the Allies were in excellent tank country, Model had nothing with which to fight them except nonmotorized infantry, which was of little value here. The Ruhr was now definitely vulnerable and, if the Allies captured this, the major industrial region in Europe, then Germany's very ability to continue the war was questionable at best.

The odds were also heavily in the Allies' favor. By September 1, they had 2 million men ashore in 38 full-strength divisions, with more arriving every week. OB West had only 700,000 men in 41 depleted and battered divisions.

Everywhere German resistance was collapsing. The British were across the Seine in strength by August 26, while Patton crossed the Meuse on August 28. Marseilles and Toulon, the major ports in southern France, fell the same day. On August 30, Amiens was lost, and the Somme River line was breached before Model could man it. That same day, British forces that were rampaging in the German rear overran the headquarters of the 7th Army and captured its talented commander, General of Panzer Troops Hans Eberbach. Dietrich, who was conferring with Eberbach at the time, narrowly escaped capture by hopping in a car and racing out of town, literally outrunning his British pursuers. Nice was liberated on September 1 and Lyons fell the next day, as the American forces pushed up the Rhone River Valley against weak opposition. Brussels was taken by the British on September 3 and Royal tankers seized the vital port of Antwerp intact on September 4. That same day, Hitler came to the conclusion that Field Marshal Model could not effectively command OB West and Army Group B at the same time. He replaced him as commander-in-chief West with Rundstedt, whom he recalled from retirement for the third time. Model retained command of Army Group B.

Then, as if by a miracle, the Allied juggernaut came to an abrupt halt.

The enemy halt was no miracle. Eisenhower's armies had simply run out of gas. No one on the Allied side had expected German resistance to collapse as it had, so the Allies had not transported enough fuel from England to continue the momentum of their pursuit. The Allied air forces had also destroyed the French railroad system, including most of the locomotives and rolling stock. These air attacks had significantly contributed to the Anglo-American victory in Normandy in June and July, but they proved to be a double-edged sword, because the Allies now needed the rail network, but it was next to useless. The galloping Allied armies were now consuming 6 million gallons of fuel every day, as well as 20,000 tons of other supplies and 2,000 tons of artillery ammunition per day. Each Allied division needed 700 tons of supplies per day to sustain the offensive. It was clear at SHAEF (Supreme Headquarters, Allied Expeditionary Force) that the pursuit could not continue in all sectors at once.

June, July, and August 1944 had been a disastrous period for the Third Reich. It had lost 55,000 men killed and 340,000 missing in the west and 215,000 killed and 627,000 missing on the Eastern Front. Counting wounded (which generally amounted to three times the number killed), the total casualties amounted to slightly more than 2 million. OB West had also lost the use of 200,000 more men, cut off in Hitler's so-called fortresses on the Atlantic coast. The 2 million plus casualties suffered from June to September were roughly equal to the losses the Wehrmacht suffered from the start of the war to February 1943, including Stalingrad. A quarter of a million horses had also been lost. Some 29 divisions had been lost or rendered impotent (including those trapped in the coastal fortresses), and 3 divisions had been disbanded in the Balkans, 2 in Italy, and 10 in the east, making the total losses for the three-month period 44 divisions. In all, the Reich would lose 106 divisions in 1944—more than it had in 1939.[27]

Field Marshal Sir Bernard Law Montgomery, the commander of the British 21st Army Group, proposed an ambitious plan to continue the drive to the Ruhr. The three divisions of the 1st Allied Airborne Army—the U.S. 101st Airborne, the U.S. 82nd Airborne, and the British 1st Airborne—would land near Eindhoven, Nijmegen, and Arnhem, respectively. This would put the Allies across the Rhine. Simultaneously, the British XXX Corps, spearheaded by the Guards Armored Division, would break through the newly committed German 1st Parachute Army (under Luftwaffe Colonel General Kurt Student) and advance rapidly northward, linking up with each airborne division in turn. Meanwhile, the British 1st Airborne Division would seize the Rhine River bridge at Arnhem, while the British 52nd (Airportable) Division landed in the Arnhem sector to reinforce the bridgehead and help continue the drive. The entire operation depended on a speedy Allied drive to Arnhem and a relatively average German reaction time in terms of speed. Much to Patton's chagrin, Eisenhower approved the plan, which was dubbed Operation Market-Garden.

Although it had the advantages of boldness and surprise, Monty's plan had a number of flaws. Most important, British intelligence was faulty. It reported that there were only a few low-grade German battalions in the Arnhem-Nijmegen area. They missed the entire II SS Panzer Corps (9th and 10th SS Panzer Divisions), which was refitting northeast of Arnhem after its battering in the Falaise Pocket. British intelligence and the Dutch resistance also failed to report that Field Marshal Model had set up its tactical headquarters at Oosterbeck, a western suburb of Arnhem, which was less than a mile from the easternmost drop zone. Secondly, the Allied advance focused on a single road. If the Germans launched rapid counterattacks against this road and cut it, the Allied advance would stall. Finally, the 1st British Airborne was to drop six to eight miles from its objective, the Arnhem bridge.

Model was eating lunch when the first wave of paratroopers floated down from the sky, about a mile from his table. The energetic field marshal left Oosterbeck a great hurry, organized the defense of Arnhem, and ordered reinforcements forward, including General of SS Willi Bittrich's II SS Panzer Corps. The German reaction was thus much more rapid than could reasonably have been expected.

Model entrusted the defense of the Arnhem bridge to a member of his operations staff, Major Ernst Schleifenbaum. His emergency battle group consisted of World War I veterans and men from 28 different commands, mostly rear-area units hurriedly armed with captured rifles and 20 rounds of ammunition. They delayed the British for a while and managed to hold part of the city, but they could not prevent the British 2nd Parachute Battalion from seizing the northern end of the bridge. Schleifenbaum's men did, however, manage to hold the southern end and repulsed several British attempts to dislodge them that night. By evening, the II SS Panzer Corps had pushed to the edge of the British drop zones, which were already under mortar fire. By nightfall, the 9th SS Panzer Division had cut the British airborne division in two, isolating the 2nd Parachute Battalion on the Arnhem bridge.

The British paratroopers were tough, exceptionally brave, and superbly trained, but these characteristics could not fully compensate for their complete lack of heavy equipment. Model and Student knew that, even in its depleted condition, the II SS Panzer Corps would destroy the British forces if they were not reinforced. To prevent the Allied rescue, Model and Student threw every ad hoc formation they could against the British XXX Corps and the two American airborne divisions. Even marginal formations cut the road and forced the American paratroopers to march and countermarch to again open the road. This took a considerable amount of time, because all recently dropped airborne divisions lacked mobility. The advance of the XXX Corps was delayed again and again. By September 20, XXX Corps had 20,000 vehicles strung out for 30 miles along a single road. Logistical problems reached nightmarish proportions as the Allies were unable to bring up bridging columns, assault boats, and other vital equipment in a timely manner, nor were they able to promptly evacuate their wounded. Meanwhile, for the men of the 2nd Parachute Battalion, time ran out.

The British resistance north of the Arnhem bridge is the stuff legends are made of, for they turned back attack after attack from elite SS troops for days. On September 20, however, they ran out of antitank ammunition and had to surrender their wounded to the Germans, to prevent them from being burned to death. The 1st, 3rd, and 11th British Parachute and 2nd South Stafford Battalions tried to rescue the wounded but, in the open terrain, were cut to ribbons by the SS troops. The combined strength of these four battalions was reduced to 400 men before the survivors made their way back to the landing zones. (A normal, full strength battalion has about 700 men.) In a similar attempt, the 10th and 156th Parachute Battalions suffered even heavier casualties.[28]

Shortly after daybreak on September 21, the survivors of the 2nd Parachute Battalion were forced to surrender. Montgomery's ambitious plan had failed. The rest of the battle centered around the Allied effort to extricate the British 1st Airborne Division from their bridgehead. The fighting finally ended on September 27. Only 2,587 of the 10,000 paratroopers were successfully evacuated. (Another 240 made their way back to Allied lines over the next few days. Most of these had been hidden by the Dutch.)

Figure 1.3
Western Front, September 5–December 14, 1944

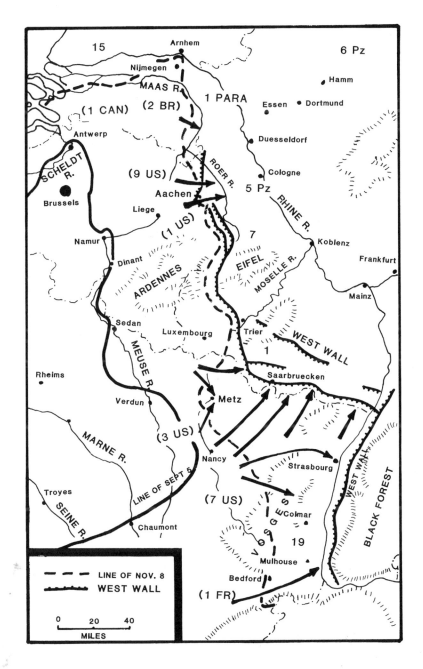

Certain popular writers (including screen writers) have downplayed or minimized Model's role in the German victory at Arnhem, presumably because he was a Nazi sympathizer. The British Official History, however, is more objective, and gives Model the lion's share of the credit for winning the battle. Because of his speedy reaction, this history points out, only 600 of the British paratroopers ever reached the bridge. Because of his immediate intervention in the battle, reinforcements converged on the British 1st Airborne much more quickly than the Allied planners thought possible. Likewise, the road to Arnhem was brought under attack much more quickly than Montgomery anticipated. Nazi sympathizer or not, Arnhem was primarily Field Marshal Model's victory.

At the Battle of Arnhem, the Allies lost their last chance for final victory in 1944 and gave Hitler the time he needed to prepare for a last, desperate counteroffensive. Meanwhile, the Allies continued to mount secondary offensives all along the front. Montgomery's army group, for example, cleared the Scheldt of German forces (making the port of Antwerp at last usable), while the U.S. 1st Army captured Aachen, fought a fruitless battle in the Huertgen Forest, and drove toward the Roer River dams. Patton—who in September was checked before the fortress city of Metz because of a lack of fuel—husbanded his resources and mounted another offensive against Army Group G in November. He overran most of Lorraine and captured Metz on November 22. Other, minor offensives tied down German forces and sapped German strength (see Figure 1.3). Had it not been for these attacks, more of Hitler's legions would have been available for the Ardennes Offensive—but that might not have been a bad thing for the Germans, as we shall see.

CHAPTER 2

Planning and Preparations

Since September, Hitler's divisions in the West had been absorbing heavy blows and generally holding their positions. Those that could not had at least succeeded in imposing significant delays on the Allies; meanwhile, the dictator himself was preparing a major counterstroke that, he hoped, would fundamentally change the course of the war and turn the tide that was now running so strongly against him.

THE PLAN

Hitler first came up with the idea of an offensive through the Ardennes during a conference at the Wolf's Lair on September 6. The first concrete step toward launching the attack was made on September 14, when Hitler ordered the creation of a new formation—Headquarters, 6th Panzer Army—to be formed under his former bodyguard, SS Colonel General Sepp Dietrich. It was duly organized in the VI Military District, mainly from elements of the former staff of the Military Governor of Belgium and Northern France; the rest of its members came from Wehrkreis XII and the Waffen-SS. The 6th Panzer Army was activated on September 24, and Dietrich assumed command two days later.[1] He was replaced as commander of the 5th Panzer Army by General of Panzer Troops Baron Hasso von Manteuffel. Hitler earmarked the 6th Panzer to direct the main blow in the upcoming offensive.

The most suitable area for the offensive, Hitler decided, was the sector that lay between Monschau (20 miles southeast of Aachen) and Echternach, a Luxembourger town on the Sure River, about 50 miles south of Monschau. This sector, occupied by the U.S. 1st Army, was held by only four infantry divisions and one armored division. Not only were the Americans thin on the ground, but the wooded areas of the Eifel (the German Ardennes) would provide ideal camouflage for the assembly of the German assault divisions. Once the breakthrough was made in this sector, according to Hitler, the drive would continue to the northwest, through the Ardennes, across the Meuse (Maas) River between Liege and Namur, and on to Antwerp. "If all goes well," Hitler proclaimed, "the offensive will set the stage for the annihilation of the bulk of 20 to 30 divisions. It will be another Dunkirk!"[2] He quickly set Colonel General Alfred Jodl, the chief of operations at OKW, and his staff to work, preparing the first draft of the operations plan, including calculation of the forces that would be required.[3] Field Marshal Wilhelm Keitel was told to prepare an overall estimation of the amount of fuel and ammunition that would be needed, and Gerd von Rundstedt was ordered to withdraw the I SS and II SS Panzer Corps, and the 1st SS, 2nd SS, 9th SS, and 12th SS Panzer Divisions, as well as Panzer Lehr, for rebuilding. They were moved east of the Rhine, to the Westphalia district, to reorganize, absorb replacements, and train for the attack. The Luftwaffe was ordered to estimate the maximum number of fighter airplanes the army could expect for air support during the offensive.

By October 8, General of Infantry Walter Buhle of the OKW staff had submitted the initial strength availability projection.[4] He estimated that the army could muster 12 panzer divisions (6 of which still needed to be refitted) by November 15. By November 20, 10 of Heinrich Himmler's newly formed *Volksgrenadier* (people's infantry) divisions would be ready for commitment. By November 30, three more would be available, and a total of 20 would be operational by December 10. By December 15, seven rocket-launcher brigades could be committed, and 13 assault gun brigades would be available by early December.

Jodl presented his concept of operations on October 11. The 6th Panzer Army (with 15th Army covering its right flank) was to launch the main attack out of the West Wall sector between Monschau on the north and Pruem on the south. It would cross the Meuse on both sides of Liege and, using the Albert Canal (which ran from Maastricht to Antwerp) to protect its right flank, would push on to the strategic objective: Antwerp. Simultaneously, the 5th Panzer Army would attack from an area between Pruem and Bitburg. It was to bypass Bastogne to the south, then turn northwest, cross the Meuse at Namur, and, bypassing Brussels, converge on Antwerp.

The OKW Operations Officer also pointed out the drawbacks of his plan. The banks of the Meuse were steep and presented a considerable barrier; bridges needed to be seized intact. In addition, the Ardennes plateau was hilly, partially forested, and cut by numerous deep gullies and small rivers. An advance through this terrain would not be easy. Furthermore, the 6th Panzer Army initially would have to cross the most difficult terrain—a dense, elevated swamp called the Hohe Venn; however,

Dietrich's army would start only about 25 miles from the Meuse, and once the Hohe Venn was crossed, the terrain would be much easier.

As usual, the infantry would attack first all along the front and score the initial breakthroughs. Then the panzer divisions would be committed through the gaps. The armor of the 6th Panzer Army would be committed in two waves. The forward panzer corps would thrust to the Meuse as quickly as possible. Advanced detachments led by the most innovative commanders would race ahead of the first wave to seize the Meuse bridges. Once the Meuse was crossed, the second wave would come abreast of the first, to start the drive on Antwerp. Jodl also suggested that the 6th Panzer Army should cover its own flank; therefore, the left-hand corps of the 15th Army should be attached to it. He stressed one point: nothing must be allowed to delay the panzer armies as they drove on the Meuse. If points of strong resistance could not be taken in the first attack, they should be bypassed and left for the following infantry divisions. Stabilizing the Western Front and bad weather, which would ground the Anglo-Saxon fighter-bombers, were prerequisites to the success of the attack, as was the necessity of keeping the lines of communications open, in spite of the Allied medium and heavy bombers.

Hitler modified the plan only slightly. He broadened the front to include the right-hand corps of the 7th Army (on the southern flank of the offensive), he concentrated the artillery, and he ordered more reserves (to be taken from the Aachen sector) to be given to 6th Panzer Army. He also gave the operation its codename, *Wacht am Rhein* (Watch on the Rhine), which suggested a defensive strategy. Later it was given the military codename *Herbstnebel* (Autumn Mist). Security precautions were so strict that just to talk about it was to risk execution. It could only be discussed via secure telephone, face-to-face, or by hand-delivered dispatches. No radio communications at all were permitted. Figure 2.1 shows the Hitler-Jodl plan for the offensive.

To lead the special detachments of picked men recommended by Jodl, Hitler went to the SS and selected two of his favorites: SS Major Otto Skorzeny and SS Lieutenant Colonel Jochen Peiper.

Skorzeny was a big man, standing six feet, four inches tall. He was born in Vienna, the then seat of the Austro-Hungarian Empire, on June 12, 1908, to a middleclass family. His father was an engineer and Otto followed in his footsteps. As an engineer student at the University of Vienna, he joined the *Schlagende Verbindungen* (a dueling society) and fought in 15 saber duels, which left his face marred with scars. He later remarked that only one of these duels was "serious" (but did not explain how one fights a nonserious duel). This fight was over a woman. Less than a month later, she announced her engagement to a lieutenant neither of the participants knew. Despite the dueling, Skorzeny survived his youth, graduated in

Figure 2.1
The Operational Plan for the Offensive

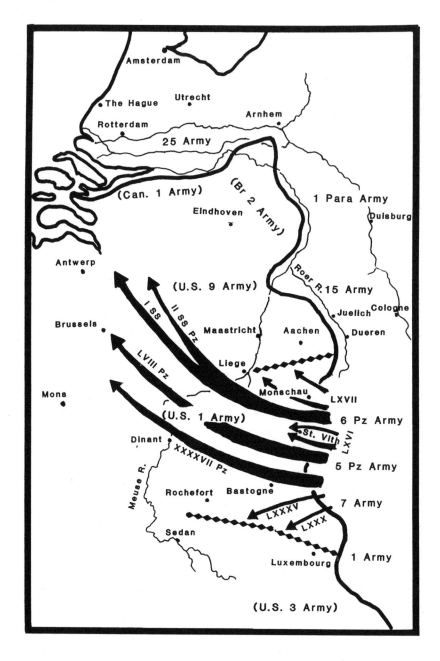

1931, and established an engineer company that became his main interest in life, along with women and car racing. He joined the Austrian Nazi Party in 1930, where he worked under the notorious Ernst Kaltenbrunner.

When World War II began, Skorzeny volunteered for fighter pilot training but was rejected because he was too old. He then joined Hitler's bodyguard unit, the Leibstandarte Adolf Hitler (LAH), which later became the 1st SS Panzer Division, as an officer-cadet. He soon impressed his superiors with his active and inquisitive mind. In 1940, as a second lieutenant of SS reserves, he designed ramps strong enough to load panzers on ships, further impressing his leaders. He fought in Holland, France, and the Balkans, where he distinguished himself by ambushing a large Yugoslav force and compelling it to surrender. He was promoted to first lieutenant in the Waffen-SS shortly thereafter.

Skorzeny went to Russia with the SS Motorized Division "Das Reich," which later became the 2nd SS Panzer Division "Das Reich." He fought in several major battles of encirclement on the Eastern Front. In December 1942, however, his luck ran out. A Soviet shell exploded behind him, and he was struck in the back of the head by shrapnel. He was sent back to Vienna to recover. Here he learned that Hitler had decided to create a new unit similar to the British commandos. He volunteered for the new command and was quickly accepted.

Skorzeny (now a captain of SS reserves) got his big chance in July 1943, when he was summoned to Fuehrer Headquarters at Rastenburg, East Prussia. Hitler was planning to rescue former Italian dictator Benito Mussolini from the anti-Fascist Italian government, which had deposed him. Hitler was personally interviewing six officers for the task of leading the rescue effort. When the dictator asked what they thought of the Italians, the other five candidates praised the Italians as gallant allies, modern day Romans, etc. The tall and physically imposing Skorzeny simply looked Hitler in the eyes and said, "Fuehrer, I am an Austrian." He got the job.

Skorzeny rescued Mussolini from a hotel in the Grand Sasso mountains in a daring gliderborne assault on September 29, 1943.[5] He became an instant celebrity and one of Hitler's favorite officers. The Fuehrer immediately rewarded him with a promotion to SS major and the Knight's Cross.

Other special missions followed, including a failed attempt at capturing the Yugoslavian guerrilla leader, Josip Tito, in November 1943. The partisan barely escaped, but the attempt set off a major battle between the SS commandos and Tito's guards, in which 213 Germans were killed, 881 were wounded, and 51 went missing. The partisans lost 6,000 men killed, wounded, and captured in the battle.

The following year, Skorzeny helped crush the Stauffenberg coup of July 20, 1944. For 36 hours, he was in physical charge of the Bendlerstrasse, the headquarters of the Replacement Army and a military complex equivalent to the Pentagon. Skorzeny, in the meantime, suppressed the Danish underground and served as chief of the SS sabotage and commando office. In October 1944, he kidnapped Miklos Horthy, the playboy son of Admiral Horthy, the regent of Hungary, who was attempting to defect from the Axis to the Soviets. When the loss of his son did not have the desired effect on the regent, Skorzeny led a bold armored raid and seized control of the government quarter in a bold *coup d'main*. Had Hungary defected, nearly 1 million German soldiers would have been cut off.

On October 21, Skorzeny reported to the Wolf's Lair following his latest successful commando mission, the seizure of the government quarter in Budapest. The Fuehrer greeted him warmly, awarded him the German Cross in Gold, and promoted him to SS lieutenant colonel. Hitler, obviously delighted, listened intently as Skorzeny described the operation in detail. When he finished his story and prepared to leave, Hitler said, "Don't go, Skorzeny. I have perhaps the most important job of your life for you. . . . In December, Germany will start a great offensive which may well decide her fate."[6] He noted that "the world thinks Germany is finished, with only the day and hour of the funeral to be named. I am going to show them how wrong they are. The corpse will rise and hurl itself at the West."[7] Then, with great relish, he described Watch on the Rhine to the tall Austrian in considerable detail, concluding by saying, "One of the most important tasks in this offensive will be entrusted to you and the units under your command, which will have to seize one or more of the bridges over the Meuse between Liege and Namur." To accomplish this task, Skorzeny and his men would wear captured American uniforms and would be equipped with captured American vehicles. At the same time, several groups of small commandos, also under Skorzeny, would infiltrate American lines, disrupting their communications and spreading fear and confusion wherever and whenever possible. Hitler told Skorzeny that his preparations were to be completed by December 2; the details he was to discuss with General Jodl, the chief of operations at OKW.

Because the time involved was so short, Skorzeny tried to protest, but Hitler brushed his objections aside. "I know that the time is very, very short, but you must do all that is humanly possible. . . . I forbid you to pass beyond the front line in person. In no circumstances must you let yourself be taken prisoner!"[8]

Skorzeny was then taken to Colonel General Heinz Guderian, the chief of staff of OKH, and later to Jodl.[9] His large unit, which was to seize the Meuse River bridges at Engis, Amay, and Huy, was designated the 150th Panzer Brigade; his small commando company was called *Einheit Steilau*. They were located at Friedental, a training base near Berlin, which was turned over to Skorzeny. Security around Friedental was excellent. It was cut off from the outside world and was guarded by Ukrainians who could not speak German. Once at Friedental, a member of Skorzeny's operation (codenamed "Greif," after a mythical bird) could even be hospitalized for any reason.

The 150th Panzer was a fairly standard armored men and consisted of two tank companies, three p ions, and three panzer reconnaissance companies neer, and support units. It was surprisingly shor equipment, probably because the combat units that had it ̶ ̶ ̶ to give it up. Skorzeny asked for 20 Sherman tanks but received only 2 (1 of which had a blown engine that could not be repaired). He asked for 30 American armored cars but got only 6. He asked for jeeps and got none at all—the German *feldgrau* liked their captured jeeps. He sent out foraging parties, however, and they located and seized 15 jeeps.

When he inspected *Einheit Steilau* units, Skorzeny was surprised and disturbed by the shortage of volunteers who were fluent in American slang. He found only 10, and they were mostly ex-sailors who had spent some time in America. Another 30 to 40 spoke English fairly well, and about 150 could speak some English with difficulty. Skorzeny divided his commando company into nine teams and instructed them to speak as little as possible. He also set up an ad hoc "School for Americans," in which the commandos were taught American habits, slang, and folkways. They also had to learn behavior modification. When an officer entered a room, the Germans habitually snapped to attention—unlike the American GIs. The Germans did not slouch like American soldiers and went to parade rest when told to relax, unlike the Americans, who actually relaxed. It took some effort to teach them how to behave like Americans. They were also taught how to spread fear and panic behind enemy lines.

Skorzeny also discovered that a strong hint concerning Operation Greif had already been leaked. The Wehrmacht sent a memo to all units, calling for volunteers who were fluent in English. They were to report to Friedental, where they would be incorporated into Skorzeny's commandos! This memo had received such widespread distribution that there was no hope that the enemy would not see it. This was a terrible security breach. Skorzeny feared the secret had been hopelessly compromised and even considered asking that the entire mission be scrubbed.

Enemy intelligence had, in fact, seen the memo. Fortunately for Skorzeny and his men, they ignored it.

Unlike Skorzeny, Hitler's other special detachment leader was no stranger to the men he would have to command—or to Skorzeny, for that matter. SS Lieutenant Colonel Joachim "Jochen" Peiper was born in Berlin on January 30, 1915, to Woldemar and Charlotte Peiper. His father fought in World War I, served in France and Turkey, and reached the rank of captain. Later he worked in the lottery business and apparently managed a tank factory during World War II. Peiper had two brothers, Hasso and

Both joined the SS. Hasso was in a Death's Head (concentration
camp guard) unit and was killed in action in 1942. Horst died in 1941—of
tuberculosis, according to the family. Rumors circulated, however, that it
was discovered that he was a homosexual and was caught by the Nazis.
According to the Nazis' idea of morality and the mindset of the SS, suicide was the only honorable way out for him, and he took it, at least
according to the rumors.

Jochen attended the Goethe Oberrealschule in Berlin and graduated in
1933. He had received an excellent education and was fluent in both
French and English. By fall he was a member of the *7th SS Reiter Standarte*
(7th SS Cavalry Regiment) and was a candidate to join the *SS-
Verfugungstruppe* (SS-VT), the first SS combat unit. By 1934 he was a full-
time SS man and had reached the rank of corporal. He volunteered for
officers' training, attended the SS Junkers' School at Brunswick, and was
commissioned *Untersturmfuehrer* (second lieutenant) on April 20, 1936
(Hitler's birthday).[10] He was assigned to the SS LAH, which was stationed
at Gross Lichterfelde in Berlin. His commanding officer was Dietrich.[11]

Peiper was short and small for an SS man: only five feet, eight inches
tall and 140 pounds. He had sharp features and long, dark hair, which he
combed straight back. He was a fanatical Nazi from the beginning. In
September 1945, his American interrogator, Major Kenneth W. Hechler,
described him as "very arrogant, typical SS man, thoroughly imbued with
the Nazi philosophy."[12] He was also very good at what he did. After the
Anschluss in 1938 (when Germany annexed Austria), he was selected by
Himmler to be one of his adjutants and his liaison officer to the SS-VT. He
accompanied Himmler's special train in the Polish campaign. Just as the
campaign ended, Jochen married Sigurd "Sigi" Hinrichsen, one of
Himmler's secretaries, who was two and half years older than he. She
would give him two daughters and one son.

Peiper accompanied Himmler to Poland again in early 1940, where he
is said to have witnessed part of the extermination of the Polish intelli-
gentsia. This story cannot be confirmed, but it is very likely that Peiper
knew of the mass murders, which were already taking place in the east.
These bothered him not at all; in fact, toleration of murder by the Nazis
seemed to have run in the family. His uncle was Field Marshal Walter
von Reichenau who, as commander of the 6th Army on the Eastern Front,
reprimanded the SS in his sector not for shooting Jews, but for expend-
ing too much ammunition when they did shoot them. He recommended
that the *Einsatzgruppen* (SS murder squads) limit themselves to two bullets per Jew.[13]

Peiper built his reputation on courage, daring, and brutality. Proud,
demanding, and arrogant, he was a fanatical Nazi and utterly contemptu-
ous of anyone who showed less military competence than himself—and
that was most people. He was obsessed with victory and reaching the

objectives assigned to him, and was as insensitive to the feeling of German generals as he was to the lives of non-German civilians or enemy prisoners of war.

Peiper got his first chance to command in Belgium when Himmler assigned him to the LAH shortly after the French campaign began in May 1940. He commanded the 11th Company. He first saw action in an assault crossing over the Aa Canal near Dunkirk on May 25. Despite being slightly wounded by shell splinters in the head, Peiper distinguished himself in the attack. For this and other actions, he was awarded both grades of the Iron Cross after the fall of Paris and was promoted to SS captain on June 1.

Later that month, Himmler recalled him to headquarters, where he again served as adjutant and liaison officer to the Waffen-SS. He became Himmler's first military adjutant on November 1—a significant promotion, for it indicates that Peiper had found favor with the Reichsfuehrer-SS. That spring, he apparently witnessed gassings in Poland.

In August 1941, Peiper again left SS headquarters and returned to the Leibstandarte, which was then fighting on the Russian Front. Peiper was again named commander of the 11th Company, III Battalion, and took part in the bitter battles between the Dnieper and the Don. Here he was again slightly wounded, this time in the right knee.

After fighting on the Eastern Front for a year, the Leibstandarte (LAH) was transferred back to France, where it was reorganized. On September 14, 1942, Peiper was given command of the III Battalion, 2nd SS Panzer Grenadier Regiment of the Leibstandarte, which was now known as the 1st SS Panzer Grenadier Division "Leibstandarte Adolf Hitler." (Later it became the 1st SS Panzer Division.) It was sent back to Russia in January 1943, where it fought in the Ukraine, including the battles around Kharkov and in the defense of the Donetz.

That winter, the army's 302nd Infantry Division was trapped on the eastern side of the frozen Donetz. Peiper rushed to the rescue with his battalion, broke through Russian lines, and covered the division's retreat across the river. After all of the infantryman had escaped, Peiper realized that the ice was too thin to support his halftracks. He then broke through Soviet lines a second time and pushed through the Soviet rear until he found a bridge. He seized it and escaped to the west. Shortly thereafter, on January 30, he was promoted to major and was awarded the Knight's Cross. He later took part in Operation Citadelle, also known as the Battle of Kursk. It was the largest tank battle in history and ended in a major defeat for Nazi Germany. From then on, all roads led back to Germany for the forces of the Third Reich.

In Russia, Peiper allegedly wiped out two Russian villages by systematically shooting every inhabitant and burning down every building. For this reason, his unit in Russia had come to be known as "the blowtorch battalion." He made it very clear that he would not let any person or thing stand in his way. Perhaps this brutality and single-mindedness of purpose is why Himmler and Hitler valued him so highly.

Peiper and the 1st SS Panzer were sent to northern Italy after Mussolini was overthrown in July 1943. In September, two of his noncommissioned officers (NCOs) were kidnapped by anti-Fascist partisans in Boves. In retaliation, the young SS major shelled the small town with 150mm self-propelled infantry guns, killing 34 people.[14]

The LAH returned to Russia a few weeks later. In November, Peiper allowed an enemy tank to come within a few feet of his position; then he personally destroyed it with a rifle grenade. "That should suffice for a close-combat badge, boys!" he joked to his men.[15] It certainly did; in fact, Peiper was decorated with the Close Combat Badge in Silver, awarded only to men who had been involved in close-quarter combat on at least 30 different occasions. He was also awarded the Oak Leaves to his Knight's Cross and promoted to SS lieutenant colonel. He was 28 years old.

Jochen Peiper and the 1st SS Panzer Division fought in a dozen more battles on the Eastern Front in the winter of 1943–44; and the division was reduced to a *kampfgruppe* (i.e., a division at approximately regimental strength). When it finally departed for France in April 1944, it had only three tanks and four assault guns left. It once had 160 tanks. Its total authorized strength was 16,000 men, but it had only 1,229 men still standing.

By the end of April, the Leibstandarte Division was in the Turnhout area of Belgium, rebuilding and preparing for the D-Day invasion. It was not committed to the Normandy fighting until July 6. Shortly before the 5th Panzer and 7th Armies were surrounded at Falaise, Peiper was wounded again—this time severely. He was evacuated to the Tegernsee Reserve Hospital in Bavaria (near his home) and did not return to duty until October. When he did, he found his regiment rebuilding in the Minden-Osnabrueck area. It had suffered heavy casualties in the retreat from France. The previous division commander, Teddy Wisch, had been seriously wounded and had been replaced by the brutal SS-Oberfuehrer Wilhelm Mohnke, who had lost a foot in the Yugoslavian campaign of 1941. He was considered too mean even in the Waffen-SS, where he was generally disliked.[16] He and Peiper, however, seem to have gotten along well.

During the early winter of 1944, many of the wounded veterans of the 1st SS Panzer Division returned to their outfit, which also absorbed thousands of replacements, most of whom were young ethnic Germans (*Volksdeutsche*) from Alsace and the eastern territories. They also received dozens of new tanks. By December 15, 1944, the 1st SS Panzer Division had 22,000 men and more than 100 tanks and assault guns.[17]

Albert Speer, the German minister of armaments and munitions, and the German war factories would also play a major (if indirect) role in the upcoming offensive. Since 1942, Speer had increased German armored production remarkably. In 1941, for example, German industry had manufactured 2,875 tanks and assault guns. In 1942, 4,300 were produced. This total rose to 6,700 in 1943, in spite of the fact that several tank factories had to be shut down and retooled to produce PzKw V and PzKw VI (Panther and Tiger) tanks. In 1944, German industry produced 11,000 PzKw IIIs, IVs, and assault guns; 1,600 tank destroyers; and 5,200 heavy tanks (Panthers and Tigers)—17,800 tanks and assault guns in all. Over the same period, the British manufactured only 5,000 tanks and the Americans produced nearly 30,000. Soviet production for 1944, on the other hand, was officially reported as 29,000 tanks, 32,000 aircraft, and 56,000 antitank guns and artillery pieces—and, in reality, must have been considerably higher. At the same time, Speer managed to increase German artillery production from 12,000 guns in 1942 to 40,600 in 1944, and antitank gun output climbed from 2,400 to 15,300 between 1942 and 1944. To achieve all of this, however, Speer necessarily had to use up Germany's stockpiles of raw materials. By September 1944, Germany's war production was already beginning to decline and would have dropped off rapidly in 1945, even without Allied air offensives and ground invasions.[18] Hitler's Ardennes campaign would be a "last chance" offensive in more ways than one.

To supply his armies and to provide more men as replacements for frontline units, Hitler widened the draft to include older and younger men, he had the rear areas combed out again, he revoked the "indispensable" draft status of many workers (much to Speer's disgust), and increased the German work week to 60 hours. As a result, the German Wehrmacht, SS, and *Volkssturm* (people's militia) had nearly 6 million men under arms by early winter. Their quality, of course, in no way measured up to that of 1940.

The three armies involved in the offensive were part of Army Group B and OB West, which would direct the actual battle (although certainly not without interference from above). Accordingly, Lieutenant General Siegfried Westphal (Rundstedt's chief of staff) and General of Infantry Hans Krebs (Model's chief) were ordered to report to Rastenburg on October 22.[19] In view of the recent defeats in the west, they expected a cool reception at best; they did not expect to be required to sign a pledge of secrecy, which stated that they would be shot if they revealed anything about what they were about to hear, other than to their commanders. At noon they were brought to the Wolf's Lair, where Hitler personally briefed them on the operation. After he finished, Jodl filled in some of the details.

Westphal returned to his headquarters, Ziegenberg Castle, near Frankfurt, and briefed his commander on the forthcoming operation.

Although Rundstedt acknowledged that the plan had "a touch of genius" in it, he considered Antwerp too ambitious an objective. After the war, he declared, "It was a nonsensical operation, and the most stupid part of it was the setting of Antwerp as a target. If we reached the Meuse we should have got down on our knees and thanked God—let alone try to reach Antwerp!"[20] At his headquarters in Krefeld-Fichtenhain (in what was formerly a hospital for recovering alcoholics), Model was less tactful. "This plan hasn't got a damn leg to stand on," he snapped.[21] After that, the reaction of the two field marshals was exactly the opposite. Rundstedt tried to convince the Fuehrer to change the objective; when that failed, he refused to have anything more to do with it and again retired to his castle, with his cigarettes, cognac, and detective novels. Field Marshal Model also considered the idea of capturing Antwerp unrealistic and never stopped trying to change Hitler's mind about the objective; but he nevertheless did everything in his power to carry out the Fuehrer's orders and make the offensive a success.

Ironically, with typical accuracy, the Allied media later attributed the entire concept to von Rundstedt and referred to it as "the Rundstedt Offensive"—much to the annoyance of the old field marshal.

Meanwhile, General of Panzer Troops Manteuffel, the commander of the 5th Panzer Army, reported to his new superior, Field Marshal Model, with considerable apprehension.[22]

Manteuffel was born on January 14, 1897, in the Imperial garrison town of Potsdam, near Berlin, the son of an army officer. He could trace his aristocratic roots back to Pomerania in 1287, and he was related to Baron Edwin von Manteuffel, a Prussian field marshal who served Kaisers Friedrich Wilhelm IV and Wilhelm I.

Manteuffel was very short—only five feet, two inches tall. He was nevertheless encouraged to follow in his father's footsteps and was educated at the Cadet Academy at Naumburg and at Berlin-Lichterfelde, Imperial Germany's West Point. He graduated in 1916, was assigned to the 3rd Brandenburg Horse Regiment, and was commissioned second lieutenant that same year. Then he was sent off to France, where he served in the cavalry squadron of the Prussian 6th Infantry Division. He fought at Verdun and was wounded when enemy shrapnel hit him in the thigh during the Battle of the Somme. Shortly thereafter he discharged himself from the hospital and returned to the front, and, in doing so, earned himself three days' detention when his deception was discovered.

Manteuffel served in the 6th Infantry Division for the rest of the war. After demobilization, he decided to leave the army and pursue a career in industry, but his uncle talked him out of it. "You must remain a soldier, for you were born one!" he declared.[23] Manteuffel then joined Freikorps von Oven, which was stationed in Berlin and commanded by a Prussian general. He applied for and was accepted into the Reichsheer in 1920.

Young Manteuffel remained in the cavalry (mainly at Rathenow and Bamberg) until 1933 and won many riding tournaments. At the end of the year, Major General Victor von Schwedler, the chief of the army personnel office (HPA), persuaded him to transfer to the panzer branch. He was promoted to captain on April 1, 1934, and was named commander of the 2nd Motorcycle Battalion at Eisenach on October 1. It was part of the 2nd Panzer Division, commanded by Colonel Heinz Guderian, which was formally activated in 1935.

Manteuffel spent the rest of his career in the *Panzerwaffe*, serving as chief training officer for *Fahnenjunkern* in the 2nd Panzer Division (1936–37), in the Panzer Inspectorate (1937–39), and in Panzer Troops Training School II at Berlin-Krampnitz (1939–41). After World War II began, he clamored for field duty and was named commander of the I/7th Rifle Regiment of the 7th Panzer Division on May 1, 1941. He took command of the 6th Rifle Regiment of the same division in August, after Colonel Erich von Unger was killed. Manteuffel led the 6th Rifle in Russia (1941–42), the 7th Rifle Brigade in Russia (1942), the ad hoc Division von Manteuffel in Tunisia (1942–43), and the 7th Panzer Division on the Eastern Front (1943). He assumed command on June 16 and was hit by 17 pieces of shrapnel from a Soviet grenade three days later, but he continued in command despite his wounds. In December, he was named commander of the elite *Grossdeutschland* Panzer Grenadier Regiment. He had been promoted rapidly: lieutenant colonel (1939), colonel (1941), major general (1943), and lieutenant general (1944).

Because of his ability and courage (he held the Knights Cross with Oak Leaves and Swords), Manteuffel became a favorite with Hitler, despite the fact that he was a professional soldier who did not share the Nazi world view and would not assist them in their crimes. He was somewhat shocked on September 1, 1944, when he was promoted to general of panzer troops and was given command of the 5th Panzer Army, which was then serving as part of Army Group G on the southern sector of the Western Front. Here he was ordered to launch a series of hasty and ill-conceived attacks in the vicinity of Luneville against the U.S. 3rd Army and was defeated by Lieutenant General George Patton. Then Manteuffel's army was then transferred to Army Group B, under the command of Field Marshal Model.

Manteuffel did not know what to expect when he entered Model's headquarters. The two men came from entirely different backgrounds and classes, and had already clashed. Their last meeting had taken place in early 1942, during the Battle of Moscow, when Manteuffel was commanding the 7th Rifle Brigade of the 7th Panzer Division. Model ordered him to attack through waist-deep snow against a strong Soviet position. Manteuffel considered the attack senseless and a useless sacrifice of life; typically, he refused to launch it. Model became absolutely livid and threatened to have Manteuffel court-martialed. Fortunately for Manteuffel, Lieutenant General Baron Hans von Funck, his divisional commander, saved him. The 7th Panzer was due to return to France for rehabilitation, so Funck placed Manteuffel in charge of the advanced party and sent him west immediately, out of Model's reach. General von Funck, however, had been retired in disgrace in September, and this time Manteuffel had no protector.[24]

Manteuffel reported with a sharp, formal salute. Model eyed him coldly. "We had difficulties in Russia," he began. Manteuffel nodded. "That is finished. We now have the same task. We are good friends."

"Good," Manteuffel replied, considerably relieved. They quickly formed a harmonious relationship based on mutual respect (both were disciplined soldiers and excellent tacticians), although they never really became friends. And Manteuffel preferred it that way. He, after all, was a baron, and Model was only the son of a school teacher.

Both Rundstedt and Model, meanwhile, came up with alternative plans. Rundstedt proposed a double envelopment, with 15th Army attacking from the north and the two panzer armies striking from the south. If they could link up in the rear of the U.S. 1st Army, approximately 15 Allied divisions would be surrounded and forced to surrender. This would be a devastating blow to Eisenhower's plans for the invasion of Nazi Germany.

Model, on the other hand, believed that—because of Germany's present lack of resources—the northern pincher (as proposed by Rundstedt) could not be made strong enough to do any good. He outlined a plan (which he codenamed *Herbstnebel*, or Autumn Fog) which would break through the Ardennes and then turn north into the rear of the U.S. 1st Army (i.e., a single envelopment). Figure 2.2 shows the "smaller solution," as opposed to Hitler's "larger solution." In the Model plan, the main attack would be directed by Manteuffel's 5th Panzer Army, instead of by Dietrich. Hitler, however, rejected both plans and insisted that his own concept be carried out.

On November 2, both Rundstedt and Model received copies of Jodl's latest version of the OKW operations plan for Watch on the Rhine. In the cover letter, the OKW chief of operations made it clear that Hitler would accept nothing less than an offensive against Antwerp. "The venture for the far flung objective is unalterable although, from a strictly technical standpoint, it appears to be disproportionate to our available forces. In our present situation, however, we must not shrink from staking everything on one card."[25] The new plan enlarged the area to be attacked on both the north and south and introduced the idea of a secondary attack. It would be conducted by Army Group H in Holland, as soon as the Allies began to throw strong forces against 6th Panzer Army. Nothing ever came of the idea. A proposed attack by elements of the 15th Army was also scrubbed.

Figure 2.2
Large vs. Small Solution

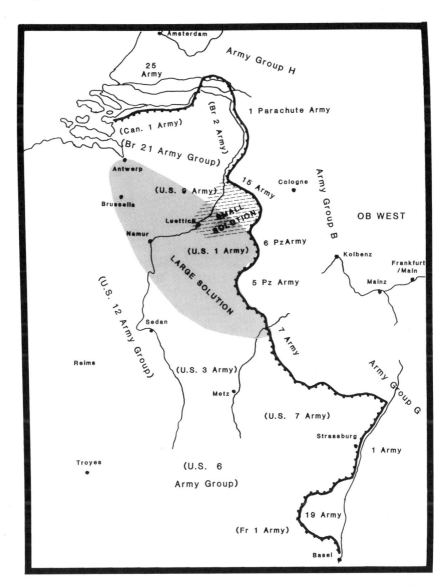

That same day, Rundstedt left for Army Group B Headquarters, where he met with Model, Westphal, Manteuffel, Dietrich, and Erich Brandenberger, the commander of the 7th Army. It was the first time the army commanders had been let in on the secret, and they were surprised that such detailed plans had been developed at OKW (i.e., at the highest level), and that it was based on such risky assumptions as weather and a strong showing by the Luftwaffe. Manteuffel offered an alternative plan (a cross between Rundstedt's plan and Model's own), through which the 5th and 6th Panzer Army would break through the Ardennes and then wheel north, while 7th Army covered their left flanks. Then the 15th Army to the north would launch a secondary thrust from the Sittard area. The two wings would link up around Tongres, northwest of Liege, surrounding 20 to 25 Anglo-American divisions in the process. On the other hand, if the Fuehrer insisted on his own plan, Manteuffel said, the 15th Army should not be committed to the offensive at all; the attack forces earmarked for it should be used to reinforce the 5th and 6th Panzer Armies.

Collectively, the plans of Rundstedt, Model, and Manteuffel became known as "the small solution." The Hitler-Jodl concept of operations became known as "the big solution." The generals' plan was brought up from time to time, almost until the eve of the offensive. Hitler rejected it every time.

On November 5, OKW ordered Rundstedt to reorganize his front in accordance with "the big solution." The 5th Panzer Army, which was defending east of Aachen at the time, was to be withdrawn, and its sector was to be taken over by 15th Army. The 6th Panzer Army was assigned to OB West (and Army Group B) effective November 10. It had already begun moving to the west with five panzer divisions—a movement that required 800 trains. Other divisions earmarked for the offensive were to be withdrawn to the Cologne-Juelich-Dueren-Bonn region for rehabilitation.

On November 7, Jodl submitted the final operations order for Watch on the Rhine. In this troop list, he placed the number of divisions available for the offensive at 38. Nine Volks artillery corps (each of about regimental strength) and seven rocket-launcher brigades would also be available. This projection was based on a best-case scenario and included six divisions (four of them panzer), which were still pinned down in defensive fighting, as well as all of the divisions of 15th Army—which Jodl very well knew would not be available for the Ardennes Offensive. Hitler must have known this as well, but he nevertheless signed the order on November 10. "Null Day" was set for December 10.

The Allied offensives of November (especially Courtney Hodges's thrusts north of the Roer) had a severe impact on *Wacht am Rhein* planning. Divisions earmarked for the offensive simply could not be taken out of the line and rehabilitated. On November 16, the long-awaited

American offensive from Aachen against Cologne began. Hitler shifted divisions from Holland to help check it, but Juelich and Dueren (both on the Roer River) were within range of U.S. artillery by November 28.

Model saw the offensive as an opportunity to pinch off the American salient formed by the attack and to trap much of the U.S. 1st Army. Given the dispositions of forces at the time, he very likely would have succeeded in inflicting a major defeat on Hodges's army. Hitler, however, rejected all of his appeals and held firmly to his own plans. "No improvisations" would be permitted.[26]

Model continued to object to the offensive almost until it was launched, because he did not believe Germany had the military resources to carry it out. On November 27, he noted that, if the offensive was halted on the Meuse, "the only result will be a bulge in the line. . . . The widely stretched flanks, especially in the south, will only invite counterattack."[27]

Manteuffel, meanwhile, put on a colonel's uniform, personally reconnoitered the American positions he was going to have to attack, and came up with some interesting observations about their habits. They considered the Ardennes a quiet sector—almost a rest and recreation area—and did not remain on alert. They usually stayed in their forward positions until an hour or so after nightfall; then they would go back to their huts in the rear. About an hour before dawn, they would return to the front. During the night, their trenches and foxholes were unmanned. Manteuffel, therefore, decided to attack without the massive artillery bombardment ordered by the Fuehrer. He figured his vanguards could cross the Our River in their assault boats before the Americans fully awoke.

Model listened to Manteuffel's ideas and found them sound. Together they went to Ziegenberg Castle, to convince Field Marshal von Rundstedt. The elder marshal was cordial but not particularly interested. He cut them off with a wave of his hand. They could do as they liked, insofar as he was concerned. To alter the OKW plan required the permission of the Fuehrer himself. Very well—they had his permission to seek an audience with the Fuehrer. If an OB West representative was needed, General Westphal could go. He would not attend the conference himself.

Model and Manteuffel had their audience at the Reichschancellery on December 2. Also present were Keitel, Jodl, and Buhle from OKW, as well as Dietrich, Westphal, and about 50 other officers. At the beginning of the conference, Hitler expressed his amazement that Rundstedt had elected not to attend. Manteuffel had his say, but Dietrich opposed his plans for the night attack. After a lengthy debate, a compromise was reached: Dietrich could have his heavy bombardment and attack at dawn; Manteuffel could use his infiltration attack in the predawn darkness without artillery preparation. Manteuffel also wanted to use indirect artificial light to support his attack through the woods east of the Our (i.e., he wanted to bounce searchlight beams off the clouds, rather than using their beams directly). When Hitler asked him how he knew he would have cloudy weather, Manteuffel reminded him that the entire offensive was predicated on the assumption that the weather would be bad. Trapped by his own words, the Fuehrer quickly backed off. Manteuffel could use "artificial moonlight" if he wanted to. Thus two radically different tactical plans evolved for the 5th and 6th Panzer Armies.

This conference, incidentally, was one of the few Dietrich attended. Apparently, he realized that he was "over his head" in his post as commander of a panzer army. He relied almost completely on his chief of staff, SS Major General Fritz Kraemer, to perform all of his higher command functions for him.[28] When Model held staff discussions, Dietrich usually sent Willi Bittrich, the commander of the II SS Panzer Corps, to represent him. Dietrich did not even attend his own 6th Panzer Army's map exercise for *Wacht am Rhein*. He did, however, support the "small solution" over Hitler's plan. Perhaps he was influenced by Kraemer, a former regular army officer who was opposed to the whole Hitler-Keitel-Jodl-Buhle cohort. Or perhaps the Oberstgruppenfuehrer—who did have a healthy dose of good Bavarian common sense—simply saw where this offensive was going and wanted as little to do with it as possible.

Toward the end of the meeting, Model again brought up the "small solution," only to hear it rejected again, with the same lengthy argument. The Allies would not be able to respond quickly to the German attack. Because a multinational coalition was involved, they would have to confer. By the time they could react in strength, the offensive would be successful: 25 to 30 Allied divisions would be destroyed, and the entire unholy alliance might shatter. Even if it did not, the Allies would not be able to regain the initiative for some time. This pause would give Germany the breathing space it needed to finish the development of her "miracle weapons," such as the jet airplane, the improved U-Boats, etc., etc. The objective, therefore, would remain Antwerp.

Three other significant points were covered at this meeting. Hitler again refused to give Brandenberger's 7th Army a panzer division, he ignored Brandenberger's request for more bridging, and he again promised that the Luftwaffe would support the offensive with 800 to 900 sorties a day. By this point in the war, however, no one really believed that Hermann Goering's air force would be of any material significance whatsoever. Their only hope was that the weather would remain poor, grounding the Allied fighter-bombers.

It is universally agreed that Keitel, the "nodding ass," submitted to Hitler's will with slave-like devotion, to the detriment both of the armed forces and the Fuehrer himself.[29] Despite his weak personality, however, it must be pointed out that he was a capable administrator. He directed the logistical build up for the Battle of the Bulge and, in this instance, his accomplishments bordered on the miraculous. With the help of the Reichsbahn and the Organization Todt (a construction and labor service), and in spite of the devastating Allied air offensive against the Ruhr, he managed to haul about 500 trainloads of equipment, fuel, and ammunition, and 1,502 troop trains across the Rhine and unload them at several different points—all without the Allies suspecting anything. So effective were his preparations that losses to Allied air attacks totaled only 8 ammunition cars in September, 11 cars of ammunition and supplies in October, and 4 cars of fuel in November. During November alone, he delivered 3,982 carloads of ammunition, fuel, rations, weapons, horses, and equipment to the assembly areas. By early December, he had eight usable railroad bridges across the Rhine, as well as eight functioning highway bridges and a dozen ferriers capable of hauling locomotives and railroad cars.[30]

Keitel had promised that an adequate supply of fuel and ammunition would be available for the offensive. On October 28, he set his objectives at 660,000 gallons of oil and almost 4 million gallons of gasoline. During the American drive against Juelich and Dueren, the daily fuel consumption of the German forces on the Western Front was 170,000 gallons each day; nevertheless, by December 15, he had 4.6 million gallons of petroleum, although (for security reasons) half of it was still on the eastern side of the Rhine. Not even all of this was available to the panzers. Here the Germans were trapped by their own security measures. They could not tell their supply staffs that an offensive was afoot without running the risk of breaching security, and if they brought up enough fuel to carry them to Antwerp, many rear echelon people would guess the truth. Because of the rugged terrain of the Ardennes, the panzers needed five fuel tanks worth of petrol to reach Antwerp. They had two when the offensive began— enough to cover 60 miles. Antwerp was 125 miles away.

Secrecy for the offensive was extremely tight. Within each army staff, only the commanding general and his chief of staff, operations officer, and one other officer were allowed in on the plan. In mid-November, General Otto von Knobelsdorf, the commander of the 1st Army, was under heavy attack by Patton's highly mobile 3rd Army east of the Saar.[31] To deal with this threat, Knobelsdorf had a few Volksgrenadier and understrength infantry divisions. His only motorized division, the 17th SS Panzer Grenadier, was in remnants and all but useless, and his only tank division, the depleted 11th Panzer, was no match for Patton's forces. Knobelsdorf therefore loudly protested the fact that he had not been given adequate armored forces. His protest was considered a breach of the security of Watch on the Rhine, and he was relieved of his command on a pretext on November 30, and replaced by General of Infantry Hans von Obstfelder, the pro-Nazi commander of the LXXXVI Corps.[32]

Despite the secrecy, all available Army Group B units conducted attack and night training exercises, on the extremely believable pretext that they might have to launch attacks on the flanks of Allied penetrations. Map exercises and exercises involving traffic management were also held, as were classes on winter warfare and traffic regulation. Unfortunately for the Wehrmacht, several divisions could not disengage from the Allied attacks to the north and south in time to be able to take advantage of these classes and exercises, but that could not be helped. Army Group B had done as much as was humanly possible to ensure that the offensive was successful, even though its commander did not really believe in it.

During the second week of December, the Wehrmacht began its final preparations for what Hitler now considered the decisive offensive of the war. Army Group B had only 22 divisions available for the attack—instead of the 38 estimated by Jodl—but it was nevertheless a formidable force. Seven of these divisions were panzer or SS panzer. On December 11, a large group of about 50 officers from Army Group B assembled at Ziegenberg, including Rundstedt, Model, Manteuffel, and Dietrich. They were relieved of their weapons and briefcases, and told to board buses, which took them via a circuitous route, designed to disorient anyone not thoroughly familiar with the area. When the buses stopped, they were led passed a double row of SS guards and into the Eagle's Nest (*Adlerhorst*), Hitler's command post, where they were soon joined by Keitel, Jodl, and the Fuehrer. It had been from here that he had directed the Ardennes offensive of 1940, which had led to the conquest of Belgium, the Netherlands, and France. He hoped that history would repeat itself in 1944.

Hitler began the meeting by paying special homage to Major Generals Baron Harald von Elverfeldt and Siegfried von Waldenburg, the commanders of the 9th and 116th Panzer Divisions, respectively.[33] They were decorated and, as a special honor, were invited to express their opinions about the condition of their units and the offensive in general. However, when the two fearless young commanders began to frankly discuss their reservations about the objectives of the campaign (although they had no knowledge of Model's "small solution"), they were quickly silenced by the Fuehrer. No modification of the grand design would be permitted.

General von Manteuffel sat next to the Fuehrer and was shocked by his physical appearance. He seemed to be "a broken man, with an unhealthy color, a caved-in appearance in his manner, with trembling hands; sitting as if the burden of responsibility seemed to oppress him, and compared to his looks in the last conference in the beginning of December, his body seemed still more decrepit and he was a man grown old."[34] Once the meeting began, however, Hitler seemed to draw additional strength from within. He spoke for two hours, raging about the political situation and the weakness of the Allied coalition, and stressing the similarities between Germany's present political situation and that of Frederick the Great, who had also struggled against a strange coalition. During his presentation,

Hitler assured the officers that Reichsmarschall Hermann Goering was going to commit 1,000 of the 3,000 operational airplanes left in the Luftwaffe to the support of the drive. Perhaps noticing the skeptical looks that flashed across many a face, he wryly added that he realized the generals did not trust Goering's figures, but he personally felt they could count on at least 800 airplanes. In addition, to make sure that they would have brought up all of the men and equipment they needed, he was postponing the attack until December 15. The next day, at a second conference with the commanders who were not present in the first meeting, he delayed the offensive until December 16. It was the last postponement.

Dietrich and Manteuffel were present at the second meeting. Hitler asked Dietrich if his army was ready.

"Not for an offensive," Dietrich replied.

"You are never satisfied," Hitler sneered.

When Manteuffel asked for additional equipment, Hitler snapped at him also. He informed the general that he had given him everything he had from the production lines and that this offensive was absorbing 80 percent of all of his new tanks, artillery, and trucks.[35]

Privately, of the senior generals of the Western Front, only Field Marshal Model gave the offensive any chance at all of succeeding—and even he conceded that the odds against it were very long indeed. "If it succeeds," he declared to his chief of staff, General of Infantry Hans Krebs, "it will be a miracle!"[36] Dietrich was more outspoken than most. "All Hitler wants me to do is to cross a river, capture Brussels, and then go on and take Antwerp!" he exclaimed. "And all this in the worst time of the year through the Ardennes, where the snow is waist deep and there isn't room to deploy four tanks abreast, let alone panzer divisions! Where it doesn't get light until eight and its dark again at four and with reformed divisions made up chiefly of kids and sick old men—and at Christmas!"

Hitler, meanwhile, had decided to send a third special force behind American lines, in the form of a parachute drop. It was to be led by Lieutenant Colonel Baron Friedrich August von der Heydte, the former leader of the 6th Parachute Regiment, who was now commanding the parachute school at Alten.

Heydte was the son of an old Bavarian Catholic aristocratic family. Born in Munich on March 30, 1907, the son of a Bavarian Army career officer, he studied law and international law at Innsbruck, Vienna, Paris, and The Hague. He received a Carnegie Fellowship in International Law and taught at Columbia University and the University of Berlin (as an assistant professor of jurisprudence). A member of the conservative Catholic political faction led by Franz von Papen, he (and others) had joined the Nazi Party in the spring of 1933, in a vain attempt to reform it from the inside into the law and order party of Germany. He joined the 15th

Cavalry (a regiment noted for its large number of Catholic officers) at Paderborn in 1935—allegedly to escape arrest after a fight with a Nazi student. His company was converted into an antitank unit later that year.

Heydte began attending a General Staff course in 1938 but rejoined his company when the war broke out. In early 1940, he was named Ia of the 246th Infantry Division. After earning the Iron Cross, 1st Class in the French campaign, he transferred to the paratroopers in August 1940.

As a captain, Heydte led the I/FJR 3 (I Battalion, 3rd Parachute Regiment) in the invasion of Crete, where he won the Knight's Cross and earned a promotion to major on August 1, 1941. Later he fought at Leningrad, where he was wounded in late 1941; with the Ramcke Brigade at El Alamein; in Italy; and in Normandy, where he commanded the 6th Parachute Regiment. He was awarded the Oak Leaves to his Knight's Cross for his part in the Battle of Arnhem. He was promoted to lieutenant colonel on August 1, 1944, and was named commander of the Battle School of the 1st Parachute Army (*Kampfschule der Fallschirmarmee*) on October 28, 1944. A quiet, thoughtful man, he did not seem like the type to be one of the leading paratrooper commanders of Nazi Germany—but he was. He was also the cousin of Claus von Stauffenberg, the leader of the July 20 anti-Nazi coup.

Early on the morning of December 8, he was ordered to report to the headquarters of Colonel General Kurt von Student, the "father" of the German parachute branch and the commander-in-chief of Army Group H.[37] "The Fuehrer has ordered a parachute attack within the framework of a powerful offensive," the excited Student began at once. "You, my dear Heydte, are ordered to carry out this task."[38]

Heydte naturally wanted to know the details of the operation, but all Student could tell him was that he would command a yet-to-be-organized *kampfgruppe* (battle group) of 900 to 1,000 men. Each regiment of the II Parachute Corps had been ordered to provide 100 of its best and most experienced paratroopers to form the new unit. Heydte asked instead to be given his old command, the 6th Parachute Regiment, whose men he knew. This would also give the attacks the advantage of unit integrity. Student, however, said this was impossible. The news of the movement of an entire parachute regiment from Holland to Germany would no doubt reach the ears of Allied intelligence and thus possibly compromise the security of the offensive. (Student unquestionably had a point here.) For the details of the operation, Heydte was to meet with General of Fliers Joseph "Beppo" Schmid, the chief of Luftwaffe Command West (formerly 3rd Air Fleet) and with Dietrich, the commander of the 6th Panzer Army, at his headquarters near Muenstereifel.

Schmid was an early Nazi who had taken part in Hitler's Beer Hall Putsch of 1923. Afterward, he joined the Reichsheer and received a commission in the infantry. He had served as chief of the Luftwaffe Military

Intelligence Branch from January 1, 1938 to November 9, 1942, during which he proved to be totally incompetent. His friend Hermann Goering (a fellow early Nazi who was now *Reichsmarschall* and commander-in-chief of the Luftwaffe) not only protected him but promoted him as well.[39] When Heydte met with him, he was commander of all Luftwaffe aviation forces on the Western Front. He was also completely inebriated. Schmid gave the parachute colonel and his immediate subordinates a broad outline of the plan, but when they started asking questions and raising objections, Schmid dismissed them rudely. But Heydte's day was just getting started. Later that morning, he met with another early Nazi, SS Colonel General Dietrich, ". . . who gave the impression of an old noncommissioned officer permanently addicted to alcohol."[40]

Baron von der Heydte looked down on Dietrich, the son of a butcher, as an uneducated street brawler, and correctly considered him unfit to command a panzer army. This opinion was strengthened during their meeting on December 8, which the burly Dietrich began by saying, "What are you parachute boys able to do?"

"Anything within reason," Heydte replied.

"All right! Take these places marked X," he said, slapping the map on his desk.

"That's unreasonable," the aristocrat replied.

"General Dietrich," his embarrassed chief of staff interrupted, "those Xs mark all the objectives [of the entire 6th Panzer Army]."

"Why didn't you tell me before?" Dietrich snapped at the capable SS-Major General Fritz Kraemer. "You have your choice, von der Heydte."

The parachute colonel selected the multiple crossroads near Baraque Michel, about seven miles north of Malmedy, Belgium. His mission would be to secure the crossroads for the 12th SS Panzer Division and the nearby bridges for the 6th Panzer Army.

"Now, you will go there and make great confusion!" Dietrich ordered. Heydte frowned.

"It's not von der Heydte's group that makes confusion," Kraemer interrupted again. "You have it mixed up with Colonel Skorzeny's Operation 'Grief.'"[41]

After he and Kraemer worked out the details of the operation, Colonel Heydte asked for details on the locations of the American strategic reserves—the forces that would likely be called on to deal with an airborne landing behind the front.

"I am not a prophet," Dietrich snapped. "You will learn earlier than I what forces the Americans will employ against you. Besides, behind their lines there are only Jewish hoodlums and bank managers."[42]

Then the baron asked for carrier pigeons, in case his radios were broken during the drop.

"Pigeons!" Dietrich laughed. "Don't be stupid! Pigeons! I'm leading my whole damn army without pigeons. You should be able to lead one kampfgruppe without a damn zoo!"

Heydte camouflaged his disgust with difficulty. Dietrich misinterpreted his silence for fear. "Don't worry," Hitler's former bodyguard smiled good-naturedly and clapped him on the back. "Take my word for it. I'll meet you personally at Baraque Michel. At noon on the first day of the attack!"[43] He went on to tell Heydte that he only had to hold out a few hours before a special kampfgruppe arrived with its new Jagdtigers and 128mm guns.

Dietrich was, in fact, opposed to the entire idea of a parachute drop. He called it "the one certain way" of alerting the Americans that they were going to attack—but he did not tell Heydte that.[44]

Heydte was even more discouraged the following morning, when he met his new command. As usual in such cases, the regiments of the II Parachute Corps had taken advantage of the opportunity to get rid of 100 of their worst troops: their criminally inclined, their physically unfit, their undisciplined brawlers, and other "problem children."

"Never during my entire career had I been in command of a unit with less fighting spirit," Heydte wrote later.[45] He acted quickly and sent 150 of the worst offenders back to their units and replaced them with volunteers from the parachute school, even though some of them had never jumped out of an airplane. By the end of the day, he had a kampfgruppe of approximately battalion strength (organized into four light parachute infantry companies), a heavy weapons company (equipped with heavy machine guns and air-droppable mortars), a signals platoon, and a supply platoon. However, he found that even his veterans were inadequately trained. Only about half had been trained to jump with weapons, and many had not jumped since the invasion of Crete in 1941. Some had not jumped since Holland (1940); only a few had ever jumped in woods or at night. The air crews scheduled to drop the kampfgruppe were no better off than the paratroopers. Two-thirds of the pilots did not have the certificates to fly the transports (old Ju-52 tri-motors) and most of the pilots and radio operators had just graduated from the training schools. For more than half of the men, this would be their first flight over enemy territory.

Heydte met his men for the first time on December 9. After they were dusted with louse repellant and vaccinated against tetanus, gas gangrene, and typhoid fever, Heydte led his advanced party to its assigned staging area, a military camp near the Senne River. He arrived at 2 A.M. and discovered that the commandant did not know he was coming and had no room for him—the entire place was full of Waffen-SS men.

A disgusted Heydte took matters into his own hands. He telephoned a friend, a pharmacist who lived in Oerlinghausen, a town located about

12 miles north of the camp. The druggist arranged emergency billets in Oerlinghasen and surrounding villages. By 10 A.M., all of the paratroopers were quartered by willing civilians. Heydte later recalled that the people of Westphalia and Lippe were happy to accommodate Wehrmacht troops but had no use for the Nazis or the SS.

After struggling with his many problems for four days, Heydte threw up his hands and took the matter to Field Marshal Model, who had originated the idea of a parachute operation in the first place. (Model, however, had suggested three dummy parachute drops—not a night jump with real men.) Heydte wanted the jump (which the troops called "Operation Suicide") cancelled.

Model had worked almost all night long on December 11–12, but he was not annoyed when he was awakened early on the morning of the 12th, and he met with Heydte immediately. He listened without speaking as the baron enumerated his many difficulties and stated his objections to committing inadequately trained air crews and paratroopers to the offensive.

Model did not insult Heydte by trying to deny or minimize a single one of his objections to the operation. "Do you give the parachute drop a 10% chance of success?" he asked, after Heydte had talked himself out.

"Yes," the baron answered.

"Then it is necessary to make the attempt," Model replied, "since the entire offensive has no more than a 10% chance of success. It must be done, since this offensive is the last remaining chance to conclude the war favorably. If we do not make the most of that 10% chance, Germany will be faced with certain defeat."[46]

Field Marshal Model had stated the conviction that was within him— the reason he labored so strenuously for an operation in which he did not believe. That was it, then. Heydte had no more objections, no more arguments. The parachute landings would have to be made, just as the offensive would have to be launched—not because it was likely to be successful—but because it was Germany's last chance.

By nightfall on December 12, most of the assault divisions had been assembled between Gemund (a town about 10 miles east of Monschau) and Bitburg, along a line running about 12 miles behind the front. The next day, Hitler gave the order for the infantry divisions to move to the next phase line, which ran about six miles behind the front. The panzer divisions, which were scheduled to join the battle only after the infantry had achieved its penetrations, remained behind the original 12-mile phase line.

During the night of December 14–15, the infantry divisions quietly moved in to their final assembly areas for the attack.

In all, Army Group B had 22 divisions for the offensive, including about 250,000 men, 2,600 pieces of artillery, and 717 panzers and self-propelled guns. Dietrich's 6th Panzer Army had nine divisions (five infantry, four panzer) and about half of the army group's panzers and self-propelled guns. Baron von Manteuffel had seven divisions (four infantry, three panzer), and about 350 tanks and assault guns. To the south, Brandenberger committed four divisions (all infantry) to the south. They had fewer than 100 assault guns between them. Contrary to the recommendation of every single major field commander involved, Brandenberger had not been given so much as a panzer brigade.

Also available for eventual commitment to the offensive were four units in OKW reserve: the 3rd Panzer Grenadier and 9th Volksgrenadier Divisions, and the elite Fuehrer Begleit and Fuehrer Grenadier Brigades.

North to south, Dietrich deployed the LXVII, I SS Panzer, and II SS Panzer Corps. General of Infantry Otto Hitzfeld's LXVII Corps (272nd and 326th Volksgrenadier Divisions) was to attack with its divisions abreast and break through in the Hohn Venn sector, along with the 277th Volksgrenadier Division of the I SS Corps. The main effort was to be made in the zone of SS Lieutenant General Hermann Priess's I SS Panzer Corps, south of the Hohn Venn, in the sector known as the Losheim Gap, where the terrain was more suitable for armor. Once the 3rd Parachute Division on the left and the 12th Volksgrenadier Division on the right broke through in the gap, Priess was to commit the 1st SS Panzer Division "Leibstandarte Adolf Hitler" (SS-Oberfuehrer Mohnke), which was to push on to the Meuse, while the infantry pushed north and west, protecting his right. To the south, Bittrich's II SS Panzer Corps (2nd and 9th SS Panzer Divisions "Das Reich" and "Hohenstauffen") was also to break through and drive on the Meuse and Antwerp, using the Albert Canal from Maastricht to Antwerp to protect its right flank. The 12th SS Panzer Division "Hitler Jugend" was to follow the 277th Volksgrenadier and help protect the right flank of the main thrust.

In the center of the German line, Manteuffel's 5th Panzer Army deployed the LXVI, LVIII Panzer, and XXXXVII Panzer Corps (north to south). On Manteuffel's northern flank lay the Schnee Eifel, a heavily wooded high ridge running generally northeast to southwest. Here, two regiments of the green U.S. 106th Infantry Division had relieved the veteran U.S. 2nd Infantry Division on December 11. Because the Schnee Eifel constituted a threat to the northern flank of the 5th Panzer Army, General of Artillery Walther Lucht's LXVI Corps was given the mission of biting it off and destroying the U.S. 106th Infantry Division.

In the main thrust of the 5th Panzer Army, Generals of Panzer Troops Walther Krueger's LXVIII Panzer Corps and Baron Heinrich von Luettwitz's XXXXVII Panzer Corps were to advance abreast to the Meuse. Krueger's corps was to cross the Our River near Lutzkampen, seize the town of Houffalize, push over the Ourthe River, and seize the Meuse River crossings between Namur and Andenne. To his south, Luettwitz's

Table 2.1
Order of Battle of OB West, December 1944

OB West: Field Marshal Gerd von Rundstedt

Army Group H[1]: Luftwaffe Colonel General Kurt Student
    1st Parachute Army: General of Paratroopers Alfred Schlemm
    15th Army: General of Infantry Gustav-Adolf von Zangen

Army Group B: Field Marshal Walter Model
    6th Panzer Army: SS Colonel General Sepp Dietrich
    5th Panzer Army: General of Panzer Troops Baron Hasso von
        Manteuffel
    7th Army: General of Panzer Troops Erich Brandenberger

Army Group G: General of Panzer Troops Hermann Balck[2]
    1st Army: General of Infantry Hans von Obstfelder

Army Group Upper Rhine[3]: Reichsfuehrer-SS Heinrich Himmler
    19th Army: General of Infantry Friedrich Wiese[4]

Notes:
[1]Activated November 11, 1944.
[2]Replaced by Colonel General Johannes Blaskowitz on December 24, 1944.
[3]Activated on or about December 15, 1944.
[4]Replaced by General of Infantry Siegfried Rasp, December 15, 1944.

Table 2.2
German Forces Engaged in the Ardennes

OKW
    Supreme Commander Adolf Hitler
    Commander-in-Chief: Field Marshal Wilhelm Keitel
    Chief of Operations: Colonel General Alfred Jodl

OKW Reserve
    3rd Panzer Grenadier Division: Major General Walter Denkert
    9th Volksgrenadier Division: Colonel Werner Kolb
    10th SS Panzer Division: SS Major General Heinz Harmel
    Fuehrer Begleit Brigade: Colonel Otto Reimer
    Fuehrer Grenadier Brigade: Colonel Hans-Joachim Kahler
    167th Volksgrenadier Division: Lieutenant General Hans-Kurt Hoecker
    6th SS Mountain Division: SS Lieutenant General Karl Brenner
    257th Volksgrenadier Division: Colonel Erich Seidel
    11th Panzer Division: Lieutenant General Wend von Wietersheim

Table 2.2 (*continued*)

OB West: Field Marshal Gerd von Rundstedt
Army Group B: Field Marshal Walter Model
6th Panzer Army: SS Colonel General Joseph Dietrich

>   LXVII Corps: General of Infantry Otto Hitzfeld
>>   272nd Volksgrenadier Division: Lieutenant General Eugen Koenig
>>   326th Volksgrenadier Division: Colonel Erwin Kaschner
>>   902nd Assault Gun Brigade
>>   394th Assault Gun Brigade
>>   17th Volks Werfer Brigade
>>   683rd Panzerjaeger Battalion
>>   405th Volksgrenadier Artillery Corps

>   I SS Panzer Corps: SS Lieutenant General Hermann Priess
>>   277th Volksgrenadier Division: Colonel Wilhelm Viebig
>>   12th Volksgrenadier Division: Major General Gerhard Engel
>>   1st SS Panzer Division: SS Oberfuehrer Wilhelm Mohnke
>>   12th SS Panzer Division: SS Colonel Hugo Kraas
>>   3rd Parachute Division: Major General Walter Wadehn
>>   150th Panzer Brigade: SS LTC Otto Skorzeny
>>   9th Volks Werfer Brigade
>>   4th Volks Werfer Brigade
>>   402nd Volks Artillery Corps
>>   388th Volks Artillery Corps
>>   501st SS Heavy Panzer Battalion

>   II SS Panzer Corps: General of SS Willi Bittrich
>>   2nd SS Panzer Division: SS Major General Heinz Lammerding
>>   9th SS Panzer Division: SS Colonel Sylvester Stadler
>>   502nd SS Werfer Battalion

Army Reserve
>   2nd Flak Division
>   519th Heavy Panzerjaeger Battalion
>   667th Assault Gun Brigade
>   653rd Heavy Panzerjaeger Battalion
>   506th Heavy Panzer Battalion

5th Panzer Army: General of Panzer Troops Baron Hasso von Manteuffel
>   LXVI Corps: General of Artillery Walter Lucht
>>   18th Volksgrenadier Division: Major General Gunther
>>   Hoffmann-Schoenborn
>>   62nd Volksgrenadier Division: Colonel Friedrich Kittel
>>   244th Assault Gun Brigade
>>   16th Volks Werfer Brigade

Table 2.2 (*continued*)

LVIII Panzer Corps: General of Panzer Troops Walter Krueger
    560th Volksgrenadier Division: Colonel Rudolf Langhaeuser
    116th Panzer Division: Major General Siegfried von Waldenburg
    401st Volks Artillery Corps
    7th Volks Werfer Brigade
    207th Combat Engineer Battalion
    1st Flak Assault Regiment

XXXXVII Panzer Corps: General of Panzer Troops Baron Heinrich von Luettwitz
    2nd Panzer Division: Colonel Meinrad von Lauchert
    Panzer Lehr Division: Lieutenant General Fritz Bayerlein
    26th Volksgrenadier Division: Colonel Heinz Kokott
    766th Volks Artillery Corps
    15th Volks Werfer Brigade

Army Reserve
    410th Volks Artillery Corps

7th Army: General of Panzer Troops Erich Brandenberger
    LXXXV Corps: General of Infantry Baptist Kniess
        5th Parachute Division: Colonel Ludwig Heilmann
        352nd Volksgrenadier Division: Colonel Erich Schmidt
        18th Volks Werfer Brigade
        406th Volks Artillery Corps
        15th Flak Regiment
        668th Heavy Panzerjaeger Battalion

    LXXX Corps: General of Infantry Franz Beyer
        276th Volksgrenadier Division: Major General Kurt Moehring
        212th Volksgrenadier Division: Lieutenant General Franz Sensfuss
        657th Heavy Panzerjaeger Battalion
        8th Volks Werfer Brigade
        408th Volks Artillery Corps

Army Group Reserve
    79th Volksgrenadier Division: Colonel Alois Weber
    11th Assault Gun Brigade

15th Army Reserve (later transferred to other armies in the Ardennes)
    9th Panzer Division: Major General Harald von Elverfeldt
    15th Panzer Grenadier Division: Colonel Hans-Joachim Deckert
    246th Volksgrenadier Division: Colonel Peter Koerte
    340th Volksgrenadier Division: Colonel Theodor Tolsdor

Figure 2.3
Dispositions, Western Front, December 15, 1944

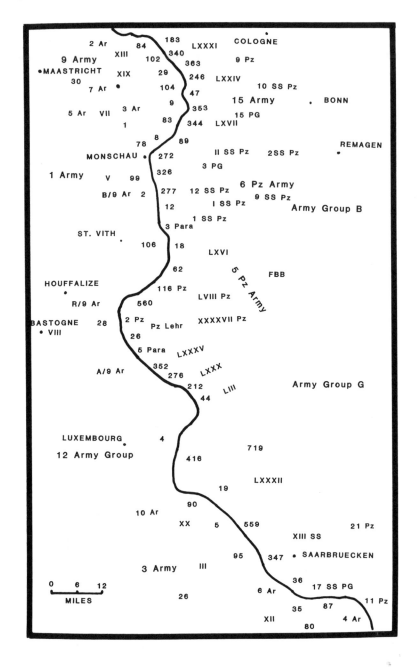

XXXXVII Panzer was to cross the Our in the Dasburg vicinity, seize Clerf, rapidly overrun the important road center of Bastogne, and push on to seize the Meuse crossings south of Namur.

On the southern flank, Brandenberger's 7th Army was given the mission of protecting Manteuffel's left by crossing the Our River near Vianden and driving along the southern flank of the XXXXVII Panzer Corps, gradually pushing his infantry divisions out to the south, to face what was believed to be negligible forces in that direction. He was ordered to threaten the city of Luxembourg if the opportunity presented itself. This mission he assigned to General of Infantry Baptist Kniess's LXXXV Corps, which controlled the 5th Parachute and 352nd Volksgrenadier Divisions. Brandenberger's other two corps (General of Cavalry Count Edwin von Rothkirch und Trach's LIII and General of Infantry Dr. Franz Beyer's LXXX) had only three Volksgrenadier divisions between them. They were ordered to demonstrate against the American forces south of the LXXX Corps. Table 2.1 shows the Order of Battle of OB West in December 1944, and Table 2.2 gives the detailed Order of Battle of the forces engaged in the Battle of the Bulge. Figure 2.3 shows the dispositions of both forces on the eve of the battle.

CHAPTER 3

The Offensive Begins

The Great Ardennes Offensive started inauspiciously. Colonel Baron von der Heydte's paratroopers did not jump because the trucks scheduled to carry them from their billets to the airfields at Paderborn and Lippspringe did not arrive. Later, Heydte learned that they had run out of gas.

North to south, the American forces in the Ardennes sector included the intermixed 99th and 2nd Infantry Divisions, the 14th Cavalry Group, the 106th Infantry Division, the 28th Infantry Division, a combat command of the 9th Armored Division, and the 4th Infantry Division. They totaled about 83,000 men. Of these, only the 2nd Division was in good condition. The 99th, 106th, and the combat command of the 9th Armored were inexperienced, and the 28th and 4th had been severely battered in the Huertgen Forest. They were in the Ardennes to rest, refit, and absorb replacements. The Americans had no idea that Hitler was about to launch a major offensive in the Ardennes.

Military intelligence officers are usually a pessimistic lot in general, but complacency was the dominant attitude up and down the American chain of command, including the front lines and the military intelligence staffs. Prisoners taken the second week of December by the U.S. 4th, 83rd, and 106th Infantry Divisions, as well as two deserters, all claimed that there would soon be a major offensive. They were ignored.

American military intelligence identified 6th Panzer Army in front of Cologne. It was assumed that its mission was defensive. This was a reasonable assumption; after all, had not the Germans just defended Aachen with great tenacity?

Prisoners from the 3rd Parachute Division informed their interrogators that the rebuilt 12th SS Panzer Division had arrived in the Eifel, as the German Ardennes was (and is) called. Their reports were also ignored.

Most seriously, on December 12, the Germans imposed radio silence throughout the Eifel sector—a sure sign that something was up. This fact was also ignored.

What was not ignored was a German deception plan called *Abwehrschlacht im Western* (the Defense Campaign in the West). Deliberately leaked into German radio traffic, which the Germans knew that the Allies would intercept, it suggested that the 6th Panzer Army had been created to launch a counterattack against the eventual Allied drive to the Rhine River. They thus explained away an entire panzer army. The leaks also stated that the 7th Army would continue to defend the Ardennes but relatively lightly. The Allies fell for the hoax. Even as late as December 15, the VIII Corps G-2 explained away an increase in German vehicle traffic noise by suggesting that they were committing new, inexperienced units to the Ardennes, to give them some frontline experience, before redeploying them to other sectors.

So certain were the American military intelligence staffs that nothing was going to happen in the Ardennes that, when it was reported that captured German soldiers had said they were going to attack, it was rejected as a mistranslation because "it's obvious they couldn't be preparing an attack."[1]

Almost alone of the senior intelligence officials, Colonel Benjamin A. "Monk" Dickson, the G-2 (chief intelligence officer) of the U.S. 1st Army, was somewhat alarmed, but even he indicated that the Germans were strengthening their defenses along the Rhine, rather than preparing for a major offensive. Then, suddenly, on the night of December 14, he declared that the Germans would attack in the Ardennes. The next day, he left for Paris for a spot of long overdue leave. He did not pass his prediction up the line to his commander, Lieutenant General Courtney Hodges, suggesting that he had little confidence in it.

Of the top intelligence officers, Major General Kenneth W. Strong, Eisenhower's G-2, came closest to grasping the true situation. In early December, he noted with concern that nine panzer divisions had disappeared from the Western Front. The following week, he wrote an intelligence summary to all top commanders, suggesting that the Germans were preparing a counteroffensive. They would attack either the Aachen salient or through the Ardennes. Eisenhower respected Strong's opinions because he himself felt concern about the thinly held Ardennes and because Strong had been right too many times. He therefore sent the G-2 to Omar Bradley's headquarters in Luxembourg. Bradley, however, had his own G-2, who had recently once again pointed out the hopelessness of the German situation. General Bradley brushed Strong off with words he would soon regret.

The offensive began at 5:30 A.M. on December 16 along an 85-mile front, from the medieval town of Echternach in the south to the resort of

Monschau (a favorite honeymoon town in happier times and one of Hitler's favorite places) in the north. In total, the Germans committed about 250,000 men, 382 tanks, 335 assault guns, and 2,623 artillery pieces to the first assault wave, while another 55,000 men with 561 tanks and assault guns waited just to the east. They constituted the second (exploitation) wave. They faced 83,000 Americans who had 242 tanks, 182 tank destroyers, and 394 pieces of artillery.

In the northern sector, the Americans were hit by a massive bombardment, featuring everything from small mortars to 14-inch railway guns. Many forward American commanders could not communicate with their battalions and regiments because their field telephone wires had been cut by the shells. They also discovered that their radios were being jammed by the recorded music of German bands. The Americans were initially unaware that a great offensive had started; they thought they had been hit by sharp, local attacks. Four hours after the battle began, General Bradley left the headquarters of his 12th Army Group in the city of Luxembourg for a visit to Eisenhower's SHAEF Headquarters, unaware that a major offensive was under way 20 miles to the north.

The German plans for the northernmost sector of the offensive had already gone astray on December 13, three days before the offensive began, when the U.S. 2nd, 9th, 78th, and 99th Infantry Divisions began an offensive toward the Roer River dams. The German plan had called for Lieutenant General Otto Hitzfeld's LXVII Corps to launch an assault between Konzen and Kalterherberg with its two divisions, the 272nd and 326th Volksgrenadier.[2] The northernmost division, Lieutenant General Eugen Koenig's 272nd VG, was tied up for four days in house-to-house fighting with the fresh U.S. 78th Infantry Division in the town of Kesternich, seven miles northeast of Monschau. Koenig could provide no help to Colonel Erwin Kaschner, whose 326th Volksgrenadier was scheduled to attack at dawn on December 16; in fact, quite the opposite was true. Kaschner had to reinforce Kesternich with two of his infantry battalions, leaving him only four battalions with which to attack.[3] To make matters worse, Hitzfeld's reinforcements had failed to arrive. Hitler had personally ordered that the 653rd Heavy Panzerjaeger Battalion—equipped with huge 70-ton Jagdtiger tank destroyers that featured 128mm guns—be attached to the LXVII Corps, to help Hitzfeld oust the Americans. The battalion, however, was traveling by rail and was stopped miles from the battlefield when an Allied air raid blew up the tracks. Because LXVII Corps did not have a single tank and neither of Hitzfeld's divisions had an assault gun, the northernmost corps in SS Colonel General Sepp Dietrich's army made little progress.

The northern sector of the American combat zone in the Ardennes belonged to Major General Walter Lauer's 99th Infantry Division, part of Major General Leonard T. Gerow's V Corps. The division had arrived only recently in Europe and was now holding a line from Monschau in the north (20 miles south of Aachen) to the Losheimergraben crossroads in the south. In his northern area, the veteran U.S. 2nd Infantry Division was attacking through his 395th Infantry Regiment toward the Roer River dams. Lauer's center regiment, the 393rd Infantry, was in a good position, but to the south his 394th Infantry Regiment was badly spread out, and his southern flank (including the road through Lanzerath) was covered by the 14th Cavalry Group, which was attached to the 106th Division of Middleton's VIII Corps. Dietrich's main attack (by the I SS Panzer Corps) was slated to go through the 394th Infantry and 14th Cavalry. I SS Panzer included (north to south) the 277th Volksgrenadier, the 12th Volksgrenadier, and the 3rd Parachute Divisions on the front line, with the 1st SS Panzer Division, the 12th SS Panzer Division, and Skorzeny's 150th Panzer Brigade in reserve.

The quality of the German infantry had declined significantly since 1940, and no better example can be cited than the 3rd Parachute Division. Led by Lieutenant General Richard Schimpf (who had recently recovered from the wounds he had suffered in the Falaise Pocket), it had lost three-fourths of its original members in Normandy and had been almost wiped out in the Mons Pocket. Its ranks had been filled by inexperienced soldiers who had about six weeks' basic training. Many of its Luftwaffe officers were hardly better; they had been pulled out of rear area staff assignments and had little or no infantry training. On December 16, the division attacked with courage but without skill, and its men were mowed down in rows. Its tactics resembled human wave assaults. Eighteen men of the Intelligence and Reconnaissance (I&R) Platoon of the 3rd Battalion, 394th U.S. Infantry Regiment, 99th Infantry Division, for example, met the attack of a reinforced battalion of the 3rd Parachute on a high knoll about 100 yards in front of Lanzerath. This was an important road junction in the Losheim Gap, a relatively open depression between the Elsenborn Ridge on the north and the Schnee Eifel to the south. It was the best tank terrain facing the American front, which is why Dietrich concentrated his panzers due east of it.

The I&R Platoon was commanded by 1st Lieutenant Lyle Bouck. The platoon's radio (and jeep) were destroyed by a shell almost immediately after the battle began. Lieutenant Bouck sent two men back to battalion headquarters on foot, asking for reinforcements or permission to withdraw. Unknown to Bouck, they never made it. They found the woods behind Lanzerath crawling with Germans and were soon having to evade German infantry. After hiding out for two days, they were captured on December 18. Meanwhile, Bouck and his men, using BARs (Browning Automatic Rifles), a 0.50 caliber machine gun, and M-1 rifles and carbines, beat back two major German attacks that morning; the dead and wounded paratroopers were pilled high along a fence in front of the

American position. One survivor recalled that it was like target practice. Hundreds of Germans were shot down. By afternoon, the entire 9th Parachute Regiment had been committed to the battle, but it was late afternoon before the detachment was overrun. One weak American platoon had delayed the entire I SS Panzer Corps's offensive for hours. (Lieutenant Bouck was awarded the Silver Star in captivity, but he did not learn of it until 1966. Later, his award was upgraded to the Distinguished Service Cross. In my opinion, he deserves the Congressional Medal of Honor.)

The tactics used at Lanzerath were not unusual. The fact that Hitler's security measures did not allow many local commanders the opportunity to conduct a proper reconnaissance was part of the problem; however, it can by no means fully explain the carelessness with which most of the German infantry advanced. Many Americans were astonished at the lack of caution the green Volksgrenadier and parachute divisions displayed in the attack. At times they advanced almost in parade-ground formations, and hundreds of them were cut down by U.S. machine guns. The U.S. 395rd Infantry Regiment, which bore the brunt of the attacks of the 326th Volksgrenadier Division, reported German infantry pushing frontal assaults with reckless abandon, to the point that German dead actually toppled into their foxholes. Just south of the 326th VG, Colonel Wilhelm Viebig's 277th Volksgrenadier Division, which had the mission of capturing the twin towns of Rocherath-Krinkelt, used similar tactics, with similar results, and in the center of the I SS Panzer, Major General Gerhard Engel's 12th Volksgrenadier Division bogged down in fruitless attacks against the 394th Regiment.

To the south, however, the story was different. Here Colonel Mark Devine's weak 14th Cavalry Group (about 900 men) faced the worst odds of any American unit on Null Day. It was attacked on the north by the bulk of the 3rd Parachute Division and on the south by the 294th and 295th Grenadier Regiments of the 18th Volksgrenadier Division. After a reconnaissance two nights earlier, patrols from the 18th Volksgrenadier Division had reported to their commander, Major General Guenter Hoffmann-Schoenborn, that they had discovered a gap of nearly two miles in the southern side of Devine's defenses, which was not occupied, at least at night. Leaving only 150 to 200 men to the east, to screen the U.S. 422nd Infantry Regiment, Hoffmann-Schoenborn struck into this gap with two regiments, supported by 40 assault guns (see Chapter VI). By nightfall, he had pushed more than two miles behind the right flank of the U.S. 423rd Infantry Regiment. The encirclement of the Schnee Eifel was already taking shape.

Meanwhile, on the southern flank of the Schnee Eifel, Major General Frederick Kittel's 62nd Volksgrenadier Division was temporarily checked by the U.S. 424th Infantry Regiment (of the 106th Division).[4] However, as the day wore on, the American commander in this sector was forced to commit all of his reserves, and one of his artillery battalions (the 591st) had been forced to fire almost all of its ammunition (more than 2,600 rounds). By nightfall, in spite of heavy casualties, the green 62nd Volksgrenadier had pushed the equally inexperienced American regiment back to the village of Winterspelt, on the road to St. Vith.

Further south, the main weight of General von Manteuffel's attack—the LVIII Panzer and XXXXVII Panzer Corps—struck the veteran U.S. 28th Infantry Division.

General of Panzer Troops Walter Krueger's LVIII Panzer Corps consisted of two divisions: the inexperienced 560th Volksgrenadier under Colonel Rudolf Bader and the veteran but depleted 116th Panzer under Siegfried von Waldenburg.[5]

The 560th was just returning to the mainland of Europe from garrison duty in Norway. One of its regiments, in fact, was still on the way. It had never seen combat. The 116th Panzer, on the other hand, had seen a great deal of fighting and had only 83 tanks out of a theoretical complement of 200. Both divisions attacked the U.S. 112th Infantry Regiment, which used captured German Westwall bunkers, pillboxes, and dragon's teeth (anti-tank obstacles) to maximum advantage. Waldenburg lost several tanks but was unable to get at the American infantry. The German infantry and panzer grenadiers continued the attack, unsupported by armor, and lost hundreds of men. The 560th nevertheless captured a stone bridge over the Our River at Ouren, only to be thrown back by an American counterattack. They also captured a partially demolished bridge near Kalborn, but it was too fragile to support anything except foot traffic. The failure of the LVIII Panzer Corps to get across the Our on the first day of the offensive was a bitter disappointment to Manteuffel, who had expected success in this sector.

The main blow came in the 10-mile sector along and behind a road known to the Americans as Skyline Drive, a highway located on a ridgeline just east of the Our River. Here the spearhead of Luettwitz's XXXXVII Panzer—the 2nd Panzer and 26th Volksgrenadier Divisions, as well as the northern part of the Panzer Lehr—struck Colonel Hurley Fuller's badly overextended 110th Infantry Regiment of the 28th Infantry Division. The battle began when the men of the two forward American battalions returned to their foxholes early in the morning and found the Germans already there: they had infiltrated across the Our River during the night. Manteuffel's tactics were working well. Despite their surprise, the U.S. troops rallied, holding off Colonel Heinz Kokott's 26th Volksgrenadier at Hosingen. As the morning progressed, however, the 26th VG bypassed Hosingen and penetrated two to three miles, as far as the American artillery positions near Bockholz. Most of the day, however, the 26th VG Division was tied up fighting the stubborn Americans in small villages east (i.e., on the wrong side) of the Our.[6]

Meanwhile, General Cota, the commander of the American division, reinforced Fuller with most of the 707th Tank Battalion, but he refused to release the II/110th Infantry, which was in divisional reserve.

December 16 was a frustrating day for Colonel Meinrad von Lauchert, the commander of the veteran 2nd Panzer Division. It was his first full day as a division commander. Manteuffel and Luettwitz had had doubts about the aggressiveness of Lauchert's predecessor, Major General Henning Schoenfeld, and relieved him of his command at the last minute.[7] No one had any doubts about Lauchert's aggressiveness. Not yet 40 years of age, he had commanded the 15th Panzer Regiment on the Eastern Front and held the Knight's Cross with Oak Leaves and Swords. Lauchert, however, had not even met some of his direct subordinates when the offensive began. His new division also had serious problems. Half of its panzer grenadier regiment (the 304th) did not have motorized vehicles. General Schoenfeld had dealt with this problem the only way he could: he mounted the men on bicycles.

Despite his problems, Colonel von Lauchert pushed the Americans back across the Our River and then led his panzer grenadiers across in assault boats, securing the west bank. Then he had to wait (impatiently) for his panzer engineers to come up through a terrible traffic jam in the rear with their bridging columns, so that his 120 tanks could cross in river. While he waited, his panzer grenadiers pushed on toward Marnach, blundering into a minefield in the process. They attacked the town but were unable to take it. Their losses were heavy and included the commander of the 304th Panzer Grenadier Regiment.

All the while, the panzer engineers were constructing bridges over the Our. Shortly before nightfall, Lauchert had a 60-ton bridge across the river at Dasburg. The tanks crossed the river that evening, and the Marnach garrison was overwhelmed by the 3rd Panzer Regiment before midnight. Lauchert and his panzers then pushed ahead to the town of Clervaux.

Fritz Bayerlein's Panzer Lehr Division also had a frustrating day. It was caught in the huge traffic jam on the inadequate roads leading to the river and then had to wait hours for a bridge to be constructed at Gemuend. It was night before this job was completed.

On the southern flank of the German offensive lay General of Panzer Troops Erich Brandenberger's 7th Army. Although Brandenberger had practically begged for a tank division, he had been given only four largely inexperienced and poorly trained marching infantry divisions. His command included General of Infantry Baptist Kniess's LXXXV Corps on the north and General of Infantry Franz Beyer's LXXX Corps on the south.[8] Altogether, Brandenberger had 60,000 men, only about 12 assault guns, and 629 guns and rocket launchers; however, he lacked trucks, prime movers for the artillery, and bridging equipment. Hitler had promised Brandenberger another 40 assault guns and ordered him to drive to the west almost to the Meuse at Gedinne, then turn and face south, to protect the southern flank of the German offensive from George S. Patton's U.S. 3rd Army. No one at 7th Army Headquarters thought this mission was possible to execute, even before the promised assault guns failed to arrive, but they resolved to do the best they could with the limited resources available.

Brandenberger's men attacked the U.S. 109th Infantry Regiment (on the right flank of the 28th Division), the 60th Armored Infantry Battalion of the 9th U.S. Armored Division near Beaufort, and the 12th Infantry Regiment of the U.S. 4th Infantry Division. His main target was the southern shoulder of the American positions, which was held by the U.S. 12th Infantry Regiment. Here, the southernmost German attack force (Lieutenant General Franz Sensfuss's 212th Volksgrenadier Division) had difficulty crossing the river, and it was almost 10 A.M. before the attack fully developed. Sensfuss's division outnumbered the Americans 10,000 to 3,000, but the U.S. divisional commander, the resourceful Major General Raymond O. Barton, reacted quickly and reinforced the 12th Infantry with an infantry battalion from his divisional reserve and elements of the 70th Tank Battalion. As we have seen, Hitler had rejected attempts by Model, Brandenberger, and Manteuffel to get a panzer division assigned to the 7th Army. Because the Americans had tanks and Sensfuss did not, and because of Barton's quick reactions, the 212th Volksgrenadier made little progress on Null Day, although it did not perform at all badly.[9] When night fell, despite heavy odds, the U.S. 12th Infantry was still holding all five of its major centers of resistance: Dickweiler, Osweiler, Echternach, Lauterborn, and Berdorf. (The next morning, Barton would throw in more reinforcements, including a battalion of the 22nd Infantry Regiment and a tank company on loan from the 9th Armored Division.)

North of the 212th, Major General Kurt Moehring's 276th VG Division took advantage of the wooded and broken terrain and thick fog to advance several miles. It was, however, stopped by tanks and armored infantry from Combat Command A (CCA) of the U.S. 9th Armored Division.

Field Marshal Model considered the 276th "a loser" and "the problem child of 7th Army."[10] Brandenberger was also not satisfied with the division, nor was he pleased with the efforts of its commander to improve it. He apparently decided on December 16 to relieve General Moehring of his command at the first convenient opportunity.

On Brandenberger's northern flank, Colonel Ludwig Heilmann's 5th Parachute Division had better success. It managed to penetrate several miles and established a bridgehead over the Our River at Vianden. All in all, however, 7th Army's progress was unsatisfactory.

The same could be said for all of Army Group B. A successful offensive depended on two factors: surprise and quick exploitation. They had achieved surprise, but quick exploitation was eluding them. The plan called for Army Group B to take one day to break through the American line and another day to cross the Ardennes. It was supposed to reach the Meuse by nightfall on the third day (although Model himself did not expect to reach the river until the fourth day). On Null Day, however, it had only achieved one breakthrough—in the Losheim Gap, north of the Schnee Eifel. It was already well behind schedule, and except for one or two places, American resistance in the Ardennes had by no means been broken.

Hitler, of course, realized none of this. Reports were flooding into Fuehrer Headquarters. German radio interceptors relayed messages of despair and near panic from trapped American units. Transmissions were intercepted in which some of the surrounded units were ordered to blow up their guns and try to escape. Other U.S. units were ordered to withdraw. There were many and obvious signs of confusion and disorder, both at the front and in lower-level headquarters. It was the first really good news Hitler had received from the Western Front in some time, and he was a happy man during the night of December 16–17.

Late that night, from his headquarters at the Eagle's Nest, he telephoned General of Panzer Troops Hermann Balck, the commander-in-chief of Army Group G, and told him: "From this day on, Balck, not a foot of ground is to be given up. Today we march!" With growing enthusiasm, Hitler explained to him that Peiper's SS kampfgruppe was well into the Losheim Gap, while Manteuffel was about to cut off the Schnee Eifel and break out to the west with his two panzer corps. He was more excited than he had been in months. "Balck," he cried, "everything has changed in the West. Success—complete success—is now in our grasp!"[11]

Hitler's enthusiastic projection was not well grounded in the facts. True, some American units had been routed, and there was confusion in their ranks. But the maximum German advance had only been about three miles, and, despite penetrations among their larger units, the Americans had generally held their positions, and the German timetable was already out of sync. Because of the lack of a breakthrough in 6th Panzer Army's sector, neither Peiper's kampfgruppe nor Skorzeny's 150th Panzer Brigade had been committed as planned, nor had Heydte's paratroopers been able to jump, and, despite all of the planning, there were serious traffic jams behind Dietrich's army.

Hitler would have been much less happy had he known of events taking place miles to the rear. By nightfall on December 16, Eisenhower and Bradley (who were dining together in Paris, in a villa previously occupied by Gerd von Rundstedt) had already been informed that eight German divisions were attacking. The two generals agreed that there was no objective worth this kind of effort in the Ardennes, or indeed east of the Meuse; however, at first, only Eisenhower seemed to have appreciated the seriousness of the situation. He told Bradley in no uncertain terms that this was not a spoiling attack, as the army group commander had suggested. He ordered Bradley to reinforce Middleton's VIII Corps in the Ardennes with the only two U.S. armored divisions presently out of the line: the 10th Armored from the south and the 7th Armored from the north. Eisenhower also ordered that the U.S. 1st Infantry Division be transferred to the Ardennes. Bradley opposed these moves, because he was sure that the offensive was a local attack only, but Eisenhower was adamant. This left only two U.S. divisions in theater reserve: the 82nd and 101st Airborne, now recuperating from the Arnhem drop near Reims, France.

Hitler had assumed that the Allies high command would work like his own command network. He was sure that Eisenhower could not shift large numbers of troops and tanks without first consulting with President Franklin D. Roosevelt in Washington and Prime Minister Winston Churchill in London. Consultations with the chiefs of staff and the Imperial General Staff would take even longer. This would give him three or more days to advance to the Meuse without a major Allied reaction. Under Eisenhower, however, SHAEF (Supreme Headquarters, Allied Expeditionary Force) did not work that way. Ike reacted within hours, not days, and made the correct moves without interference from amateurs in Washington or London. Although he did not realize it, Hitler's plan was fatally flawed from the first day.

CHAPTER 4

The Battle on the Northern Flank

According to the plan, the 3rd Parachute and 12th Volksgrenadier Divisions were supposed to break through the thin American line covering the northern sector of the Losheim Gap. Oberfuehrer Wilhelm Mohnke's 1st SS Panzer Division would then drive through the gap, advance rapidly to the Meuse River and capture the bridges in the vicinity of Huy, about 50 miles from the jump-off point, by the end of the second day of the offensive. From there, the four tank divisions of the 6th Panzer Army would continue the advance to Antwerp.

Mohnke divided his division into four battle groups (kampfgruppen or KGs), each based on a parent unit. KG Peiper was the augmented 1st SS Panzer Regiment, KG Hansen (under SS Lieutenant Colonel Max Hansen) was built around the 1st SS Panzer Grenadier Regiment, KG Sandig (under SS Lieutenant Colonel Rudolf Sandig) formed around the 2nd SS Panzer Grenadier Regiment, and KG Knittel's core unit was Major Gustav Knittel's 1st SS Panzer Reconnaissance Battalion.[1] The division would be spearheaded by KG Peiper, which included I Battalion of SS Lieutenant Colonel Jochen Peiper's own 1st SS Panzer Regiment (two companies), equipped with Panthers; 6 and 7 Companies, 1st SS Panzer Regiment, equipped with Panzer Mark IVs; 9 Company (9/1st SS Panzer Regiment), the engineer company; and 10/1st SS Panzer, the self-propelled anti-aircraft company. KG Peiper also included the 501st SS Heavy Panzer Battalion, equipped with Tigers and monstrous 72-ton Royal Tigers, the largest tank used in World War II, as well as III Battalion, 2nd SS Panzer Grenadier Regiment; 3/1st SS Panzer Engineers; and 84th Flak Battalion, a Luftwaffe unit. In all, he had approximately 90 panzers (including 20 Tigers, 35 Panthers, and 35 PzKw IVs) and 4,000 men.

Peiper did not like the plan from the beginning. He felt his designated route of advance, from Honsfeld, to Baugnez, to Ligneuville, and to Stavelot on the Ambleve River, was better suited for bicycles than panzers. Also, the schedule called for him to reach the Meuse in two days, which he considered impossible.[2] He was in the process of objecting to everything when Mohnke told him that the plan and his route of advance had been personally selected by the Fuehrer himself and could not be changed. Then he learned that two trainloads of fuel intended for Lieutenant General Hermann Priess's I SS Panzer Corps had not arrived, and he would have to capture gasoline from the Americans to continue his drive. Priess had learned from spies that the Americans probably had large fuel dumps at Buellingen, Stavelot, and Spa, generally north of the main line of advance. Priess decided to capture them and passed the information on to his subordinates but kept this intended diversion from higher headquarters.

Much to Peiper's disgust, Skorzeny's 150th Panzer Brigade was placed next to his own kampfgruppe. Its assignment was to race for the Meuse once Peiper broke through. Peiper, however, intended to handle this mission alone. He commented that Skorzeny and his men might as well have stayed at home.[3]

On December 16, everything went wrong in the zone of the I SS Panzer Corps. As we have seen, the poor quality 3rd Parachute Division was stopped on Null Day, so Peiper was left fuming in the area, unable to join the battle. He expected the parachute infantry to penetrate the American lines by 7 A.M. and to clear the mines from the road between Losheim and Losheimergraben. Then the engineers were to replace a destroyed overpass by noon. If they did so, Peiper guaranteed that he would reach the Meuse by midnight—or by early morning on December 17 at the latest. But as of noon, nothing had happened. At midday, Priess, the commander of the I SS Panzer Corps, signaled Peiper directly: "Turn west to Lanzerath. 3rd Parachute Division has been stopped. Take over and get them moving again."[4]

Peiper tried to reach his new area of operations but was seriously delayed by a massive traffic jam on the narrow Ardennes roads in the zone of the 12th Volksgrenadier Division. The main road west had to accommodate not only the 12th VG and the 3rd Parachute Divisions, but also the 391 guns and rocket launchers of the 388th and 402nd *Volksartillerie* Corps and the 49th and 9th *Volkswerfer* (People's Rocket Launcher) Brigades, most of which were horse drawn.[5] The impatient and angry SS colonel ordered his tanks to push on ruthlessly, running down anything that got in their way. Trucks, Volkswagens, and horse-drawn artillery scattered into the ditches in the face of the Tigers, which ignored the curses of the army officers and drivers. Peiper ultimately discovered that the cause of the delay was a wrecked bridge, which had been demolished by the Germans in their retreat that fall. None of the staff officers had taken this into account when they planned the advance. An angry and upset Peiper found a detour around the downed bridge and finally reached the rear area of the 3rd Parachute Division. Then there was an explosion. Mines! The 3rd Parachute had failed to clear the road of its own mines! According to several historians, Peiper was unwilling to delay until his engineers could be brought up, so he ruthlessly pushed through the minefield, using his own tanks. The 1st SS Panzer Regiment lost five tanks and five other vehicles, deliberately sacrificed by their own commander, according to those who accept this version of the story. "Needless to say nothing of the sort happened," British Major General Michael Reynolds wrote later.[6] According to Reynolds and also Ralf Tiemann, one of the 1st SS Panzer Division's historians, the pioneers of Lieutenant Rumpf's 9th Company/1st SS Panzer Engineer Battalion came up and cleared the mines.[7] The version of events presented by General Reynolds and Herr Tiemann seems far more likely to this historian; in any case, by all accounts, Peiper was in a very bad mood when he approached Lanzerath, just before midnight. He found the town occupied by the 9th Parachute Regiment, which had posted no sentries and sent him no guides.

In Lanzerath, Peiper made short work of Colonel Hermann von Hoffmann, the commander of the 9th Parachute Regiment. Hoffmann, who had spent most of the war in the Air Ministry, outranked him, but Peiper, who was an SS officer with the Knight's Cross with Oak Leaves and a favorite of the Fuehrer, carried much more weight, and they both knew it. Peiper listened as the colonel told him that the woods ahead were full of Americans in pillboxes, covered by minefields and automatic weapons. Peiper asked if the colonel had seen them himself. No, but he had received a report to this effect from one of his battalion commanders. Peiper investigated. The battalion commander had not seen the Americans himself but had received the intelligence report from a company commander. Then he discovered that the company commander had not personally reconnoitered the area either, but had accepted the word of some of his inexperienced men. Completely disgusted, Peiper demanded and got the regiment attached to his battle group; it would support the night attack that he was about to launch on Buchholz Station. The attack took place before 4 A.M. on Sunday, December 17. Resistance was light; Buchholz was a walkover.

About all that initially stood in Peiper's way at this moment were some odds and ends of various American units and part of Colonel Mark Devine's 14th Cavalry Group (18th and 32nd Squadrons)—1,500 men in all, equipped with armored cars, half-tracks, 17 light Stuart tanks, and six 75mm assault guns. (The Stuart, incidentally, was a good reconnaissance vehicle but was next to useless in a tank battle against German panzers. For this reason, throughout this book, the author counts only Shermans and not Stuarts when taking account of U.S. tank strength.) To the American rear and scattered all over the map lay the four battalions of Colonel Wallis Anderson's U.S. 1111th Engineer Combat Group, which would make life much more difficult for Peiper than would the routed and demoralized cavalry group.

Figure 4.1
KG Peiper's Advance

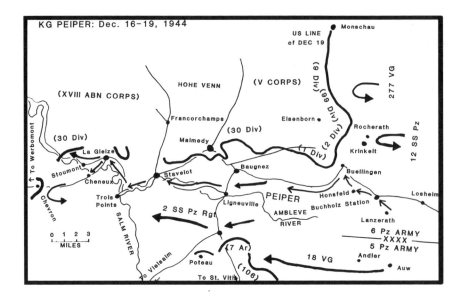

For Peiper, the next objective was the town on Honsfeld. It was garrisoned primarily by service units of the U.S. 99th Infantry Division, which provided amenities (such as hot showers and food) for frontline troops who had temporarily been given a break. After the offensive began, an American captain had created an ad hoc rifle company to defend the town. It was made up of service troops and stragglers, as well as a few antitank troops from the 14th Cavalry Group.

Heading west toward Honsfeld, Peiper found the roads filled with retreating U.S. Army vehicles, also heading west. Peiper simply fell in behind one of these columns and entered Honsfeld with the Americans, passing by two tank destroyers, which were not manned. When they realized that the kampfgruppe was among them, the U.S. soldiers scattered. Peiper captured 50 reconnaissance vehicles, half-tracks, and trucks, along with 15 or 16 tank destroyers.[8] He turned the town over to the commander of the I Battalion, 9th Parachute, along with about 150 prisoners, and told him to mop up and await orders from his own regiment. (The 9th Parachute, meanwhile, took dozens of other prisoners.) Peiper retained about a battalion of paratroopers, however, and used them as infantry in support of his tanks. He was now on his own, in the forefront of the 6th Panzer Army. Figure 4.1 shows the route of Peiper's advance.

After Peiper left Honsfeld, a second SS echelon arrived. One SS officer lined up eight prisoners (some of whom were barefoot and in their underwear) and had them shot. Another group shot four American soldiers and ran over a fifth with a tank. One young girl volunteered to guide the SS to their next objective, the village of Buellingen. The SS apparently suspected she was trying to deceive them. They shot her seven times in the back.

Peiper's orders now dictated that he travel due west over bad secondary roads toward Schoppen; however, he was almost out of gas, so he took the road north to Buellingen, even though it was in the zone of the 12th SS Panzer Division. (The road assignments in the zone of the 6th Panzer Army were directional only; division commanders were at liberty to take other routes, if they considered it appropriate.)[9] The Quartermaster Company of the U.S. 2nd Infantry Division was lining up for breakfast when Peiper appeared, seemingly out of nowhere. Meeting almost no resistance, he quickly overran the small American garrison, destroyed 12 American artillery spotter and liaison airplanes on the ground, and captured more than 70 prisoners and about 50,000 gallons of gasoline. He ordered his prisoners to fill his tanks and then pushed on again, to the west.[10]

Meanwhile, at the Headquarters of the 1st U.S. Army in Spa, General Courtney Hodges had been unperturbed on the first day of the Battle of the Bulge. It took some time for the news of the offensive to reach him. When it did, he assumed that it was a diversionary attack, designed to draw him away from his Roer River offensive. Bradley also showed no undue concern, thinking that the German offensive would soon peter out because of a lack of resources. Major General Gerow, the commander of the V Corps, was not as sanguine as his superiors. On December 16, he had asked Hodges's permission to deal with the crisis in his sector as he saw fit. Hodges did not initially agree but gradually began to realize that the Ardennes Offensive was not a diversion. During the night of December 16–17, acting on orders from General Eisenhower, he assigned the 1st Infantry Division (then resting behind the front at Aachen) to the V Corps and, just before dawn on December 17, agreed to let Gerow act on his own initiative. General Gerow immediately cancelled the U.S. 2nd Infantry Division's attack toward Wahlerscheid.

Leonard T. Gerow was a Southern officer and gentleman who had been raised in the traditions of General Robert E. Lee, perhaps the most brilliant commander in American history. In 1862, Lee won one of his many victories by deliberately falling back to Marye's Heights, south of Fredericksburg, Virginia, from whence he slaughtered the vastly superior forces of his less-astute opponents with relative ease. Gerow now imitated that strategy. His Marye's Heights was Elsenborn Ridge, a very strong position about six miles behind the present front. Gerow's position, however, was even more difficult than that faced by Lee in 1862, because he had to first extricate 18 intermingled infantry battalions, some of which were in danger of being cut off.

Gerow temporarily placed Major General Walter M. Robertson in charge of both the 2nd and 99th Infantry Divisions, while he sorted out logistical problems, reinforcements, and organized the defense of Elsenborn Ridge.[11] He also had to guard against the possibility that Colonel Peiper (who was somewhere beyond his right flank) would turn north. (One of Peiper's reconnaissance companies did push to within 600 yards of the 2nd Division's Command Post before it was driven off by an infantry battalion.)

Colonel Wilhelm Viebig's 277th Volksgrenadier Division had been given the task of capturing the twin towns, but its mission exceeded its strength.[12] Strangely enough, Sepp Dietrich, the least capable of the senior German commanders, realized this even before the battle began. He appealed to Hitler to let him lead the advance with his armor. The Fuehrer overruled his former bodyguard and insisted that the infantry spearhead the attack. This decision not only led to heavy losses in the inexperienced people's grenadier units but also resulted in unnecessary traffic congestion and massive traffic jams.

It is interesting to speculate what might have happened had Dietrich gotten his way. The Panthers and SS panzer grenadiers would almost certainly have gained more ground than the inexperienced infantry and quite possibly would have captured the vital Elsenborn Ridge before the Americans manned it. Had they done so, the battle would have developed much differently than it did, and the northern shoulder of the German offensive might not have been blocked. Without the infantry clogging the roads with their horse-drawn vehicles, the Germans might have been able to get their fuel trucks to their panzers, 6th Panzer Army's advance might not have stalled out, and Army Group B's offensive might not have been channelized so quickly, despite Eisenhower's incredibly rapid reaction. From there, anything is possible, but history is full of interesting "might have beens." Figure 4.2 shows the Battle of Elsenborn Ridge as it actually developed.

Robertson, the soft-spoken, highly competent commander of the U.S. 2nd Infantry Division, executed a brilliant retrograde, leap-frogging his battalions back toward the twin towns of Rocherath and Krinkelt, in spite of attacks from the 277th and 12th Volksgrenadier Divisions. Losses on both sides were severe, and a great many American vehicles became stuck in the mud and had to be abandoned. The U.S. 394th Infantry Regiment was smashed by the 12th Volksgrenadier, and a battalion of the 38th Infantry Regiment was "practically annihilated" by the 277th VG.[13]

General Robertson nevertheless pulled it off, partially because the inexperienced men of the U.S. 99th Infantry Division fought much better than anyone expected. Dietrich, for example, threw the veteran 12th Volksgrenadier against it near Losheimergraben, an important road junction on the southern flank of the V Corps line. The 12th was considered the

Figure 4.2
Elsenborn Ridge

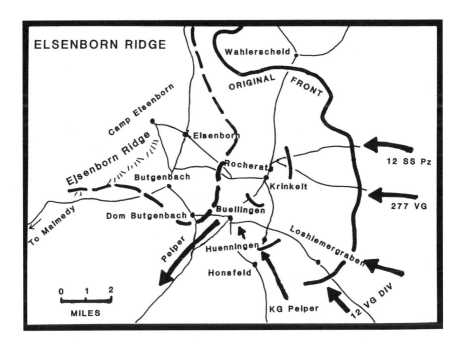

best infantry division in the 6th Panzer Army, and it was well led by Major General Gerhard Engel, Hitler's former adjutant, but it could only gain a quarter of a mile against the stubborn 99th, which turned it back in heavy, close-quarter fighting.[14]

Early in the afternoon, because of the heavy casualties in his assault divisions, Dietrich decided to commit armor in the form of SS Colonel Hugo Kraas's 12th SS Panzer Division against Robertson's northern flank, although a breakthrough had not yet been achieved.[15] Most of the tanks of the SS Panzer Division "Hitler Youth" were promptly bogged down in the mud, but the young panzer grenadiers managed to push the Americans back, and the entire V Corps position was in danger when night fell. During the night of December 17–18, tanks from the 12th SS (now extricated from the mud) broke through the U.S. line and pushed into Krinkelt, only to be expelled by a hasty counterattack. The following morning, Tigers from the 12th SS pushed into Rocherath, only to be repulsed by artillery fire from Elsenborn Ridge, by bazooka fire and men hurling antitank mines, and by Americans who poured gasoline on the tanks and then set them on fire. The 12th SS Panzer Division "Hitler Youth" lost 67 of its 136 tanks in the first three days of the battles for Krinkelt and Rocherath. The fighting was fierce and, because the American soldiers had heard that the SS were shooting captives, few prisoners were taken by either side.

American casualties were also heavy. The U.S. 393rd Infantry Regiment of the 99th Infantry Division, for example, lost 1,357 men, the 394th Infantry Regiment lost 1,198 men, and the 395th Infantry Regiment lost 422 men. The Table of Organization and Equipment (TOE) strength of a U.S. infantry regiment was 3,163 men. The 1st Battalion of the 393rd was especially hard hit and lost 72 percent of its men.[16]

By nightfall on December 18, however, General Robertson had completed his complicated maneuver, and Army Group B had ordered Dietrich to abandon his tank attacks on the twin towns. During the night of December 18, despite the protests of General Priess, he swung the Hitler Youth Division to the south, in an attempt to reach the Malmedy road. This maneuver also failed because the U.S. 1st Infantry Division had arrived by now and blocked this route.

With the 12th SS Division withdrawn from his front, Robertson completed the withdrawal to Elsenborn Ridge on December 19 with few difficulties. Meanwhile, Hodges had again reinforced Gerow, this time with the veteran U.S. 9th Infantry Division, one of the best units in the American army. Losses had been high but, with the 1st, 2nd, 9th, and 99th Infantry Divisions on and around Elsenborn Ridge, the northern shoulder of the front was secure.

The 6th Panzer Army had five major routes of advance, which were called *Rollbahnen.* Rollbahn A was on the north and Rollbahn E was the southernmost route of advance of 6th Panzer Army. Gerow's stand effectively blocked Rollbahnen A, B, and C. Peiper was advancing along Rollbahn D. Figure 4.3 shows the main march routes to the Meuse for all of Army Group B.

Hitler naturally could not resist reinforcing failure. He sent Major General Walter Denkett's 3rd Panzer Grenadier Division into action at Rocherath-Krinkelt on December 19, but it was also turned back. North of the twin towns, Lieutenant General Otto Hitzfeld's LXVII Corps launched weak attacks with Lieutenant General Eugen Koenig's 272nd Volksgrenadier Division and Colonel Erwin Kaschner's 326th VG Division. These were relatively easily defeated. Hitler also tried to commit the II SS Panzer Corps to the south, but the advance stalled for lack of fuel before the SS men could even reach the battlefield.

The 6th Panzer Army continued to attack it for days, but only succeeded in lengthening its casualty lists. Gerow easily turned back every attack, just as the Master had done at Fredericksburg in 1862. Robert E. Lee would have been proud of him.

And what had happened to the paratroop drop, which had been designed to delay the American reinforcements, coming down from the north?

Figure 4.3
Main March Routes to the Meuse

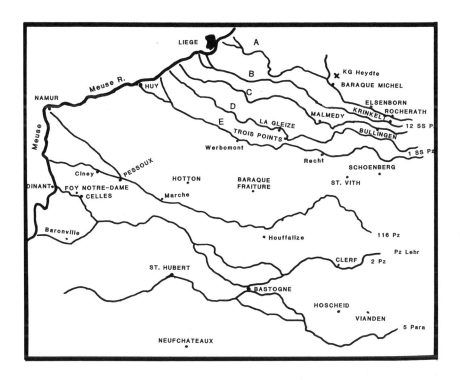

As we have read, Baron von der Heydte's kampfgruppe had been unable to jump on schedule during the night of December 15–16, because the trucks slated to carry it to the airfields had failed to arrive because they had no gas. During the following day, word came through from 6th Panzer Army that the attack had not gone as expected; the drop was rescheduled for the same place on the night of December 16–17, in spite of terrible weather conditions. Heydte was very concerned. The wind velocity was reported at 20 feet per second—barely within tolerance—and the colonel suspected the report was erroneous. He was right. The velocity was actually 50 feet per second—far too high for a night jump into a forest.

The operation ran into problems almost immediately. Most of the experienced jumpmasters of 1940 and 1941 had been killed or captured in Crete, Normandy, Brest, or on the Russian Front. (Germany had no jumpmasters with experience in night combat jumps, because this was its first [and only] nighttime combat jump of the war.) The inexperienced jumpmasters, who did not realize the strength of the headwinds the Junkers were bucking, gave the order to jump according to the clock. About 200 men landed in the Bonn area, well behind German lines. When the other airplanes crossed Allied lines, they were met by a hail of antiaircraft fire. Several airplanes were shot down and the formations were scattered.[17]

At 3 A.M. on December 17, Colonel Heydte jumped at exactly the right place, but only 10 of his 111 remaining Ju-52s and Ju-88s followed suit. Upon reaching his assembly point at 3:50 A.M., Heydte found only six men. An hour later, only 20 more had shown up. The colonel knew that the drop had failed. In all, only 35 airplanes had dropped their paratroopers in the Hohe Venn sector—300 men in all. Heydte could only assemble 150 of them. They could do little other than spread alarm in the American rear and capture an occasional solitary message carrier and a few light vehicles. (He captured more than 30 Americans in this manner.) Realizing that he could not possibly hold the vital road junction with so few men, Heydte hid his command nearby and awaited the arrival of the panzers. It was a frustrating wait. For five days he watched three fresh American divisions roll passed, on their way to stem the German tide. At one point, a U.S. motorized column from the 26th Infantry Regiment, 1st Infantry Division, spotted Heydte and some of his men. They waved, and the Germans waved back. The Americans continued on their way without slowing down or firing a shot—they had bigger fish to fry elsewhere. Heydte's troops, however, accomplished more than they knew. Not knowing KG Heydte's true situation or strength, and possibly fearing more parachute drops, the U.S. V Corps was forced to keep the U.S. 18th Infantry Regiment of the 1st Infantry Division (3,000 men) and CCA of the 3rd Armored Division (thousands of men and about 100 tanks) in the Eupen area, to protect its rear from German paratroopers, despite the fact that they were needed at the front. They remained there until December 20. Then they came looking for Heydte and his men.

KG Heydte might have done some more good for the Reich by informing Model about the fresh American reinforcements heading for the front, except for the fact that it had lost all of its radios in the initial drop. The entire signals detachment had landed in front of surprised German grenadiers near Monschau, and they were indeed fortunate that they were not shot by their own comrades. No doubt Heydte bitterly recalled Dietrich's answer when he had asked for carrier pigeons. Regardless, neither 6th Panzer Army nor Army Group B had any clue as to what had happened to Heydte and his men. As far as higher headquarters were concerned, they had simply disappeared.

Finally, on the morning of December 20, an American battle group, supported by tanks, arrived in the area. It was obvious that they were looking for paratroopers. Heydte decided he could wait no longer. About noon, he freed his prisoners after entrusting them with his own wounded and injured, disbanded his command, ordered the men to break into groups of three, and to try to make their way back to German lines. About a third of them (around 100 men) actually made it.

Baron von der Heydte himself was in poor shape. In an earlier training accident, he had shattered his left forearm and injured his right arm, and neither had healed. He nevertheless set out with his second-in-command and a dispatch runner. They slept in the forests during the day and hiked toward Monschau, at the northern end of the Ardennes, during the night. Dietrich was supposed to have captured the town during the first day of the offensive. Heydte had no way of knowing that it was still in American hands. After they reached the outskirts of the town and learned the true situation, the Baron decided that he could go no further. He sent his two comrades on their way, while he limped into Monschau and entered one of the first houses. The family was sympathetic to Germany and the son of the house was proud of his Hitler Youth uniform. Heydte was unimpressed. He sent a note to the American commander in the town (part of the 395th Infantry Regiment), stating that he wished to surrender.

This ended the last German airborne operation of the war.

In the meantime, American generals and operations officers guessed that, in spite of the relatively good roads radiating out of Malmedy, the greater threat was St. Vith. They ordered it reinforced with parts of the 7th Armored Division, which were until then driving to join the 106th Infantry Division. This left only Lieutenant Colonel David E. Pergrin's 291st Engineer Combat Battalion to hold Malmedy. He immediately set up roadblocks along several routes and at the major intersections in the villages of Ambleve, La Gleize, Stavelot, and Trois Ponts.

Feeling very isolated (as indeed he was), Colonel Pergrin begged passing units to stop and help him defend the town. The 38th Armored Infantry Battalion (of Combat Command B, CCB, 7th Armored Division), among others, refused and continued on to St. Vith. Battery B of the 285th Field Artillery Observation Battalion also stopped and conferred with Pergrin but decided to continue on to St. Vith. Pergrin warned them to take a different route because German tanks had been spotted nearby. They ignored him.

At noon on December 17, while the bulk of the 6th Panzer Army was stalled in the Elsenborn Ridge sector, SS Colonel Peiper's kampfgruppe approached Baugnez, a six-house hamlet less than two miles from Malmedy, with SS Major Josef Diefenthal's III/2nd Panzer Grenadier Regiment at the point. Had he arrived a short time before, he would have barreled straight into Combat Command R (CCR) of 7th Armored Division, and the entire course of the battle might have developed differently. As it was, however, Peiper ran into Battery B of the 285th Artillery. As soon as they saw Battery B, the SS opened fire. Confusion and panic broke out in the American ranks. Vehicles were abandoned in the middle of the road, and some of the men ran into a nearby woods, from which they eventually made good their escape. Others took cover in the ditches, where they were captured by the SS men. In all, more than 150 men were taken prisoner. They were gathered in a field south of Baugnez, where, without warning, they were fired upon by the SS. The first to fire was SS Private First Class Georg Fleps (of the 7th Company, 1st SS Panzer Regiment), a *Volksdeutsch* (racial German) whose family had left Swabia for the Seven Mountains region of Rumania in the Middle Ages. (Many of the Volksdeutsche SS were more fanatical than the native born Germans—or "more Catholic than the Pope," as the Europeans say.) His shots signaled the beginning of the "Malmedy Massacre." The SS were seized with what author Charles Whiting later described as an "atavistic fury." The Germans called this type of frenzy *Blutrausch* (roughly translatable as "an intoxication of the blood"). Some of the running Americans reached the nearby woods and escaped. Others escaped by feigning death. Those who were caught playing dead were shot through the head with pistols or machine pistols. In all, 72 men were fatally wounded. Another 14 were hunted down and killed in the immediate vicinity.

This was not the only atrocity that was laid at the door of Peiper and his men. According to the U.S. Official History, they murdered approximately 300 American POWs and at least 100 Belgian civilians in 12 separate incidents during the Battle of the Bulge.[18] Both of these figures appear to be conservative. Even the mothers of German soldiers were not spared. Madame Adel Bodarwe, a widow whose son had been drafted into the German Army, operated a small cafe almost at the sight of the massacre. She witnessed the atrocity and disappeared that same day. She has not been heard from since.

About 2:30 P.M., approximately an hour and a half after the murders, a patrol from the U.S. 291st Engineers discovered the bodies, and news of the atrocity spread through American ranks like wildfire. Surrender now became a risky business for any German, but especially so for members of the SS. There had been incidents of SS men shooting their prisoners in Normandy, and many SS prisoners had already been shot as a result; the Canadians and SS seem to have been particularly keen on shooting each other after they surrendered, but, after Malmedy, American atrocities against SS prisoners increased markedly.

History has not proven beyond a shadow of a doubt that Colonel Peiper ordered or sanctioned the murders, but he had been at the site shortly before the shooting began. He was not present when the crime was carried out and, after the war, some apologists have suggested that Peiper was not aware that his men were shooting prisoners. This may be true, but I seriously doubt it. The 1st SS Panzer Regiment was too disciplined a unit to commit a dozen atrocities without its commander being aware of it and at least acquiescing to it. One or two I could perhaps believe, but a dozen or more? No. The SS simply did not work that way.

From Baugnez, the road led straight down a steep hill to the town of Malmedy, two miles away. The southern fork of the road, however, turned sharply to the left, toward Ligneuville and St. Vith, one of the major road and railroad junctions in the Ardennes. Peiper's objective was Ligneuville, so he bypassed Malmedy. From Ligneuville, he was to turn off and begin the steep climb westward, up a third-class road to the town of Stavelot and the bridge across the Ambleve, the first water barrier on his way to the Meuse. Peiper attacked Ligneuville at 2 P.M. The town was defended by elements of the U.S. 14th Tank Battalion—mostly service units—some anti-aircraft gunners and a handful of supply troops from the 9th Armored Division. The Americans nevertheless put up stiff resistance and knocked out a Panther, severely burning Peiper's good friend, SS Lieutenant Arndt Fischer, in the process. The SS knocked out two Shermans (which had been left with a maintenance unit and were undergoing repairs) and an assault gun.

Ligneuville was the site of the headquarters of U.S. Brigadier General Edward W. Timberlake's 49th Anti-Aircraft Brigade. Timberlake was in the middle of lunch in the Hotel du Moulin when Peiper surprised him. There was panic in the hotel, and Timberlake and his staff barely had time to flee in the direction of Vielsalm; they even left their war maps behind. Peiper, however, was disappointed. He later complained that he was late and only managed to capture their lunch.

The SS shot up several American supply trucks as they left Ligneuville and took at least 22 prisoners. Shortly thereafter, SS Sergeant Paul Ochmann of Peiper's headquarters company marched eight American POWs from the 843rd Tank Battalion into the middle of the village street, where he shot them with his machine pistol.

Meanwhile, south of Malmedy, on Peiper's left flank, the Fuehrer Begleit Brigade and elements of the 18th Volksgrenadier Division forced back the remnants of the U.S. 14th Cavalry Group, freeing Peiper's left.

That evening, Colonel Peiper approached Stavelot, a medieval town of some 5,000 people. Located in the valley of the Ambleve, it was surrounded by high, sparsely wooded cliffs. Most of the town was located on the northern bank, but a single row of houses was located on the southern bank. On the last bend of the road before Stavelot, the lead panzer hit a mine and was knocked out. (Some sources say that it was hit by a bazooka round.) Through his field glasses, Peiper could see American trucks. They were members of a supply unit of the 7th Armored Division and were heading for St. Vith, but Peiper did not know that. Stavelot was virtually undefended. Thinking that the town was full of Americans, Peiper halted his advance and sent a panzer company to scout the road south of the Ambleve to the bridge at Trois Ponts. If he could take that bridge, he would not need the one at Stavelot.

By this time, Peiper was nearing exhaustion. He had not slept for 40 hours. Perhaps this was the reason behind his decision to try to take the bridge at Trois Ponts via a secondary road first, and then to attack Stavelot the following morning if that failed. In any case, it turned out to be a fatal decision. Peiper went to bed, and the rest of the regiment followed his example and fell asleep almost instantly. Many of the SS men had not slept in three days. Little did Peiper dream that Stavelot was his for the taking. The only combat unit in the town was a single squad of the 291st Engineer Combat Battalion (13 men!), and it was not yet prepared to blow the bridge. Trois Ponts was also vulnerable at that moment, but not by the secondary road, as Peiper had hoped. It was impassable to tanks. He would have to attack through Stavelot.

During the night, Colonel Pergrin reinforced Stavelot with other elements of his U.S. 291st Engineer Combat Battalion, as well as parts of the 202nd and 51st Engineer Combat Battalions, a tank destroyer (TD) platoon, and some armored infantry. The engineers, meanwhile, rigged the bridge for demolition.

That same day, December 17, Manteuffel, Dietrich, and a group of their officers met at Manderfeld, the headquarters of the I SS Panzer Corps (and the former command post of the U.S. 14th Cavalry Group). They decided to abandon the idea of driving to the Meuse in one fell swoop. Operation Grief, Skorzeny's reckless thrust to the river, was cancelled, because the mass panic it needed to succeed simply was not present. Skorzeny therefore recommended that Dietrich renounce his original plan of using the 150th Panzer to seize the Meuse crossing and employ the brigade as a regular tank unit. Dietrich agreed. The most important part of Operation Grief was over before it had begun.

In the other part of Operation Grief, the commando teams of the Einheit Steilau were almost unbelievably successful in spreading confusion, fear, and panic in the American rear. Skorzeny estimated that six to eight of his nine teams successfully made their way behind U.S. lines, and they did damage out of all proportion to their numbers. One team switched road signs and sent an entire American regiment rushing in the wrong direction. Others blocked off key road junctions and thoroughly disrupted traffic simply by using white tape—the engineers' standard warning for minefields. One team member told an American officer such a horrifying tale of German successes just down the road that he abandoned the town he was holding. Two groups were caught: one after it had reached the Meuse, the other near Liege. Even then they continued to do damage. Under interrogation, one member "revealed" that Skorzeny and a special commando party were on their way to Paris. There they would rendezvous at the famous Cafe de la Paix and proceed to SHAEF

Headquarters at Versailles, where they would assassinate Dwight D. Eisenhower himself! General Eisenhower was virtually held prisoner by his own security people for the next few days while they tried to chase down Skorzeny, who was not even in the same country as Ike.

Elsewhere, the Americans developed their own code system, by which they asked questions no German was likely to know, such as who won the World Series, what was the name of Mickey Mouse's girlfriend, or what was the name of Li'l Abner's hometown. One American brigadier general (Bruce C. Clarke) incorrectly stated that the Chicago Cubs baseball team was in the American League and was held in custody for five hours. The American Military Police (MPs) who held him ignored his pleas, informing him that only a Kraut would make a mistake like that!

Not even British Field Marshal Montgomery was exempt from the new system. He was halted by an U.S. guard, but arrogantly told the young man that he would not put up with such nonsense, and ordered his driver to proceed, regardless of what the guard said. As his car began to speed away, the angry guard opened fire and shot out his tires. Naturally, General Eisenhower got a great deal of pleasure from the incident and even went so far as to proclaim that this was the best thing for which Skorzeny had ever been responsible.

The captured commandos, of course, were executed as spies. Before their executions, one team had a last request. They wanted to hear a group of captured German nurses, who were being held in a nearby cell, sing Christmas carols. The request was granted. They were shot the next day. Their last words (spoken by Gunter Billing) were "Es lebe unser Fuehrer, Adolf Hitler" (Long live our Fuehrer, Adolf Hitler).

Meanwhile, on December 17, Eisenhower released the 101st and 82nd Airborne Divisions for use in the Ardennes. The next day, General Hodges ordered the U.S. 30th Infantry Division, which had been resting in the Aachen sector, into the area, and Eisenhower sent the headquarters of the U.S. XVIII Airborne Corps from England to Belgium and placed it at the disposal of Hodges. The American generals were particularly concerned that Stavelot and Malmedy not be lost. If they fell, the Germans would be in a position to capture the Headquarters of the 1st U.S. Army, as well as 2.5 million gallons of fuel, lying in the fur forests between Spa and Ambleve.

CHAPTER 5

The Destruction of KG Peiper

Shortly after midnight on December 18, Peiper received word from one of Skorzeny's commandos (a naval lieutenant) that the main body of the 1st SS Panzer Division was bogged down in the mud of the Ardennes forests. They had taken secondary roads that could not accommodate heavy tanks; in addition, they were meeting heavy resistance everywhere. Peiper could expect no reinforcements that day or for the foreseeable future. The SS colonel had already been experiencing a sense of loneliness, because both his flanks and rear were badly exposed. Now he felt a sense of defeat, as if the big offensive had already failed.

During the night of December 17–18, the Americans reinforced Stavelot with a task force from the U.S. 526th Armored Infantry Battalion under Major Paul Solis, as well as several engineer units (Chapter IV). The 526th included two platoons of towed 3-inch antitank guns, three 57mm AT guns, and a few Sherman tanks. Peiper attacked just before dawn with the Panthers of 1st Company, 1st SS Panzer Regiment (1/1st SS Panzer), followed by Captain Josef Diefenthal's III Battalion, 2nd SS Panzer Grenadier Regiment (III/2nd SS Panzer Grenadier). Lieutenant Krenser, the commander of the 1st Company, was badly wounded almost immediately. Peiper replaced him with Lieutenant Hennecke and continued the advance. Hennecke ordered his first two panzers to rush the bridge at full speed. The lead tank was hit by a Sherman, but its momentum was so great that it barreled through the antitank obstacle in front of the bridge and careened into two Shermans, damaging them both. The burning Panther then came to rest; every member of the crew was dead.

Meanwhile, the second Panther roared over the bridge, followed by the panzer grenadiers and the rest of Hennecke's panzers. The Americans engineers pushed their detonators, but nothing happened. This failure was later attributed to two strangers in U.S. uniforms who assisted in placing the charges. They were apparently from Skorzeny's commandos and were there to sabotage the detonation mechanism. In any case, the SS took the bridge intact. The Americans abandoned their antitank guns and pulled back to the center of the town, where a wild fight began. It was almost 10 A.M. before the German spearhead was through Stavelot. Because speed was essential, Peiper decided not to wait until all of the resistance at Stavelot had been mopped up before proceeding, in spite of the jam in his rear. Hoping that the 3rd Parachute Division would soon arrive in Stavelot, he headed west, toward Trois Ponts.

It should be noted here that the 30-ton M-4 Sherman—the main battle tank of the United States Army—was distinctly inferior to the German Panther. Its 75mm main battle gun was of relatively low velocity and could not penetrate the armor of the Panther or the Tiger. On the other hand, the Tiger, Panther, and Panzer Mark IV (PzKw IV) could pierce its frontal armor, and the Sherman had an unfortunate tendency to catch on fire when hit, earning it the nickname "Ronson," after a popular cigarette lighter of the day. It also had a high silhouette, making it much easier to spot and hit than a German assault gun. On the other hand, it was much more mechanically reliable than the Tiger. It was also easier to mass produce, and its numerical superiority turned the tide in more than one battle. Each U.S. armored division had a TOE strength of 186 Shermans, and even American infantry divisions had a TOE strength of 53. In late 1944, most American divisions were at their full TOE strength in tanks, which was not the case with the German Army.

The most numerous German tank on the Western Front was the PzKw IV, which had been in production since 1940 and was a workhorse. It was mechanically reliable and had a high velocity 75mm gun, which was superior to the Sherman's gun. It was, however, lighter than the Sherman (weighing 23 to 25 tons, depending on the model) and was generally considered only slightly better than the American M-4.

The overall best tank of the war was the PzKw V Panther. It weighed 45 tons, was highly maneuverable, and had a very effective 75mm main battle gun. It was also very dependable mechanically.

The famous PzKw VI Tiger tank threw fear into American ranks because it was both huge and deadly. A typical Tiger weighed 60 to 62 tons, although the Tiger II (*Koenigstiger* or King Tiger) weighed up to 72 tons. The Tiger fired a deadly 88mm gun and had extremely thick armor. Unless a Sherman could hit it from the rear, American shells usually just bounced off the Tiger. The PzKw VI, however, had some serious drawbacks. It was slow, underpowered, had poor maneuverability, and weighed so much that few bridges could support it. It was also mechanically unsound. Even in this, the fifth year of the war, more Tigers were lost to mechanical breakdowns than to combat damage. Equally serious in the Battle of the Bulge was its awful fuel economy. The Wehrmacht lost more Tigers in the final stages of the battle to empty gas tanks than to American attacks—ground or air. They simply ran out of fuel and had to be abandoned.

Shortly after Peiper left Stavelot, what was left of Major Solis's American task force withdrew along the Malmedy Road, toward Fuel Depot Number 3, the gas dump at Francorchamps, about two miles north of Stavelot. Peiper bypassed it because he did not know it was there. In some written accounts, and in a popular movie, the Americans at Francorchamps destroyed Peiper's tanks by rolling barrels of fuel on them. This never happened. It makes for a pretty good movie, though.

In the meantime, the SS committed another atrocity at Stavelot. Apparently one or more civilians fired on some SS men near the town, and a group of Belgians, armed with shotguns, did threaten SS Corporal Edmund Tomczak, who had been wounded and temporarily captured. Although the SS would have been perfectly justified—both morally and legally—in executing the shotgun-carrying civilians, there is no excuse for what happened next. They took out 130 civilians and shot them. The dead included 60 men, 47 women, and 23 children. The oldest was 78; the youngest was a nine-month-old baby. When one of the condemned women cried and protested that they were only innocent civilians, one of the SS men shrugged his shoulders and said: "The innocent must pay for those who are guilty. The people of Stavelot have been harboring American soldiers."[1]

Trois Ponts got its name from its two bridges over the Salm River and one over the Ambleve. If Peiper could seize these bridges, he would have an almost unobstructed path to the Meuse. The village was defended by elements of the U.S. 51st Engineer Battalion under Major Robert Yates, plus a 57mm antitank gun and crew, and stragglers from the U.S. 7th Armored Division. Yates had 120 engineers, armed with eight bazookas and four 50-caliber heavy machine guns.

Just before noon, the vanguard of KG Peiper arrived with 19 Panthers. The SS engineers cleared the mines the Americans had laid and the tanks pushed forward. The 57mm gun knocked a track off of the first Panther, but the second scored a direct hit on the gun, killing its entire crew. As the SS men neared the bridge, however, the Americans blew it up in their faces.

Peiper was furious. "Those damned engineers! Those damned engineers!" he cried again and again. "If we had captured the bridge at Trois Ponts intact and had had enough fuel," he declared later, "it would have been a simple matter to drive through to the Meuse River early that day."[2] He realized now that there was only one possible route available to him: the road to the right, leading through the steep gorges of the Ambleve to the mountain village of La Gleize, where he hoped the bridges were strong enough to bear the 72 tons of his Royal Tigers. He did not know it, but he was driving into a trap from which most of his command would not escape.

On the morning of December 18, Peiper's latest advance caused a near panic at the Headquarters of the 1st U.S. Army, when it was learned that an unidentified German armored column had broken through Stavelot and was now heading in the general direction of Spa. General Hodges, who at the time was meeting with General Gavin, had originally planned to use the 82nd Airborne at Houffalize, to fill the gap between St. Vith and Bastogne. Now he ordered Gavin to concentrate his division in the vicinity of Werbomont, to stop the German panzer force from heading west down the valley of the Ambleve toward the Meuse. Then Hodges abandoned the town of Spa and moved his headquarters to the Hotel des Bains in Chaudfontaine (near Liege), 15 miles farther to the rear.

That afternoon, Peiper advanced down the winding, hilly road through La Gleize, a village of small stone houses, grouped around a little church. The most prominent building was the Chateau du Froide Cour. Meanwhile, in spite of the poor weather, P-47 Thunderbolts from the U.S. 365th Fighter Group appeared and strafed and bombed Peiper's entire column, which was now 20 miles long, with machine guns and 500-pound bombs. Much of the column was trapped on the winding mountain roads and the troops, especially those who had only served in Russia (and that was many of them), were badly shaken.

The bombing cost Peiper two hours and 10 vehicles. Angry and impatient, he got the column moving again, toward Werbomont, five or six miles away. He hoped to find the bridge at the hamlet of Neufmoulin intact.

The Neufmoulin bridge crossed the small but unfordable Lienne River. At nightfall, just as Peiper arrived, a detachment from the U.S. 291st Engineer Battalion blew it sky high. Peiper had no choice but to return the way he came. In the growing darkness, a small column of half-tracks from the 2nd SS Panzer Grenadier Regiment found an intact bridge that could handle Tiger tanks. The column pushed up the road, only to run into an American ambush, set by the newly arrived 2nd Battalion, 119th Infantry Regiment (30th Infantry Division), which was led by Major Hal McCown. They knocked out five half-tracks, and the survivors retreated the way they had come.

Meanwhile, another battalion of the 30th Infantry Division (1/117th Infantry Regiment) arrived on the battlefield and immediately attacked Stavelot, despite the fact that it had no artillery support. It did, however, have a platoon of towed 3-inch antitank guns and the support of Jabos from the U.S. IX Tactical Air Command. By evening, the Americans had taken all of the town except the vital bridge. It was defended by the 2nd Company of the I Battalion/2nd SS Panzer Grenadier Regiment (KG Sandig) and a single Tiger, which defied every effort to knock it out.

Peiper had left only a small rearguard at Stavelot because he believed that the 3rd Parachute Division would close up rapidly and protect his rear, but it did not. He was now in serious trouble. KG Peiper was now virtually surrounded in La Gleize. In and around the village, he had an intact battalion of Panzer IVs and Panthers, supported by SS Major Diefenthal's grenadiers. A short distance to his rear, he had a battalion of Tigers, a motorized anti-aircraft battalion, and a battery of 105mm self-propelled guns. In all, he had about 3,000 men and 200 armored vehicles.

On the morning of December 19, there was fighting in the Ambeleve sector from one end to the other. The Americans at Stavelot had at last taken the vital bridge, severing the lifeline of KG Peiper. At noon, SS Lieutenant Colonel Rudolf Sandig, the commander of the 2nd SS Panzer Grenadier Regiment, rallied every unit he could get his hands on and launched a desperate counterattack. Six Tiger tanks pushed toward the bridge, while a dozen or so assault boats plunged into the river, 100 yards away. From the heights above the town, a battery of American artillery (which had arrived during the night) blasted the amphibious attack to bits. The Tiger attack was halted when the leading PzKw VI was blown up on the bridge. There were no survivors.

In the meantime, Peiper had learned of the disaster at Stavelot, so he ordered SS Major Gustav Knittel, the commander of the 1st SS Panzer Reconnaissance Battalion, to turn around and recapture the bridge. Simultaneously, KG Sandig would attack from the south. Knittel advanced with light armored vehicles, a few tanks, and some self-propelled artillery. His attack ran into a whirlwind of American artillery fire and was smashed. Knittel lost more than 300 killed, wounded, or missing—more than a third of his force.

On the southern bank of the Ambleve, KG Sandig was also checked with severe losses. The other battle group of the 1st SS Panzer Division, KG Hansen, was far to the rear around Recht and was battling with CCR of the U.S. 7th Armored Division. Mohnke now ordered KG Hansen to advance down Rollbahn E to Trois Points, in another effort to assist Peiper. Hansen turned the battle in the Recht sector over to SS Oberfuehrer Sylvester Stadler's 9th SS Panzer Division, which was far behind schedule and was just now arriving on the battlefield *on foot*. It and the other division of the II SS Panzer Corps, the 2nd SS Panzer Division "Das Reich," ran out of gas before they could reach the front. Without their panzers and assault guns, they would not make much of an impression on the U.S. 7th Armored Division.

While Knittel's attack was being repulsed and with the noose tightening around his command, Peiper was forced to deal with yet another battalion of the U.S. 30th Infantry Division, which had taken the key village of Stoumont, 1.5 miles west-southwest of La Gleize, the day before. Peiper struck just after dawn, spearheaded by three Tigers and screened by a fog that limited visibility to 50 yards. The American defenders broke immediately, uncovering the eight towed antitank guns. The gunners quickly joined the fleeing infantry, and the SS penetrated into the eastern side of the village and captured the AT guns without a fight. In the streets, American bazooka crews knocked out two Tigers but could not stop the attack. By noon Stoumont was in German hands, and the Americans had lost 267 men killed or captured.

Peiper, in the meantime, was looking for a way out of the trap. He knew that if he could capture Targnon, a small town about one mile west of where the Lienne flows into the Ambleve, he could turn southwest onto a fairly good road along the west bank of the Lienne. From here he could perhaps take Chevron and finally be able to break out of the Ambleve Valley. First, however, he would have to oust the Americans from the Stoumont Railroad Station, about a mile from the town, at the end of a steep, curving road.

The station was defended by the U.S. 119th Infantry Regiment and 10 Shermans. Just as the attack began, a company from the 740th Tank Battalion arrived. It surprised the Panthers and knocked out several of them. The German commander withdrew to Stoumont, where Peiper concurred with his actions. He was almost out of fuel and could not waste any more in a tank battle. He now concluded that he no longer had enough fuel to reach the bridges west of Stoumont, so he hedgehogged. He posted the I/lst SS Panzer Regiment at Stoumont, the II/lst SS Panzer Regiment at La Gleize, and elements of the 2nd SS Panzer Grenadier Regiment and the 84th Light Flak Battalion at Cheneux. His five 105mm guns and six 150mm infantry guns were now almost out of ammunition. So were his tanks. Peiper ordered his panzer commanders not to fire on American armored vehicles unless they were fairly certain of scoring a first-round "kill."

In the meantime, Lieutenant General Matthew Ridgway, the commander of the U.S. XVIII Airborne Corps, took charge of the battle. His missions were to block any further advance by KG Peiper and to bridge the 20-mile gap between the U.S. V and VIII Corps. His forces included the 30th Infantry and 82nd Airborne Divisions, plus CCB of the U.S. 3rd Armored Division, which was coming down from the north. His first priority was to surround the SS battle group.

Peiper's situation was desperate. Dietrich's 6th Panzer Army had still not succeeded in broadening the breakthrough sufficiently for the second wave of armor to push ahead, and Gerow continued to hold Elsenborn Ridge, effectively strangling the German offensive in the northern sector.

Early on the morning of Wednesday, December 20, SS Colonel Sandig made another attempt to retake Stavelot. His infantry went forward before dawn, hoping to cross the river before daylight. Elements of the U.S. 743rd Tank Battalion, supported by infantry, fired incendiary shells into the line of houses on the German side of the river, silhouetting the SS men in the stream. They were slaughtered; at least 40 SS were killed.

Sandig ordered direct tank fire on the American positions nearest the river. The American infantrymen, who had given away their positions when they shot up the SS assault force, were forced to give way, and Sandig captured the first row of houses. Then the Americans counterattacked in force and pushed the Germans back across the Ambleve. By 7:30 A.M., the U.S. line on the south side of the river had been reestablished, and Stavelot remained firmly in American hands.

Meanwhile, a task force under the command of Brigadier General William Harrison (the assistant commander of the U.S. 30th Infantry Division) and a task force from the CCB of the U.S. 3rd Armored Division tried to retake Stoumont. The key position in the German defenses was St. Edouard's Sanatorium, the largest building in the town. It was built like a fortress and dominated the main road, just at the edge of the town. The battle raged all day long, but the American attack finally stalled on the slope of the hill, about 200 yards from the Sanatorium, after losing five Sherman tanks and almost 200 men. There, under the cover of fog, two U.S. infantry companies dug in to await nightfall and the next order to attack. Meanwhile, the Shermans from CCB scattered Knittel's reconnaissance battalion and relieved Major Yates's engineers, who had been holding out for three days against the constant efforts of the SS recon troops to penetrate their lines. Yates had less than 100 men left. The American task force continued to push down the Ambleve toward Stavelot, when it ran into an SS ambush. All six Shermans in the point were hit immediately. The SS detachment that sprang the ambush was well dug in and had three heavy tanks and six antitank guns. Seeing the narrow road was blocked by burning Shermans and a determined enemy, the Americans pulled back. Another U.S. task force pushed to within two miles of La Gleize, but it was beaten back by KG Peiper. Although he was now practically immobilized by a lack of fuel, Peiper had served notice that he was not going to give up easily.

Gavin's 82nd Airborne Division joined the battle in strength that day and attacked the I/2nd SS Panzer Grenadier Regiment and 84th Light Flak Battalion at Cheneux, which was located on the Ambleve, southeast of Stoumont. The fighting was bitter and lasted well into the night. Gavin's 504th Gliderborne Infantry Regiment was driven back three times. On the fourth attempt, it established a toehold in Cheneux. That night, the Americans besieging Stoumont launched another attack, and, supported by several Shermans, managed to capture the first floor of the Sanatorium. Just before midnight, the SS in Stoumont launched a desperate counterattack. Yelling, screaming, and firing their weapons wildly, they rushed down the hill to St. Edouard's. Cannon fire from panzers in hidden positions just above the building rocked the Sanatorium, which took hit after hit. The German infantry got near enough to the Shermans to use their Panzerfausts, and soon four American tanks were burning. The rest retreated, leaving the GIs in the Sanatorium without armored support. Then the Tigers attacked. Most of the Americans in the building surrendered, although a few managed to escape.

Early on the afternoon of December 20, Oberfuehrer Mohnke at last came up and managed to cross the Ambleve between Trois Ponts and Stavelot. His main unit, SS Colonel Max Hansen's 1st SS Panzer Grenadier Regiment, took advantage of fog and crossed at Petit-Spai. The 1st SS Panzer Engineer Battalion quickly threw a light bridge across the river, and Mohnke's remaining panzers began to cross.

To Hansen's front lay the U.S. 505th Parachute Infantry Regiment, waiting for the SS in snow-filled foxholes. They were supported by about 40 Sherman tanks from the CCB. Hansen's attack pushed forward with great determination and forced the Americans to retreat with severe casualties. Then, suddenly, the bridge Mohnke was using to get his armor across the river collapsed after only a handful of tanks had crossed. Frantically he called for his combat engineers, who were soon working in waist-deep freezing water. Then the U.S. artillery opened up on them, and 20 or more were killed or wounded. Mohnke's forces pulled out until the fog returned a short time later. Meanwhile, Hansen's attack petered out. By late afternoon, the Leibstandarte Division's attempt to rescue KG Peiper had been halted miles from Peiper's perimeter.

It should be noted here that the superiority of American artillery was a major contributing factor to our victory in the Ardennes, just as it was in virtually every victory won in the European Theater of Operations. American artillery fire support was always lavish but, by December 20, German fire support was sparse. This was due to a lack of gasoline, a shortage of prime movers, and, especially, the poor road network. Much of the German artillery had simply been left behind since December 16, and that which was moved forward was often not adequately resupplied with shells or gas.

On December 21, Mohnke signaled Peiper to hold on and revealed his latest plans for rescuing the trapped battle group. Peiper, however, no longer believed he would arrive in time. He therefore decided to contract his perimeter during the night and defend only the hilltop village of La Gleize and the bridgehead at Cheneux. Meanwhile, the battles of Stoumont and Cheneux continued. General Harrison attacked the Sanatorium from the west with two battalions, supported by tanks, while Major McCown's 2nd Battalion/119th Infantry Regiment circled cross-country to cut the road to the east that linked Stoumont and La Gleize.

In the meantime, the German tanks fell back a short distance. Peiper sent the tough Major Werner Poetschke, a Knight of the Iron Cross, to stop the retreat. Armed with a panzerfaust, the major went from panzer to panzer, warning each tank commander in turn that he would personally destroy them if they retreated so much as a meter.

As was the case the day before, the Americans pushed slowly up the hill and captured the first floor of the Sanatorium. Just as had been the case the day before, the SS counterattacked with their Tigers, and the Amis quickly pulled out of the building. Meanwhile, McCown cut the Stoumont-La Gleize road without any trouble, but the major himself pushed too far forward and was captured. Now, leaderless, the 2nd Battalion fell back to its starting point.

To the south, the Battle of Cheneux finally reached its climax, as a battalion of glider troops stormed the village in savage fighting. Most of the SS defenders were killed, and Major Wolf's 84th Light Flak Battalion ceased to exist. The Americans captured 14 flak wagons and a battery of 105mm howitzers, but 225 men were killed and wounded in the process. Of the two main assault companies, B Company had only 18 men left, and every officer was a casualty. C Company had three officers and 38 men left.[3]

That night, as planned, Peiper pulled back his perimeter to La Gleize, leaving only a rearguard in Stoumont. Meanwhile, XVIII Airborne Corps planned another series of attacks for the next day.

La Gleize was a village of 30-odd houses and consisted of two streets, including a school and a church on the village square and a couple of modest hotels. Peiper set up his command post in the basement of the school, while the Americans began an artillery bombardment that would continue until the end of the battle.

The Battle of Stoumont continued throughout the night of December 21–22. It began to snow at dawn and soon a blizzard was raging. Under the cover of the snow, a company of Shermans pushed up the hill to the Sanatorium and began to fire into it at almost point-blank range. The SS men continued to fight for about an hour; then the survivors sneaked away, leaving behind only their dead, dying, and badly wounded. Of the 150 houses in the village, 140 had been rendered uninhabitable or had been completely destroyed during the battle.

Meanwhile, SS General Priess, the commander of the I SS Panzer Corps, had been trying to convince Dietrich and Kraemer to pull Peiper out of the cauldron while he still had the strength to fight his way out. His suggestion had been forwarded to Fuehrer Headquarters, but had been turned down. All Priess could get Dietrich to do was to promise to have the Luftwaffe air-drop supplies to the encircled kampfgruppe during the night of December 22–23. At this point, Priess gave up. He knew that Peiper was being sacrificed for an objective that was no longer realistic.

Inside La Gleize, KG Peiper was suffering its heaviest casualties of the campaign at the hand of the American artillery. That afternoon, he signaled Mohnke that he was almost out of ammunition and requested permission to break out. He received no answer.

Just before midnight, 22 German airplanes dropped supplies (mainly ammunition and gasoline) to the trapped battle group. Rumors ran wild in Allied ranks that the SS were being reinforced by paratroopers. General Harrison, however, suspected the truth and did not let the drop divert his attention or alter his plans. Peiper's men, meanwhile, were only able to recover about 10 percent of the supplies that were dropped.

The morning of December 23 broke clear and cold. It was perfect weather—for the Allies. The long-grounded fighter-bombers ran wild throughout the Ardennes sector and did not neglect Battle Group Peiper. The American artillery, meanwhile, began to shell the trapped SS men with proximity shells—an American secret weapon that had first been used against Skorzeny's 150th Panzer Brigade two days earlier (see Chapter IX). They allowed the Americans to detonate shells above ground level, without explosion by contact. They inflicted "catastrophic casualties" on the Germans and drove the SS into the cellars (except for those inside the tanks).[4] When the artillery bombardment lifted, the American infantry advanced, confident that the back of the German defense had been broken. Almost immediately they ran into a minefield. The Sherman tanks crossed the minefield without infantry support, but two were quickly knocked out by the Tigers. The rest retreated rapidly. Task Force Harrison had been repulsed.

Late that afternoon, the Amis advanced again and fought their way into the outskirts of La Gleize. They were met with fire from heavy machine guns and 20mm flak guns. This ended the American attacks for the day. American artillery, however, continued to pound La Gleize. In six days, the divisional artillery of the U.S. 30th Infantry alone fired more than 57,000 rounds. La Gleize was reduced to rubble.

Peiper, meanwhile, was determined to break out. His objective was the German lines on the other side of the Ambleve, somewhere in the vicinity of Stavelot. He planned to leave his equipment behind. Fortunately for him, the nearby terrain was rugged and heavily wooded, favoring escape. Oberfuehrer Mohnke approved the breakout attempt via radio at 5 P.M., but only if Peiper could bring out his vehicles. Furious, Peiper decided to ignore Mohnke and to break out anyway.

Late that evening, along the Trois Ponts road, the bulk of Captain Koblenz's reconnaissance company (half of Knittel's battalion) was captured, along with Koblenz himself. It was the second major subordinate unit of Peiper's battle group that had been destroyed, and it reinforced the colonel's determination to break out, no matter what.

The survivors of KG Peiper slipped out of La Gleize between 2 A.M. and 3 A.M. on Sunday, December 24, and made their way in small groups down the slope that led out of the village in the direction of the Ambleve. Only 800 out of the original 4,000 men were left. They left behind 300 wounded.

About 4:30 A.M., the SS rearguard (about 50 men) blew up the panzers and the equipment. German losses in La Gleize totaled 28 tanks, 70 half-tracks, and 25 artillery pieces, with more in the surrounding countryside. That morning, Task Force Harrison cautiously entered the ruined village. The SS rearguard surrendered without a fight. It also gave up about 150 American prisoners, some of whom were wounded. Major McCown was the only prisoner unaccounted for; he was still with Peiper.

A few days later, an American tank recovery team began removing the damaged and abandoned German armor. The innkeeper's wife, Jenny Geenen, however, had a feeling for history and decided that La Gleize should keep at least one memorial to the battle. She approached the Americans and offered them a bottle of cognac in exchange for a King Tiger tank. They accepted with audacity. This Tiger still guards the eastern approaches to the village, just as it did in 1944.[5]

By nightfall on December 24–25, what was left of the kampfgruppe had covered more than 20 miles, despite rations limited to a handful of hard biscuits and a few shots of cognac. Shortly after nightfall they crossed the Ambleve over a small wooden bridge and found themselves in a thickly wooded area, through which elements of the 82nd Airborne were moving. There were several skirmishes, and McCown managed to escape in the confusion. Years later, he reached the rank of major general.

Early on Christmas morning, December 25, the survivors of KG Peiper swam the icy Salm River and made contact with the 1st SS Panzer Division, four miles east of the U.S. 82nd Airborne. They were welcomed as victors by their comrades. The next day, the exhausted remnants of the 1st SS Panzer Regiment were sent to St. Vith, to rest and reequip.

Hitler's best hope of reaching Antwerp had been broken before it reached the Meuse.

General of Panzer Troops Baron Hasso von Manteuffel, the commander of the 5th Panzer Army during the Ardennes Offensive. He later commanded the 3rd Panzer Army on the Eastern Front (1945) (U.S. National Archives).

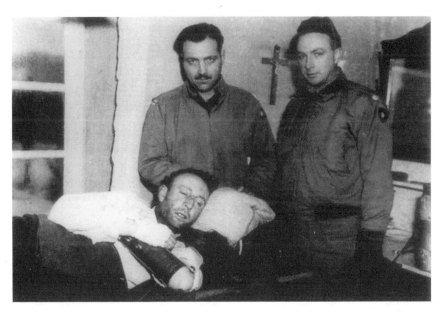

Colonel Baron Friedrich von der Heydte, commander of the German airborne forces during the Battle of the Bulge, shortly after he surrendered to American forces at Monschua (U.S. National Archives).

A Panzer Mark V "Panther" tank. More reliable mechanically than the Tiger, it was considered by many to be the best tank produced during World War II (U.S. Army Institute of Military History).

A German paratrooper bails out, date unknown (U.S. Army Institute of Military History).

Some of the American dead, murdered at Malmedy by Kampfgruppe Peiper in December 1944. This photograph was taken by U.S. Lieutenant Colonel Williams some time after the massacre.

SS Colonel General Sepp Dietrich (top), the commander of the 6th Panzer Army, speaking with Field Marshal Model during the Battle of the Bulge, December 1944. Dietrich did not handle his forces well during this battle and was easily out-performed by his neighboring army, the 5th Panzer under Baron Hasso von Manteuffel (U.S. Army Institute of Military History).

An American Sherman tank rolls past a knocked-out German PzKw IV during the Battle of the Bulge, December 1944. This Mark IV was abandoned after its right track was destroyed. Although mechanically reliable and easy to mass produce, the Sherman was considered inferior to most German tanks in 1944–45 (U.S. Army Institute of Military History).

Field Marshal Walter Model speaking with a soldier during the Battle of the Bulge (U.S. Army Institute of Military History).

Colonel General Albert Jodl, the chief of operations of the High Command of the Armed Forces. Jodl and his staff did much of the planning for the Ardennes Offensive. Jodl is seen here on his way to formally surrender to General Eisenhower in May 1945. He was executed as a major war criminal at Nuremberg the following year (U.S. Army Institute of Military History).

A StuG assault gun. Built on a PzMk III chassis and relatively easy to manufacture, this type of assault gun was used extensively by the Germans during the Ardennes offensive and was often quite successful, especially in an infantry support role (U.S. National Archives).

The village of Foy after the battle (U.S. Army Signal Corps Photo).

The U.S. 26th Infantry Regiment of the 1st Infantry Division, moving up to Bullingen in the early stages of the Battle of the Bulge (U.S. Army Signal Corps Photo).

British Field Marshal Sir Bernard Law Montgomery with Lieutenant General Simpson, the commander of the U.S. 9th Army. Much to the chagrin of Generals Bradley and Patton, Eisenhower assigned control of the U.S. 1st Army to Monty during the Battle of the Bulge (U.S. Army Institute of Military History).

German soldiers take boots off of dead American soldiers during the Battle of the Bulge. Note that censors have covered the road signs so that the location is not known (U.S. National Archives).

Hitler with his favorite commando, SS Colonel Otto Skorzeny. Skorzeny—who rescued Mussolini in 1943—commanded the 150th Panzer Brigade during the Battle of the Bulge (U.S. National Archives).

Field Marshal Model (left) with Major General Gerhard Engel (1906–76), the commander of the 12th Volksgrenadier Division. Engel was Hitler's army adjutant from 1938 to September 1943, when he became so excited by a Hitler speech that he volunteered for frontline duty. He successively commanded the 27th Infantry Regiment, 12th Volksgrenadier Division, and Division Ulrich von Hutten (April 12, 1945–end). He was promoted to lieutenant general on April 1, 1945 (U.S. Army Institute of Military History).

An SS man calls for his comrade to advance during the Battle of Poteau, 1944 (U.S. National Archives).

A member of the 1st SS Panzer Division during the Battle of the Bulge (U.S. National Archives).

A meeting in orange grove in Sicily, July 25, 1943. Troy Middleton (left), the commander of the 45th Infantry Division, discusses the situation with Lieutenant General Omar Bradley (center), the II Corps commander, and Lieutenant General George S. Patton (right), the commander of the U.S. 7th Army. A year and a half later, the three were fighting together in the Battle of the Bulge, during which Middleton commanded the VIII Corps, Patton the 3rd Army, and Bradley the 12th Army Group (U.S. Army Institute of Military History).

General Dwight D. Eisenhower, the Supreme Allied Commander in Europe. General Bradley is in the back of the jeep (U.S. National Archives).

A dead German *Landser* in the Ardennes, December 1944. A Landser was the companion in misfortune to the American G.I. or the British Tommy (U.S. National Archives).

U.S. Major General James M. Gavin, 1944. Born in 1907, the son of unwed Irish immigrants, he was placed in an orphanage between the ages of one and two. Eventually adopted, he enlisted in the army when he was 17 to escape the Pennsylvania coal mines. He performed so well and showed such promise that he was selected for West Point. As a junior officer, young Gavin devoted himself to the study of Great Captains, especially Caesar, Alexander the Great, Napoleon, Robert E. Lee, and Thomas J. "Stonewall" Jackson. He was a major force in the development of the U.S. airborne force and its doctrines. During the Ardennes Offensive, Gavin served as acting commander of the XVIII Airborne Corps and commander of the 82nd Airborne Division. Later promoted to lieutenant general, he wrote *On to Berlin* and *Airborne Warfare,* as well as numerous articles. After retiring from the army, he served as an advisor to President Kennedy and as U.S. ambassador to France. An early critic of the Vietnam War, he died in Baltimore in 1990, at age 82 (U.S. National Archives).

A towed German howitzer in the Ardennes, 1944 (U.S. National Archives).

Montgomery and Patton exchange insincerities. The two famous Allied commanders were rivals who could not stand each other. This photo was taken in Sicily, 1943 (U.S. National Archives).

German guards march American prisoners captured in the Battle of the Bulge to the P.O.W. compounds (U.S. Army Institute of Military History).

Luftwaffe troops undergoing rifle instruction, date unknown. Many of these troops were incorporated into Luftwaffe Field divisions, where they were led by air forces officers and performed badly in infantry combat. Later, many of them were incorporated into units such as the 18th Volksgrenadier Division, where they did much better under more capable army commanders (U.S. Army Institute of Military History).

Equipment formerly belonging to the 2nd Panzer Division, abandoned after the Battle of Celles and captured by the U.S. 2nd Armored Division, December 1944 (U.S. Army Signal Corps Photo).

CHAPTER 6

The Schnee Eifel

The greatest military disaster the United States suffered in the European Theater of Operations during World War II occurred during the Battle of the Bulge. Remarkably, it was not inflicted upon the American army by the fanatical SS soldiers, elite paratroopers, Skorzeny's commandos, or by Baron von Manteuffel's vaunted panzer troops. The defeat was administered by the 18th Volksgrenadier Division, which was one of the least elite formations in the German Wehrmacht. It was, in fact, considered well below average in the autumn of 1944, as far as German divisions were concerned. Only its commander was above the ordinary.

The division began its existence as the 18th Luftwaffe Field Division, which was formed from excess air force personnel in Soissons at the end of 1942. In early 1943, it was transported to the Channel coast, and guarded the Dunkirk sector until November 1, 1943, when it was incorporated into the army as *Feld-Div. 18 (L).*[1] A nonmotorized or "marching" infantry unit, it fought in the Battle of Normandy in June 1944, where it performed poorly and was routed by the British within 24 hours of being committed to action. So great were its casualties that it had to be temporarily absorbed by the 21st Panzer Division. In August 1944, the 18th Luftwaffe Field was again smashed during the retreat to the Seine. It lost about 80 percent of its men, a corresponding amount of its equipment, and almost all of its vehicles. It was sent to Kolding, Denmark, to rebuild. On September 9, 1944, it was redesignated and became the 18th Volksgrenadier Division. Six days later, its new commander arrived. His name was Guenther Hoffmann-Schoenborn.

Colonel Hoffmann-Schoenborn was the descendant of a military family. His father, Georg, was a lieutenant colonel, and his father-in-law was a major. He was born in Posen an der Warthe (now part of Poland) on May 1,

1905. He entered the Reichsheer (the 100,000 man army allowed to Germany by the Treaty of Versailles) on April 1, 1924, as a *Fahnenjunker* in the 3rd Artillery Regiment. As was typical in the Reichsheer, the training period was long and thorough, and promotions were slow. Hoffmann did not receive his commission until February 1, 1928. He was promoted to first lieutenant in 1931 and to captain in 1935.[2]

Although parts of his personnel record are no longer legible, it appears that Hoffmann spent his entire pre-1937 career in the artillery. This included a four-month special communications course at the Artillery School at Jueterbog and a six-month tour of duty as a battery commander in a heavy artillery unit (150mm guns) (1934–35). Meanwhile, he married on April 22, 1933. Frau Franz Hoffmann gave him a son, Wolfgang, on February 27, 1934, and a daughter, Renate, 17 months later. A second son, Guenter, was born about 1941.

When World War II broke out, Captain Hoffmann was given command of the 2nd Battery of the I/42nd Artillery, a heavy artillery battalion of 150mm guns that formed part of the defenses of the Western Front while Hitler's armies overran Poland. On October 13, 1939, after the fall of Warsaw, young Hoffmann was named commander of the 730th Heavy Artillery Battalion, a motorized unit then forming in the Duesseldorf area of Wehrkreis VI. In April 1940, the Staff, 730th Heavy Artillery was redesignated Staff, 777th Heavy Artillery, and its batteries were sent to other units. Meanwhile, Hoffmann and his headquarters were transferred to Dortmund, where they took charge of three batteries of 210mm mortars from three different Wehrkreise. Unfortunately, the records do not indicate which advanced combat unit or units this General Headquarters outfit was attached to during the French campaign, but it no doubt saw significant fighting. Hoffmann-Schoenborn was decorated with the Iron Cross, 2nd Class on May 31. He received the Iron Cross, 1st Class three weeks later.

In the summer of 1940, after the fall of France, Hoffmann's career took a significant upward turn when he was selected to attend a special officers' course on assault gun training. The main weapon of the assault gun force was essentially a turret-less Panzer Mark III tank, generally armed with a 75mm gun, which had a very limited traverse. (Because of its lack of a turret, the assault gun was not classified as a tank.) In his book, *Panzer Leader*, Colonel General Heinz Guderian, the "father" of the blitzkrieg, expressed indignation concerning how the assault gun force (which was a subdivision of the artillery inspectorate) should have been placed under his own panzer inspectorate, but was not.[3] Any honest historian, however, must admit that Hitler was occasionally right about some things (as Harry Truman said, "even a blind hog finds an acorn once in a while"), and it is hard to argue with the record of success of the assault guns. From June 22, 1941, to January 1944, they destroyed 20,000 enemy armored vehicles on the Eastern Front alone—probably more than a dozen times their own peak strength.[4]

Hoffmann reported to the 2nd Artillery Lehr Regiment at Jueterbog on August 14, 1940, and underwent training as an assault gun officer and commander. On October 1, 1940, also at Jueterbog, he assumed command of the 191st Assault Artillery Battalion, which was activated that same day. The three-battery unit was redesignated 191st Assault Gun Battalion on February 7, 1941, without any changes being made to its table of organization. Hoffmann, meanwhile, was promoted to major on December 1, 1940.[5]

Early in 1941, the new battalion was loaded on trains and traveled southeast to the vital Ploesti oilfields in Rumania (via Vienna, Budapest and Bucharest), which were then being threatened by Joseph Stalin and the Soviet Union. In late March, the 191st was hurriedly sent to southern Bulgaria, because Hitler had decided to invade Yugoslavia and Greece. The Balkan campaign began on April 6.

Hoffmann-Schoenborn first distinguished himself in the Balkans. Attached to the 5th Mountain Division of the XVIII Mountain Corps, his battalion attacked the Greek Army, spearheaded the German 12th Army's breakthrough of the Metaxas Line, and was largely responsible for the surrender of the Greek forces at Salonika. The 191st then took part in the pursuit of the Greco-British forces as far as Thermopylen. On May 13, the battalion was recalled to the north, where the bulk of the German Wehrmacht was assembling to invade Russia. The 191st lost 15 killed and 37 wounded during the Balkan campaign. The next day, May 14, Hoffmann-Schoenborn was decorated with the Knight's Cross.[6]

Hoffmann's battalion was initially assigned to Field Marshal Walter von Reichenau's 6th Army for Operation Barbarossa, as the invasion of the Soviet Union was codenamed. It was later part of Colonel General Ewald von Kleist's 1st Panzer Group (later Army) and the 4th Army and, at various times in 1941, was attached to the 98th Infantry Division, the 111th Infantry Division, the 75th Infantry Division, the III Motorized Corps, the LV Corps, the 4th Army, and the 3rd Motorized Division. It was considered a shock unit and took part in almost every major action fought by Army Group South until the Battle of Moscow, when it was assigned to Army Group Center. Hoffmann was within 30 miles of the Soviet capital on December 2, 1941, fighting Russian T-34 tanks, when three machine gun bullets ripped through his arm, ending his combat career for some time. For his part in the forcing of the Dnieper and in the Battle of the Kiev (where 667,000 of Stalin's soldiers were captured), Hoffmann-Schoernborn became the 49th recipient of the Oak Leaves to the Knight's Cross on December 31, 1941. He was still in the hospital at the time.

On March 1, 1942, after a period of wounded leave, Major Hoffmann returned to active duty as commander of the III Battalion, 29th Motorized Lehr Regiment at Jueterbog. The III/29th was part of the Replacement

Army and was engaged in training replacements and new units for the field armies. Many of its officers had been wounded on the Eastern Front and were not yet ready to return to Russia.

Hoffmann proved to be an excellent assault gun unit training officer. He was promoted to lieutenant colonel in 1942, was given command of the 2nd Motorized Lehr Regiment at Jueterbog on December 1, 1942, and became commandant of the Assault Gun School at Burg on August 1, 1943. He was promoted to full colonel on November 1, 1943. In August and September, 1944, he attended a brief Division Commanders' Course at Hirschberg, Silesia, and was then given command of the 18th Volksgrenadier Division in Denmark.

Hoffmann's new command was a poorly equipped "People's Infantry" unit. It included a core of 2,500 men from the original 18th Luftwaffe Field Division, 3,000 men from naval and other air force units, and 5,000 men from the Replacement Army. These men included what Hitler called "rear area swine," combed out from various establishments in the zone of the interior, and the so-called "indispensables," who had previously held important positions in German industry. Very few of these men were recent draftees, and "the personnel of the division could scarcely be described as young," Lieutenant Colonel Dietrich Moll, the Ia (chief of operations) of the division recalled. "Not many of its officers or men had seen much action . . . Germany was in her sixth year of war, yet few men of this division had campaign ribbons or decorations."[7] (German divisions had no chief of staff so, as Ia, Moll actually functioned as the de facto chief of staff. Moll's unpublished manuscript is the source of much of this chapter.)[8]

The 18th VG's general lack of experience is probably why a proven training master like Hoffmann was selected to command it. Throughout his career, Hoffmann was known for his efficiency and energy, and he was a proven training officer. He now set about his new task with a vengeance. Any officers who were not capable of keeping up with the requirements of the live-wire colonel were summarily relieved of their duties. This included most of the original Luftwaffe officers assigned to the division. Hoffmann, however, showed a definite skill in choosing capable replacements, and soon the efficiency of the new division improved markedly.

By October 15, the 18th Volksgrenadier was nearly at full strength and had most of its equipment. Training, in general, was proceeding at least at a satisfactory rate; all units had undergone field training exercises; and the former airmen and sailors were at least familiar with their new mission, weapons, and equipment. Training in communications, however, was inadequate and would remain so. Light machine gun training was also behind schedule. The division had received the guns, but an Allied air raid on the Hamburg supply depot had destroyed the mounts before they could be shipped. The horse artillery regiment was also not yet ready and, instead of the antitank and anti-aircraft battalions some divisions had, Hoffmann only had a single AT company (equipped with 75mm guns) and one anti-aircraft company, which was outfitted with 37mm guns. Later, a motorized antitank company and an AT battalion head-quarters arrived, but the division still had only 21 antitank guns. More serious still was the fact that each of his three rifle regiments was only authorized two battalions of infantry. The divisional supply regiment—which included a veterinary company, a butcher platoon, a motor trans-port company, a bakery company, ammunition columns and various supply units—was desperately short of personnel. Its only motor transport company had a carrying capacity of 120 tons. This proved to be insufficient, especially because its vehicles were old and in poor condition. Several soon broke down and could not be repaired due to a lack of spare parts. The divi-sional bakery company and butcher platoon, on the other hand, would keep the 18th well provisioned throughout the offensive. Despite its defi-ciencies, Colonel Hoffmann reported that the division was ready to assume a limited defense mission. Table 6.1 shows the division's order of battle.

A week later, on October 22, Hoffmann and Moll met with General of Artillery Walter Lucht, the commander of the LXVI Corps, at Gerolstein, 30 miles west of Koblenz.[9] Hoffmann was informed that his division would take over a quiet sector in the Ardennes, relieving SS Major General Heinz Lammerding's 2nd SS Panzer Division "Das Reich."[10] The advance parties of the 18th Volksgrenadier left Denmark that same day. None of those involved knew that the 2nd SS was being withdrawn so that it could be rebuilt for Hitler's winter offensive.

The relief of the SS division took place without any particular difficulties. Most of the initial movement of the 18th VG took place by rail, but there was only one Allied air attack on its trains. This took place at Marburg and resulted in several casualties and some loss of equipment. The division's units detrucked at dawn or dusk, when American air activity was slack. The relief was well-planned, followed inconspicuous routes, selected and used assembly areas, and provided guides to every unit from regimental headquarters to infantry squad. Lammerding (a much less capable com-mander than Hoffmann) put pressure on the soldiers to effect a speedy relief; Colonel Hoffmann, however, insisted that everything proceed sys-tematically, even if it took a couple of extra days and annoyed the SS gen-eral. Even so, the relief was completed by October 30, and was not noticed by the Americans.

The Schnee Eifel (Snow Mountains) was collectively the most significant terrain feature in division's new sector. The West Wall (called the "Siegfried Line" by the Allies but not by the Germans) ran along the prominent Schnee Eifel Ridge. This position had been captured by the Americans in September, so they held the dominant position, and much of the area

Table 6.1
Organization of the 18th Volksgrenadier Division

Divisional Commander: Major General Hoffmann-Schoenborn
Divisional Headquarters

    Ia (Operations Officer): Lieutenant Colonel (GS) Dietrich Moll
    Ic (Chief Intelligence Officer): Captain von der Lieth
    Ib (Supply Officer): Major (GS) Ruschke
    IIa (Personnel Officer): Major Krummbiegel

293rd Infantry Regiment: Lieutenant Colonel Witte
294th Infantry Regiment: Lieutenant Colonel Drueke
295th Infantry Regiment: Lieutenant Colonel Otto, later Lieutenant Colonel
    Klimke
1818th Artillery Regiment: Lieutenant Colonel Hadenfeldt

    I Battalion: Captain Bleiffert
    II Battalion: Captain Albers
    III Battalion: Captain Schwars (killed in action)
    IV Battalion: Captain Oehme

1818th Reconnaissance Company
1818th Anti-Tank Battalion: Captain Rennhack
1818th Engineer Battalion: Captain Kuhr
1818th Signal Battalion: Captain Baron von Adrian
1818th Supply Regiment
18th Division Training School: Major von Blomberg
Division Surgeon: Major Dr. Kleyser

---

could be seen from their observation posts. Hoffmann nevertheless felt that the German position was secure because the sector was thickly wooded (making it unlikely that the U.S. forces would employ tanks), observation was difficult, and no good roads went into the area. Also, the SS division had constructed strong positions in the forward zones, which the 18th now occupied. The sector, however, was too long. According to German peacetime doctrine and wartime experience, the largest amount of frontage that a single division could expect to hold against a determined attack was nine kilometers (about six miles). Hoffmann's sector was 19 kilometers (about 12 miles) long. Accordingly, he could not occupy the position in depth nor establish reserves. All three of his rifle regiments had to be put on the front line, along with his engineer battalion. Even so, it was not possible to establish a continuous trench line. The division had to prepare a number of strongpoints in depth, and the ground between them had to be covered by patrols.

The six weeks the 18th Volksgrenadier Division spent in the "quiet sector" proved to be of immense benefit to it in the upcoming battle. With the assistance of the LXVI Corps, it set up a Division Training School five miles northeast of Stadtkyll and engaged in training whenever possible. It also became accustomed to enemy fire, learned to use camouflage effectively, established an efficient signals network, and conducted reconnaissance and combat patrols from the first night it was committed. It was, in fact, because of this patrolling and its detailed knowledge of the American positions (including the "soft spots" in the U.S. line) that the 18th was selected to participate in the Battle of the Bulge.

In November, the division was ordered to extend its sector four kilometers (about 2.5 miles) to the left, stretching its line even more thinly. In early December, as the 5th Panzer Army prepared for the Ardennes offensive, it was ordered to relieve the 277th Volksgrenadier Division and extend its sector nine kilometers (six miles) to the right, to the southern edge of Neuhof. This gave it a sector 32 kilometers (20 miles) long. To cover this front, Hoffmann ordered the 294th Infantry Regiment to shift from the center to the right and assigned his antitank company to it. An American attack in the center at this time would have met little resistance. Fortunately for the Germans, none was launched.

Relations between the Headquarters of the 18th Volksgrenadier and that of the LXVI Corps were not particularly good. The corps lacked depth and sufficient units, and often assigned tasks to the 18th; the division lost an artillery battalion, its 75mm antitank company, the division's training school, and part of the motorized ambulance platoon, all of which were assigned to positions outside of the division's sector. Hoffmann, however, was considered something of a "golden boy" and was favored by the Nazis. He went over General Lucht's head through "special channels" and appealed to Reichsfuehrer-SS Heinrich Himmler, who had been commander-in-chief of the Replacement Army since the failure of the July 20 attempt on Hitler's life. The division's detached units were soon returned to the 18th VG.

Initially, the 18th VG faced the U.S. 28th and 90th Infantry Divisions. Just before the start of the offensive, the sector was taken over by the inexperienced U.S. 106th Infantry Division, which was nicknamed "the Golden Lions."

Colonel Moll and his officers had a generally favorable impression of the Americans they faced. They compared favorably to the Germans in terms of physical stamina, and "were exceptionally well trained in military security," the Ia recalled. "They had been taught to give only their name, rank, and serial number, when captured, and to refer to the Geneva Convention. Since the Germans rigidly adhered to that convention," Colonel Moll wrote, "any attempt at using force to gain further information was out of the question." (This comment, unfortunately, did not apply to *all* German units in the Battle of the Bulge, but at least the captives of regular German Army units such as the 18th Volksgrenadier were generally treated properly.) "Prisoners," the colonel added, "tended to grow more talkative . . . if it was possible to make them divulge the name of their home town or if the name of their commander had already been learned. Then they assumed that the division was already well informed and did not mind giving additional details."[11] Thus, the Germans were able to learn that the American main line of resistance extended along the line Roth-Kobacheid to the Schnee Eifel Ridge and from there to Bleialf. They had two regiments on the line and one in reserve.

Colonel Moll had one negative comment about the Americans. "One significant enemy characteristic was his strong aversion to night fighting. After dark the enemy even disliked to patrol behind his own lines."[12] The main method of defense, in fact, consisted of laying down a more or less constant artillery fire. The U.S. Army regularly dropped 2,000 to 3,000 rounds a day on the 18th Volksgrenadier Division and most of it was quite accurate. Firing began regularly at 8 A.M. and ended at 5 P.M., with very few rounds being fired at night. American artillery spotter aircraft appeared regularly after 9 A.M. and disappeared at noon. They would reappear about 1 P.M. (after lunch) and continue to fly over the 18th sector until 5 P.M., when they left for the day. This American predictably had not changed since the Battle of Sicily and allowed the Germans to work unimpeded at night and would lead to significantly longer American casualty lists than was absolutely necessary.

During the six weeks they spent on the "quiet front," casualties among the men of the 18th Volksgrenadier were normal. They lost 110 men killed or captured, as well as 450 wounded or reported sick. They received no replacements; nevertheless, their morale improved significantly during this period. Colonel Moll recalled: "Although the men knew the situation was serious, they still believed that the war might have a favorable outcome. Increased combat experience brought greater self-assurance and a belief that they were a fair match for the enemy."[13] Because of this and other factors, Colonel Hoffmann reported his division as ready for limited attack missions. He did, however, stipulate that the division's lack of mobility in the infantry regiments (because of a lack of cross-country vehicles, wreckers, and supply vehicles) made it unfit for a deep drive into American territory.

Only 32 men deserted to the Americans during the quiet front period. "This," Moll said, "was a remarkably low figure." About half of the deserters were from the *Volksliste* III—ethnic or partial ethnic Germans living outside Germany who had been vested with German citizenship for a probationary period. They were liable for military service but could not be promoted above the rank of private first class. Their loyalty to the

Third Reich was questionable at best, many were anti-Nazi, and ever
body understood the motive behind their desertions. The other half was
composed of men who, until recently, were well-paid "indispensable"
employees in industry. They deserted, as Moll wrote, "not because of anti-
Nazi feelings or because they anticipated the loss of the war, but because
they were afraid to fight."[14]

Hoffmann was also outraged by these desertions and issued the following order to the troops. In it, he showed his pro-Nazi leanings:

Traitors from our ranks have deserted to the enemy. Their names are [six names
are listed] . . .

These bastards have given away important military secrets. . . . Deceitful Jewish
mud slingers taunt you with their pamphlets and try to entice you into becoming
bastards also. Let them spew their poison!

We stand watch over Germany's frontier. Death and destruction to all enemies
who tread on German soil.

As for the contemptible traitors who have forgotten their honor, rest assured the
division will see to it that they never see home and loved ones again. Their families will have to atone for their treason. The destiny of a people has never
depended on traitors and bastards. The true German soldier was and is the best
in the world. Unwavering behind him is the Fatherland.

And at the end is our Victory.

Long live Germany! Heil the Fuehrer![15]

Hoffmann was not only outraged for morale reasons—he was also
angry for good, solid military reasons. Every time there was a desertion,
the accuracy of enemy artillery fire improved significantly. Roll-call areas
and supply facilities were always hard hit within 24 hours, along with
company and platoon headquarters, field kitchens, and messenger routes,
indicating that the deserters told the Americans everything they knew.
Later, after his men captured the G-2 (military intelligence) files of the
U.S. 106th Infantry Division, this impression was confirmed.

After a year in grade as a colonel, Hoffmann-Schoenborn was promoted
to major general, effective December 1, 1944. That same day he met with
General Lucht at the LXVI Command Post at Gerolstein. Here the 18th
Volksgrenadier Division was given the mission of surrounding the bulk of
the U.S. 2nd Infantry Division on the Schnee Eifel, as well as crossing the
Our River at Schoenberg. Then, remarkably enough, it was given a third
mission: "advance with all mobile forces along the Our River road toward
St. Vith, which will be taken by surprise assault."[16] For this offensive, the
244th Assault Gun Brigade and another medium artillery battalion was
assigned to the division.

In retrospect, the third mission assigned to the 18th VG (the capture of
St. Vith) clearly exceeded its capabilities. Neither Hoffmann nor Moll

ne, however, because they thought the objective might
ugh they knew it would be very difficult.

wo weeks, LXVI Corps pulled out several infantry
ort training courses in attack techniques, including live
on exercises. Although normally very critical of the leadership
the LXVI Corps, Colonel Moll noted: "This training proved of great
importance to the success of the initial penetration. Units were not only
instructed in how to attack, but a number of other deficiencies were cor-
rected. Men were checked for proper equipment and taught to avoid
noise in manipulating it."[17]

The regimental commanders of the 18th Volksgrenadier Division were
informed of the upcoming offense on December 10. The troops were not
to be informed until the night before the attack.

U.S. Major General Troy Middleton, the commander of the U.S. VIII
Corps, was concerned that the two forward regiments in the Schnee Eifel
were too far east and thus in a potentially dangerous position. He
requested permission to pull them back 10 miles, but the U.S. 1st Army
rejected the idea because it would involve giving up a portion of the West
Wall and an excellent defensive position to the Germans.

Meanwhile, the U.S. 106th Infantry Division relieved the 2nd Infantry
in the Schnee Eifel.

The new unit was totally green and had been sent to the Ardennes (like
the 18th Volksgrenadier) to get some experience in a relatively quiet sector. It was, however, in an exposed position and without adequate
reserves. It was also in no way prepared for what it was about to face.

Hoffmann's men quickly realized that something was up on the other
side. Enemy artillery fire increased markedly and American infantry
was behaving differently and awkwardly. Patrols soon brought in prisoners, which confirmed that was a new division on the Schnee Eifel. The
forward observers of the LXVI Corps observation battalion, meanwhile,
did an excellent job of identifying the locations of the American artillery,
which was concentrated in the Schlausenbach-Muetzenich-Amelscheid
area.

Because of the terrain, Hoffmann considered the right half of the division's area more favorable to a major offensive, because the attack forces
would initially travel through the open ground of the southern extremity
of the Losheim Gap; from there, the Our River Valley could be reached by
a relatively short advance. Also, reconnaissance patrols had already identified a weak spot in the American line. The German officers assumed that
they had found a unit boundary. Such places were almost always weak
spots. (They were right. They had, in fact, located the boundary between
the U.S. 106th Infantry Division and the 14th Cavalry Group.)

The attack from the German left flank was much weaker than that of
the right. It would have to pierce the U.S. line at the southern edge of the

village of Bleialf, where the Alf River would have to be crossed. Here they would have to cross a hill exposed to American fire. Worst still, terrain would not permit the artillery to follow the infantry and support the advance.

"The division commander knew that his objectives could be reached only by ruthlessly concentrating all available forces and by exploiting the enemy's weak spot and the few advantages of the terrain," Colonel Moll wrote later.[18] With that in mind, Hoffmann divided his division into two assault groups. On the right flank, he concentrated the 294th and 295th Infantry Regiments on the front line. Behind it at Steinberg lay an ad hoc mobile battalion, KG Rennhack, consisting of the 1818th Engineer Battalion, the 1818th Reconnaissance Company, and a mobile engineer company, all under the command of Captain Rennhack. After the 295th Infantry Regiment reached Verschneid, Rennhack was to advance toward Andler, secure the Our Valley, and push on to St. Vith. One battalion of the 1818th Artillery Regiment was assigned to support the left flank. Lieutenant Colonel Witte commanded the left assault group; Hoffmann himself commanded the right.

On the German left, the 293rd Regiment assembled south of Brandscheid, with the objectives of capturing Bleialf and then pushing on to seize the bridge at Schoenberg. Most of the 466th Artillery Command (the LXVI Corps artillery) took up positions southwest of Pruem to support it with their heavier guns. Because of the poor terrain here, a military police unit was attached to KG Witte to enforce strict traffic control.

To have adequate assault forces on his flanks, Hoffmann had to resort to drastic measures. He stripped his entire center of combat formations and assigned the defense of the middle of his line to the Divisional Training School under Major von Blomberg. At that time, the school was teaching small NCO classes—about 150 to 200 men in all. They were given the task of screening the entire Schnee Eifel sector. These men were tough and capable, but they could not be expected to hold off a determined American attack of greater than company strength. Hoffman, however, was gambling that no such attack would be launched.

He was right.

Because of the difficult terrain, Hoffmann did not believe he could capture Schoenberg until December 17. As long as the Americans held out in the Schnee Eifel-Andler-Schoenberg area, only limited forces would be available for forcing the Our Valley. The division, he said, could not be expected to reach St. Vith and the Wallerode hills before December 18.

The unit commanders of the 18th assembled at the division's command post on December 10 and were told of the planned attack. They were ordered to submit their written orders and plans by December 13, so that they could be reviewed. Meanwhile, to overcome the American tank obstacles on the main line of resistance (MLR), the engineers constructed a well-camouflaged bridge to facilitate the advance.

Nerves were tense as zero-hour approached. On the night of December 14, elements of the 2nd Panzer Division moved westward along the main highway from Buedesheim to its assembly areas. "The noise of the armor could be heard for miles," Moll recalled.[19] The division now doubted that surprise could be attained—and it should not have been. But when an officer from the 106th Division's G-2 (military intelligence) section reported to his superiors at VIII Corps, he was told, "Don't be so jumpy. The Krauts are only playing phonograph records to scare you newcomers."[20] A similar report from the 99th Infantry Division was dismissed in the same peremptorily manner.

The following night, on the very eve of the offensive, the 244th Assault Gun Brigade arrived and assembled northeast of Ormont, behind the right attack group. The 18th VG Division now had about 40 assault guns for the attack.

"Each man now reflected on the chance for success," Moll recalled. "Spirits were generally high. Germany could still muster reserves. Everyone felt that the end had not yet come, in spite of what the enemy stated daily in his propaganda leaflets. Probably none of those on the front line knew that the attack was a last, desperate attempt."[21]

In the Ardennes, the morning of December 16 was dark and hazy. The division's advanced patrols crossed the MLR at 4 A.M. A special assault company, equipped only for close combat, spearheaded the attack of each regiment. They moved out at 5 A.M. At 5:30 A.M., just beyond the division's right flank, a massive artillery bombardment suddenly opened up. It was the Artillery Command, I SS Panzer Corps, supporting its forward units. All attempts at stealth and secrecy ceased immediately. The cat was out of the bag!

Colonel Moll remained at the 18th Volksgrenadier Division's Command Post, about a half a mile south of the village of Ormont, while Hoffmann-Schoenborn personally directed the assault gun brigade. Moll waited nervously as reports slowly trickled in. In the thick fog, the 294th became disoriented and marched for Krewinkel instead of Weckerath. The 295th, however, passed north of Roth without making contact with the Golden Lions, and, to the south, the 293rd Infantry crossed the MLR south of Brandscheid and entered the woods to the west.

No battle sounds could be heard at the division's command post and Colonel Moll was worried that the Americans had learned of the attack and had pulled back without being detected. By 9 A.M., however, it was obvious to the troops at the front that the enemy had been taken by surprise. By mid-morning, the 294th was back on track and had crossed a deep valley a mile northeast of Auw, while the vanguard 295th Regiment was advancing west of Roth and was heading for Kobscheid, and while other elements of the 295th dealt with American resistance at Roth. Because of the poor road network, both regiments were short of heavy weapons, which could not keep up with the advance. Most of the fighting was being done by the infantrymen and the assault gun brigade.

Because of an almost total lack of American reaction, Colonel Moll still believed that the Americans had withdrawn from the Schnee Eifel. Consequently, Major von Blomberg ordered several thrusts by combat patrols from the Training School. To Moll's surprise, all of these were quickly turned back by the Americans, in some cases with severe losses. The forward regiments of the U.S. 106th Infantry Division were clearly still in place.

By noon, it was obvious that the division was going to have to control the road running from the Schnee Eifel Forest Station to Roth and Auw, if it were to continue the pace of its advance. Auw was captured by the 294th late on the afternoon of December 16, while both Roth and Kobscheid were encircled by the 295th Infantry but could not be captured. The effort to encircle the 106th Division was clearly in jeopardy. Meanwhile, to the left, Witte's 293rd Infantry Regiment had captured Oberlascheid (west of the Americans in the Schnee Eifel), but it had been checked in the woods and had not captured Bleialf, its objective for the day. Also disconcerting was the fact that the I SS Panzer Corps—the right adjacent unit to the 18th Volksgrenadier Division—had gained little ground. This was serious to Hoffmann and his men, because its right flank would be seriously exposed if it continued. The young major general, however, decided to ignore the risk and proceed. That night, he decided to commit his mobile reserves. He ordered Captain Rennhack and his mobile battalion to cross the MLR at dawn and push toward Andler, behind the advancing 294th Infantry Regiment. He was then to advance along the Our Valley to the bridge at Schoenberg, thus completing the right pincher of the encirclement. Hoffmann himself would lead the attack in the Andler sector with a battalion of the 294th.

Hoffmann's orders had the desired effect on December 17. He personally led the attack that captured Wascheid and reached the Our Valley. He also captured the bridge at Andler intact. Rennhack came up as planned and headed down the valley, into the rear of the U.S. 422nd and 423rd Infantry Regiments, accompanied by Hoffmann and the 244th Assault Gun Brigade. The American command seemed paralyzed as they drove into their rear. Figure 6.1 shows the Battle of the Schnee Eifel.

Resistance at Roth was overcome by the 295th Infantry Regiment that morning, so that the vehicles carrying the heavy weapons could now move forward. Colonel Otto then turned his attention to Kobscheid, where resistance had stiffened.

Meanwhile, to the south, Colonel Witte managed to get the advance of his 293rd Infantry Regiment moving forward again. Early that morning, he launched a strong assault on Bleialf, which was defended by an ad hoc

Figure 6.1
The Battle of the Schnee Eifel

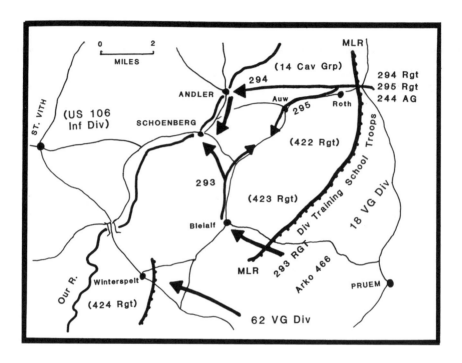

battle group from the U.S. 423rd Infantry Regiment. The German grenadiers advanced "with considerable elan"[22] and quickly took the town, effectively breaking through the American line in the process. They then turned northwest and headed for Schoenberg, against weakening American resistance. Witte's main problem was delays caused by groups of Americans who realized that they were in danger of being encircled and were now trying to escape to the west. Some of them succeeded in doing so, but the trap was closing. The American positions had now been completely broken through on both flanks. The mobile battalion and assault gun brigade—personally led by General Hoffmann—reached Schoenberg shortly before noon and captured the bridge intact. By early afternoon, the encirclement was complete.

"The behavior of the enemy on the second day of the attack was wholly incomprehensible," Colonel Moll recalled. "In the main, he did nothing. However, localized resistance was stubborn and eliminated only with difficulty. That is to say, the Americans fought bravely wherever fighting actually occurred. But their tactics were unsystematic."[23]

That night, the spearhead of the 18th Volksgrenadier barreled through the American rear and overran the service battery of the 589th Field Artillery Battalion. The acting battalion commander, Major Arthur C. Parker, ordered the other three units of the battalion (Headquarters Company and Batteries A and B) to make a run to the west, through Schoenberg to St. Vith. It was almost too late. Battery B ran into an ambush and was practically destroyed. It lost all of its guns. The other two units were also largely destroyed. Only remnants escaped through the darkness.

By dusk on December 17, the mobile elements of the 18th VG Division (followed by the marching infantry of the 294th Regiment) had captured Sets and had reached Wallerode Muehle, 2.5 miles east of St. Vith. But, despite the success of the combat units of the division, its rear area was in considerable disarray. Because of the poor roads, many of its vehicles had bogged down at the Schnee Eifel Forest Station, and traffic congestion here and elsewhere could not be controlled. Many vehicles were still mired in the mud. The continued American resistance in the Schnee Eifel prevented the use of the better road from Pruem to Sellerich to Bleialf, and the 1818th Artillery Regiment was busy helping the infantry wipe out the Schnee Eifel Pocket. It was impossible, therefore, to move artillery or heavy weapons forward to support the drive on St. Vith.

Both Model and von Manteuffel were unhappy with the huge traffic jam on the road to Schoenberg and both turned up at LXVI Corps and 18th Volksgrenadier's headquarters to try to straighten out the mess. Neither had any success.

With the division conducting two widely separated major operations at once—the elimination of the Schnee Eifel Pocket and the drive on St. Vith—Hoffmann divided the command functions of the 18th Volksgrenadier Division in two. He placed his Ia, Colonel Moll, in charge of finishing off the two regiments of the U.S. 106th Infantry Division in the Schnee Eifel, while he retained command of the mobile units driving on St. Vith. The colonel controlled the 293rd and 295th Infantry Regiments, the newly attached 669th Ost Battalion (made up of former POWs from the Soviet Union), all of the artillery, most of the support and supply units, and a few assault guns, left behind by Hoffmann. On December 18, the third day of the attack, Moll would experience considerably more success than his chief.

On the morning of the 18th, resistance in the Schnee Eifel Pocket crumbled. "The enemy still showed surprisingly little initiative," Colonel Moll wrote. "The impression persisted that the Americans, having been cut off from the rear, considered any further efforts to be hopeless." By the end of the day, effective American resistance was deteriorating rapidly. Moll inspected the American positions and found that " . . . the Americans were fighting a 'rich man's war.' Weapons and equipment were excellent, each improvised bunker had its own telephone and cooking facilities, while the officers' suitcases even contained uniforms for Sunday promenades."[24] Moll then placed Lieutenant Colonel Witte in charge of mopping up operations in the wooded area southeast of Schoenberg. Witte controlled his own regiment, a single battalion from the 1818th Artillery Regiment, and a few attached engineers and signals troops. Moll ordered all other units, as well as supply and ammunition columns, to head for the St. Vith sector. Because of the poor road network, traffic congestion, and competition for road space from other units (most notably Colonel Remer's Fuehrer *Begleit* [Escort] Brigade), it would take days—not hours—for them to reach the front.

With the U.S. 7th Armored Division fighting for its life at St. Vith and with General Middleton desperately trying to organize the defenses of Bastogne, 20 miles west of the original front line, the U.S. VIII Corps forgot all thought of rescuing the two demoralized infantry regiments trapped in the Schnee Eifel. The Germans had almost forgotten about them as well. They knew that soon they would run out of food and would be forced to surrender. Until then, a single battalion of German artillery continued to pound the Schnee Eifel. The American artillery, which was already out of ammunition, could not reply.

On December 18, the two trapped regiments of the 106th received orders to attack to their rear. About dark, Colonel Charles Cavender, the commander of the U.S. 423rd Infantry Regiment, received orders to take Schoenberg itself. As night fell, he and his men trekked through the Alf Valley. His trucks and command jeeps bogged down in the mud, and many weapons were lost. Confusion reigned on the American side. Nevertheless, the regiment—spearheaded by its 1st Battalion—launched a night attack. Unfortunately for the Americans, Lieutenant Colonel William H. Craig, the commander of the 1st Battalion, was killed almost immediately by a German artillery shell, and the attack lost its direction. A German counterattack confounded the confusion.

The Americans were now low on ammunition. All they had was what they personally carried with them. Machine gun and mortar ammunition was almost exhausted. The two trapped regiments had appealed for aerial resupply on the afternoon of the 17th, stating that they needed 200,000 rounds each of M-1 rifle and .30 caliber machine gun ammunition and 1,000 bazooka rockets. They also asked for mortar shells, bandages, plasma, and other supplies. But air force bureaucracy had grounded the C-47s. A second mission was requested. This time the C-47s landed at a field in Belgium, but no fighter protection was available and no map coordinates for the scheduled drop were provided. Once again, the mission was scrubbed.

Despite its difficulties, the U.S. 422nd Infantry Regiment attacked toward Schoenberg on the morning of December 19. It very quickly came under machine gun and artillery fire from several directions. Part of its 1st Battalion was overrun by assault guns and part of it was cut off and captured. The other two battalions continued to attack, but German artillery fire knocked out most of their remaining mortars and machine guns. The 423rd suffered heavy casualties and became very disorganized. The Germans captured about 3,000 prisoners that morning.

After that, Colonel George Descheneaux, the commander of the 422nd Infantry, decided to surrender. He had not been able to get food or ammunition for four days. He conferred with Colonel Cavender, who also decided to capitulate. It was all over on the 20th. General Jodl was surprised that two regiments could not hold out longer. General Middleton expressed a similar opinion. But they were green troops, cut off in their first battle. Veteran troops would no doubt have held out longer. In any case, about 8,000 men were captured; only about 200 escaped. It was the largest mass surrender of American soldiers in the European war and their greatest defeat. And it was administered by a unit and a commander no one had ever heard of.

CHAPTER 7

St. Vith

And what was happening in the zone of the 5th Panzer Army, while Dietrich was being frustrated at Elsenborn Ridge and KG Peiper was being slaughtered at La Gleize?

Very simply, its offensive became the major offensive; General Manteuffel developed his secondary attack into the primary thrust upon which Nazi Germany based all of its hopes.

On December 16, as we have seen, Manteuffel began his advance with three corps attacking on line: Lucht's LXVI, Krueger's LVIII Panzer, and von Luettwitz's XXXXVII Panzer (north to south). Lucht's initial mission was to bite off the Schnee Eifel, destroy the two American regiments there, and capture St. Vith, while Krueger and Luettwitz drove on to the Meuse.

The American commanders were taken totally by surprise, not just in the zone of the 5th Panzer Army but all along the line and at every level of command. Only a few days before the offensive began, General Bradley, the commander of the U.S. 12th Army Group, said to the press: "If the other fellow only would hit us now! We could kill more Germans with a good deal less effort if they'd only climb out of their holes and come after us for a change!"

He got his wish; however, as we have seen, Eisenhower reacted more quickly than the Fuehrer or his advisors at OKW thought possible.

Eisenhower's strategy for dealing with Model's offensive came straight out of a World War I battle manual: (1) reinforce the shoulders north and south of the breakthrough area to constrict the breakthrough as much as possible; (2) simultaneously, delay the enemy's advance as much as possible by using mines, blowing up bridges, and denying him access to key intersections and towns; (3) set up a secondary blocking position behind the threatened sector to provide a defense-in-depth and to check the offensive, if possible; and (4) accumulate reserves, especially on the shoulders, to launch a decisive counteroffensive.

Eisenhower threw delaying forces into the battle with incredible speed. Before the first day of the battle was over, Major General Alan W. Jones, the commander of the U.S. 106th Infantry Division, had been reinforced with Brigadier General William M. Hoge's CCB of the U.S. 9th Armored Division. Jones planned to use it in an attack toward Schoenberg, to rescue the two trapped regiments. That evening, General Middleton, the commander of the VIII Corps, promised Jones further reinforcements, in the form of the 7th Armored Division. At this point, however, the Americans made a major mistake. The two generals had a bad telephone connection and contact between them was lost before they could complete their conversation. Jones understood Middleton to say that the 7th Armored would arrive at St. Vith (Jones's headquarters) at about 7 A.M. on December 17. But this was not Middleton's intent. The division was located in the Maastricht area in the Netherlands, about 90 miles away, and had only just been alerted. There was no way it could move that far, that fast. It did not even begin its move until 4 A.M. on the 17th. Jones, however, based all of his plans on December 16 on the assumption that the 7th Armored would be in St. Vith the following morning. He cancelled Hoge's attack toward the Schnee Eifel and committed it to the south, where his other regiment, the 424th Infantry, was under heavy attack from Kittel's 62nd Volksgrenadier Division at Winterspelt. (Until then, Hoge's 27th Armored Infantry Battalion and most of his 14th Tank Battalion were trying to keep a corridor open to the Schnee Eifel.) This set the stage for the greatest single disaster the U.S. Army suffered in the European Theater in World War II, as it left Hoffmann and the 18th Volksgrenadier Division free to deal with the Americans on the Schnee Eifel (Chapter VI).

Meantime, the U.S. 75th Infantry, 17th Airborne, and 11th Armored Divisions were just arriving on the European mainland. Eisenhower promptly ordered them to the Ardennes, along with every General Headquarters (GHQ) unit he could lay his hands on. These included six engineer regiments or groups and several field artillery battalions. Among other things, the engineers were ordered to prepare to blow the Meuse River bridges. Finally, the U.S. 9th Army (led by Lieutenant General William H. Simpson), operating to the north, was ordered to send his reserves to Hodges's 1st Army in the Ardennes, and General Patton was instructed to prepare to counterattack the German right (southern) flank with three full divisions.

In the meantime, the 7th Armored Division was in no hurry to get to the front. Acting on orders from General Eisenhower, Bradley telephoned Brigadier General Robert Hasbrouck, the commander of the 7th Armored, and alerted his division for an immediate move to Bastogne. This conversation took place at 5:30 P.M. on December 16. Bradley, however, was still skeptical that this was truly a major offensive and did not impress Hasbrouck with the gravity of the situation. Hasbrouck ordered Brigadier

General Bruce Clarke, the commander of CCB, to move his command as soon as he got road clearance. He also ordered Clarke himself to go to Bastogne and meet with General Troy Middleton, the commander of the U.S. VIII Corps, to learn the true situation.

Clarke met with Middleton at 4 A.M. on December 17. The corps commander told him that a penetration threatened the U.S. 106th Infantry Division, but details were vague. He ordered Clarke and the 7th Armored Division to go to St. Vith and help General Jones. Clearly, neither Middleton nor his staff yet appreciated the seriousness of the situation. Neither did Clarke, who went to bed. He did not learn until later that CCB did not begin its march until just before dawn. Even then it could only move very slowly.

On December 17, CCB struggled to reach St. Vith over roads clogged with refugees and fleeing troops from the 14th Cavalry Group, VIII Corps Artillery units, rear-area troops from the 106th Infantry, and other routed units. It would take the 31st Tank Battalion, the advanced guard of the division, three hours to cover the last 2.5 miles to St. Vith. By that time, night had fallen on the 17th, and Lucht and Hoffmann had tightened their grip on the Schnee Eifel.

KG Peiper also slowed the advance of the 7th Armored on December 17 by cutting its easternmost road south of Malmedy—one of the two north-south routes leading to St. Vith. Shortly thereafter, Colonel Church M. Matthews, the division's chief of operations, topped a hill south of Baugney and ran right into a column of SS. His driver hit the brakes but was shot before he could turn around. The colonel jumped out of the car and, ignoring an angry shout in German, ran up a hill, toward the safety of a thick cluster of fur trees, about 200 yards away. He never made it. Several bullets from SS machine guns cut him down, killing the U.S. 7th Armored Division's most important staff officer.

The Germans scored a significant victory over the defenders of St. Vith on the American left flank on December 17. That afternoon, CCR and elements of CCB, 7th Armored Division, set up defensive positions around Recht. About nightfall, they were attacked by the spearhead of KG Hansen, including the Jagdpanzers of SS Major Rettlinger's 1st SS Assault Gun Battalion (*Sturmgeschuetzabteilung der 1. SS Panzerdivision*). Karl Rettlinger was tough, even by SS standards—although he was not murderous. He had been with the Leibstandarte since 1933 and had won the Knight's Cross for personally destroying 30 Russian tanks on the Eastern Front, including six in a single attack. He also wore the Wound Badge in Gold, which was only awarded to men who had been wounded five times or more. Supported by the grenadiers of the I/1st SS Panzer Grenadier Regiment, Rettlinger ousted the Americans from the town after a 45-minute battle and forced them to retreat down the road that led to the village of Poteau, seriously endangering the left flank and rear of the St. Vith defenses. They left behind at least four burning Shermans.[1]

That evening, Colonel Devine of the 14th Cavalry Group, along with a small escort, left Poteau and headed for St. Vith, in an attempt to see General Jones, the commander of the 106th Infantry Division. They ran into a German panzer detachment instead, and every vehicle they had was shot up or destroyed. Devine and two of his officers reached St. Vith on foot, where General Jones did not believe that they had encountered German tanks so far in his left rear. He relieved Devine of his command. Because the executive officer of the 14th Cavalry, Lieutenant Colonel Augustine Duggan, had been missing in action at Recht, command devolved on Lieutenant Colonel Damon, the commander of the 18th Squadron.[2]

To the southeast of St. Vith, meanwhile, with a considerable amount of artillery support, the U.S. 27th Armored Infantry Battalion and most of the 14th Tank Battalion of Hoge's CCB, U.S. 9th Armored Division, counterattacked the 62nd Volksgrenadier Division near the village of Steinebrueck, on the Our River, southeast of St. Vith. They inflicted severe losses on the German infantry but then, on orders from General Jones, withdrew as night fell.

All day on December 17, Manteuffel's troops were pouring into the breaches in the Allied line and, by 2:30 P.M., had pushed to within three miles of St. Vith. General Jones, who was suffering from despair and stress, seemed to have given up. He had already handed the defense of the town over to Lieutenant Colonel Thomas Riggs and later (at 12:30 P.M. on December 17) to Brigadier General Clarke, the commander of CCB of the 7th Armored Division. Initially, Riggs had little to defend it with. His own 81st Engineer Combat Battalion had already been smashed and had only 110 survivors. The 168th Engineer Combat Battalion could muster only 350 men, plus a little artillery and some headquarters troops from the 106th Infantry Division. He set up his main defenses on the high ground known as "the Pruemerberg," about a mile east of St. Vith.

Clarke's arrival did not initially improve the situation, for he only had his two aides and his driver with him. His tanks and armored infantry would not arrive in strength until well after nightfall. All he had with which to hold the vital town was Riggs's battle group. Fortunately for the Americans, the Germans did not pursue rapidly and launch a hasty attack on St. Vith. They missed a golden opportunity.[3]

This was not the fault of General Baron Hasso von Manteuffel. He intended to attack the town on the morning of December 18 with the 18th and 62nd Volksgrenadier Divisions and Colonel Otto-Ernst Remer's elite Fuehrer Begleit Brigade, which he had just received from OKW reserve.[4] Unfortunately for him, 5th Panzer Army was also plagued by massive traffic jams in the rear, and the inadequate Ardennes-Eifel road network, and the stubbornness of isolated American detachments did not help. A single German panzer division typically included more than 2,000 vehicles (2,600 if it was at full strength) and only 200 could be pushed into a mile of road. The traffic gridlock meant that the fuel trucks could not reach the spearheads, which often ran out of gas, which in turn stalled the other vehicles in the column.

This is exactly what happened to Remer's Fuehrer Begleit Brigade. Its supply columns were tangled with those of the 9th SS Panzer and 18th Volksgrenadier Divisions, and it simply ran out of gas—on the third day of the offensive! The next day, the 9th SS Panzer only had enough fuel to move its reconnaissance battalion and, further north, the 134 tanks and assault guns of the 2nd SS Panzer Division were also immobilized due to a lack of fuel. Things would become even worse from December 19 on through the end of the battle. Because of Gerow's masterful defense at Elsenborn Ridge, Dietrich was forced to sideslip to the south. As a result, his traffic became intermixed with Manteuffel's, causing even greater headaches.

Brigadier General Hasbrouck, the commander of the 7th Armored, arrived in the St. Vith sector during the night with the bulk of his division. At 2 A.M. on the morning of December 18, however, KG Hansen (the reinforced 1st SS Panzer Grenadier Regiment of the 1st SS Panzer Division) struck from the north against the ill-fated remnants of the 14th Cavalry and CCB, northwest of St. Vith. It then pushed on to the southwest and into the town of Poteau, where—after daybreak on December 18—it was heavily engaged by CCR (temporarily under the command of Colonel Fred Warren) of the 7th Armored. While the battle of Poteau raged, the vital Vielsalm-St. Vith road was unusable by the Americans (see Figure 7.1). Because this road was critical to the defense of St. Vith, Hasbrouck rushed an entire combat command (CCA under Colonel Dwight A. Rosembaun) to the sector and retook Poteau in bitter fighting. Fortunately for the defenders of St. Vith, Poteau was located near the border of the 5th and 6th Panzer Armies, and these two forces had radically different missions, insofar as St. Vith was concerned. Fifth Panzer Army wanted to seize the town for its road network; 6th Panzer Army was only interested in moving west. As a result, Oberfuehrer Mohnke's division did not try to develop its threat against the left flank of St. Vith, although there was heavy fighting north of Poteau for two more days. Much to his annoyance, SS Lieutenant Colonel Max Hansen received orders to abandon Poteau, but hold Recht, to keep the Born-Kaiserbarracke-Ligneville road open for the 9th SS Panzer Division "Hohenstaufen," which was coming up slowly from the east, crippled by fuel shortages. Max Hansen was completely disgusted. He felt (probably correctly) that he could have pushed all the way to Vielsalm, which would have isolated the U.S. 7th Armored and 106th Infantry Divisions, as well as CCB of the 9th Armored Division, at St. Vith. Another opportunity was wasted.

In the meantime, the U.S. 424th Infantry Regiment and CCB of the 9th Armored Division retreated into the St. Vith defensive line, which was shaped like a 15-mile-long horseshoe. Figure 7.1 shows the Battle of St. Vith.

Figure 7.1
The Battle of St. Vith

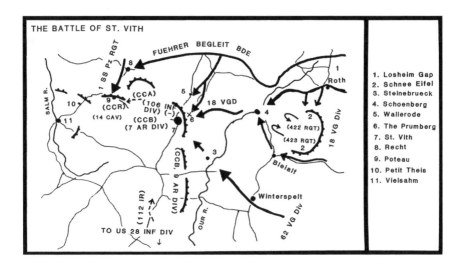

According to the German plan, St. Vith was supposed to be the main effort of Hoffmann's 18th Volksgrenadier Division on December 19, but it spent the day struggling forward, followed by Remer's Fuehrer Escort Brigade. The mobile battalion reached a point near Wallerode (in front of St. Vith), while, immediately to the south, the 294th Infantry Regiment made it as far as the Pruemberg. Neither had any artillery. The 294th Regiment attacked anyway, but it was repulsed by American tanks and artillery.

In the meantime, beginning on December 19, far to the rear of the U.S. 1st Army, an event of potentially great importance was taking place. On the orders of Field Marshal Sir Bernard Law Montgomery, the vanguards of General Sir Brian Horrock's British XXX Corps were quietly beginning to take up blocking positions on the west bank of the Meuse. This corps was very strong and included the Guards Armoured Division; the 6th Parachute Division; the 43rd, 51st, and 53rd Infantry Divisions; the 6th Guards Armoured Brigade; and the 29th, 33rd, and 34th Armoured Brigades. Montgomery was beginning the process of establishing a second line of defense for the Allies. It would not be needed, as we shall see, and only one of its brigades would be heavily engaged, but knowing that it existed had to make the American generals in Versailles and the Ardennes feel better.

Sometimes, Monty was a better ally than most American authors (then and now) give him credit for being.

Because of their supply problems, the Germans confined themselves to probes on December 19. On the 20th, however, Krueger's LVIII Panzer Corps began to turn the flank of the St. Vith defenses to the south, while (south of it) the 2nd Panzer and 560th Volksgrenadier Divisions bypassed the town and headed for Bastogne (Figure 7.1). St. Vith was left to General Lucht and the LXVI Corps.

December 20, the fifth day of the attack, was a frustrating day for Baron von Manteuffel and Field Marshal Model. Both turned up at the command post of the 18th Volksgrenadier Division, where they attempted to get the offensive going again. But American resistance had stiffened to the point where an attack without direct artillery support was doomed from the outset, and Hoffmann was unable to get his artillery and heavy weapons forward because the narrow road was clogged by the Fuehrer Escort Brigade. In places, Remer's tanks blocked the road completely. It was nightfall before Hoffmann could get all three of his infantry regiments abreast of each other—and still the artillery had not arrived. Elements of a supporting rocket launcher brigade and the artillery of the 62nd Volksgrenadier Division, however, did reach firing positions near the American line.

The long-awaited main attack began at 11 A.M. on December 21. General Lucht informed his divisional and brigade commanders and their operations officers that St. Vith was to be taken that day, regardless of cost. Preceded by an artillery bombardment, the 18th and 62nd Volksgrenadier Divisions launched a series of furious attacks against the U.S. line. The 18th Volksgrenadier was stopped in heavy fighting and Lieutenant Colonel Otto, the commander of the 295th Infantry Regiment, was seriously wounded. The 62nd Volksgrenadier Division, however, pushed back the U.S. 424th Infantry Regiment, which was reinforced at Neubrueck with the 27th Armored Infantry Battalion and the 14th Tank Battalion. The 62nd Volksgrenadier nevertheless stormed the village and overran the command post of the 27th Armored Infantry. The battalion commander, Lieutenant Colonel Fred Cummings, resisted fiercely, and shot down about 20 grenadiers before he was overwhelmed and captured.

Wave after wave of German troops hurled themselves at the American positions, supported by the tanks of the Fuehrer Begleit Brigade, which captured the important position of Nieder Emmels, just north of St. Vith. OKW—which realized that no unit west of St. Vith could be effectively supplied until the road junctions in the town were secured—ordered 6th Panzer Army to support the attack. Accordingly, Dietrich sent strong elements of Bittrich's II SS Panzer Corps to strike the northern third of the American line. Casualties were heavy on both sides, but, by nightfall, the American line had been penetrated in three places. At 8 P.M., the U.S. 38th Armored Infantry Battalion was overwhelmed. Only 100 of its original

1,142 men were fit to fight when its acting commander learned that there were Tigers and Panthers behind him. He ordered the unit to disband and break out to the west in groups of five or six. At that point, with panzers in the streets of St. Vith, General Clarke ordered his men to fall back and reestablish a line west of the town.

It was already too late for Colonel Riggs's U.S. 81st and 168th Engineer Battalions and his supporting armor on the Pruemerberg, the high ground a mile east of St. Vith. That evening six Tigers from the Fuehrer Begleit Brigade advanced but were blocked by five Shermans. At the last moment, the Germans fired high-intensity flares, which temporarily blinded the American tankers, just as the Tigers got within the effective range of their 88mm main battle guns. They quickly knocked out all five tanks before the Americans could recover. Then Hoffmann's Volksgrenadiers overran the Pruemerberg. Riggs's men headed for the woods and tried to escape. Some of them did, but many, including Colonel Riggs himself, were captured.

With the American line broken, Colonel Remer quickly moved in for the kill. The Fuehrer Begleit Brigade poured into St. Vith and captured the town at 9:30 P.M. on December 21, although scattered fighting continued until midnight.[5]

With St. Vith in his hands, General Lucht continued to press his attack all along the line. At 2 A.M. on December 22, north of St. Vith, a battle group from Hitler's escort brigade launched a tank attack against the town of Rodt. Resistance was fierce, but Remer's men took the town shortly before noon, splitting CCA of the 7th Armored from Clarke's CCB.

Meanwhile, the U.S. XVIII Airborne Corps arrived from England and took charge of several widely scattered formations, including the 7th Armored Division and its attached units west of St. Vith. General Ridgway ordered Hasbrouck to take up an oval-shaped defensive perimeter nearly 10 miles across between St. Vith and Vielsalm, an area the Americans soon dubbed "the fortified goose egg." He told Hasbrouck to hold it until help could arrive; his men would be reinforced by air drop until then.

Neither Hasbrouck nor Clarke thought much of the scheme, because their troops were exhausted and the area had only one adequate road—hardly a suitable place for an armored defense. They tried to carry out Ridgway's order nevertheless, but Lucht's grenadiers, moving through the dense forests, penetrated their perimeter almost at will. That morning, Hasbrouck sent Ridgway a message: "In my opinion if we don't get out of here and up north of the 82nd before night, we will not have a 7th Armored Division left."[6]

Ridgway considered Hasbrouck unduly pessimistic. Meanwhile, however, Field Marshal Montgomery had taken charge of the U.S. 1st Army on December 20, including the northern half of "the Bulge" (much to the chagrin of General Bradley). Although he was somewhat reluctant to interfere in American affairs, Monty had considerably more experience in armored warfare than Ridgway and realized that Hasbrouck was probably right in wanting to get out of the "goose egg"; regardless, he did not want to run the risk of losing the 7th Armored. He overruled Ridgway and ordered Hasbrouck to withdraw.

There was considerable question as to whether the division could escape with its equipment or not. But the Americans were lucky. On December 22, the Germans continued to wrestle with traffic control problems, as the artillery and supply columns of the 18th Volksgrenadier were tangled with the tanks of Remer's brigade and Dietrich's panzer army, as well as with the guns of the rocket brigade and anti-aircraft units. "In the midst of this mass of vehicles," Colonel Moll recalled, "which for periods of half an hour often moved neither forward nor backward, stood the staff car of Generalfeldmarschall Model, who at last elected to walk." When he finally arrived at the command post of the 18th Volksgrenadier Division, General Hoffmann received a blistering reprimand.

Colonel Moll wrote:

A traffic tie-up of disastrous proportions developed. Since the attack had begun, the military police detachment of the division had been working day and night to untangle the traffic congestion. However, the detachment was not equal to its task . . . To straighten out the confusion . . . every staff officer of the division, including even the veterinary officer, stood from 24 to 36 hours in the streets, attempting to get the vehicles moving again.

Reprimands given the division by the army group commander were not justified, as higher headquarters was clearly at fault. The lack of orders resulted in a delay of at least 36 hours in the conduct of operations. . . .

By evening of 23 December the traffic tie-up east of St. Vith still had not been untangled . . . Artillery pieces badly needed for the expected fighting in the Salm sector were still bogged down on the road between Schoenberg and St. Vith. The Operations Officer [i.e., Moll himself] was once more ordered to try to get these units moving. Driving up the road behind the Pruemberg, he found the same situation as on the day before. The road was completely blocked, largely by tanks and motorized columns of the right adjacent unit, which did not properly belong in the division's zone of attack. Attempts to get the traffic moving failed because the SS refused to take orders from an Army officer. SS traffic police stopped vehicles of the division, making some of them drive into the ditch to allow SS columns to pass.

The picture was one of complete disorder, brought about by incompetence and a breakdown of authority. Only by on-the-spot court-martials could the situation have been cleared up.

By the end of the day the division artillery was finally moved out of St. Vith. The disastrous traffic tie-up, however, meant a further delay in the attack. For several days afterward tanks, other vehicles and a bridge column in St. Vith crowded against the right side of the road, unable to rejoin their unit.[7]

December 23 broke clear and very cold. Allied fighter bombers were out in strength and—even more important—the dirt roads in the "fortified goose egg" froze. The 7th Armored, as well as disintegrated elements of the 28th Infantry Division, the 9th Armored Division, and the 424th Infantry Regiment, were able to escape with negligible losses in men and equipment, despite the efforts of the Fuehrer Begleit Brigade to disrupt the withdrawal. Even so, the defenders of St. Vith lost 6,000 men out of a total of 22,000 engaged. The 7th Armored alone lost 3,400 men and at least 88 tanks and 25 armored cars.[8]

To date, Manteuffel had practically destroyed the U.S. 106th and 28th Infantry Divisions and the 14th Cavalry Group; he had also smashed the 7th Armored and CCB of the 9th Armored. But he was six days behind schedule for reaching the Meuse, and Eisenhower, Bradley, and Montgomery were flooding the Ardennes with reinforcements. West of the Meuse, Montgomery had already brought down part of the British XXX Corps and ordered it to guard the Meuse River crossings, thus forming a second line of defenses. Meanwhile, the focal point of the battle shifted yet again, from St. Vith to the town of Bastogne.

CHAPTER 8

The Siege of Bastogne

The main strike force of Manteuffel's 5th Panzer Army was General of Panzer Troops Baron Heinrich von Luettwitz's XXXXVII Panzer Corps, which included the 2nd Panzer Division, the Panzer Lehr Division, the 26th Volksgrenadier Division, the 15th *Volks Werfer* (People's Rocket Launcher) Brigade, the 600th Combat Engineer Battalion and the 182nd Flak Assault Battalion. It also had the 559th *Panzerjaeger* (Tank Destroyer) Battalion with 19 Jagdpanzers and the 243rd Assault Gun Brigade with 18 StuG assault guns. Initially, the 559th Panzerjaeger and the 243rd AG were attached to the Panzer Lehr. On December 16, the 2nd Panzer had 26 PzKw IVs, 49 Panthers, and 45 assault guns; the 26th VG had 14 tank destroyers; and Panzer Lehr had 30 PzKw IVs, 23 Panthers, and 14 tank destroyers—not counting attached units. Because of the restricted road network, Panzer Lehr was initially placed in reserve. That day, Luettwitz attacked with the 2nd Panzer and 26th Volksgrenadier Divisions. They were still more than a match for their opponents—the men of the U.S. 28th Infantry Division—who were spread far too thinly along the Our River.

The U.S. 28th Infantry Division included (north to south) the 112th, 110th, and 109th Infantry Regiments. It also included the 630th Tank Destroyer Battalion, the 687th Field Artillery Battalion, and the 707th Tank Battalion. Behind the 28th Division lay CCR of the U.S. 9th Armored Division, which was part of VIII Corps's reserve.

The XXXXVII Panzer Corps was not the only enemy the overextended 28th faced on December 16–17. Its northernmost regiment, the 112th, was attacked by General of Panzer Troops Walter Krueger's LVIII Panzer Corps, which included the 560th Volksgrenadier Division (Colonel Rudolf Langhaeuser) and the 116th Panzer Division (Major General Siegfried von Waldenburg), which had 26 PzKw IVs, 43 Panthers, and 13 IV tank destroyers.

To the south, the U.S. 109th Infantry Regiment of the 28th Division was struck on December 16 by the 5th Parachute Division, the 352nd Volksgrenadier Division (both of General of Infantry Baptist Kniess's LXXXV Corps of the 7th Army), and two regiments of the hapless 276th Volksgrenadier Division of General of Infantry Franz Beyer's LXXX Corps.

Each line regiment of the American 28th Division had one or more major towns to defend. The 112th on the north blocked the German approach to the important road junction of Houffalize, while the 109th to the south defended Vianden and Diekirch. The 110th Infantry Regiment, however, had the most important task—bar the German way to the town of Clerf near the front and the vital crossroads of Bastogne, some 20 miles to the rear.

The battle was a mismatch from the beginning.

South of St. Vith, Luettwitz's XXXXVII Panzer Corps's first objective was the town of Clerf, which was defended by elements of Colonel Fuller's 110th Infantry Regiment, reinforced by a few tanks from the 9th Armored Division.

Major General Norman Cota, the commander of the 28th, ordered Fuller to hold the town at all costs. "No one comes back!" he ordered, emphatically.

"No one comes back," the tough Colonel Fuller repeated.

Very few did. His battalions were pinned down and gradually crushed by Colonel Meinrad von Lauchert's 2nd Panzer Division. At 6 P.M. on December 17, the German tanks broke into Clerf, and a panzer rolled up to the Claravallis Hotel, where Fuller had located his command post, and fired into it at point-blank range. Fuller's staff fought off the German infantry for about a half an hour, but the panzers wrecked the hotel, which was soon literally coming down around Fuller's ears. He and the surviving members of his staff ducked out the back door and tried to escape to the west, but most of them did not make it. Colonel Fuller, who tried to infiltrate through the woods with a blinded soldier holding on to his belt, was captured. The next day, 102 members of the Headquarters Company surrendered, and the 110th Infantry ceased to exist.

With his center smashed, Cota rapidly lost control of his division. His southernmost regiment, the 109th Infantry, was pushed south, into the zone of the 4th Infantry Division of Patton's 3rd Army, which temporarily absorbed it. To the north, the destruction of the 110th cut off the 112th Infantry Regiment from his parent division. With the Germans behind it to the south, the regiment retreated into the St. Vith line, where it was greeted as a welcome reinforcement. Cota and his staff retreated to the west, a headquarters without a command. The U.S. 28th Infantry Division had been eliminated as an effective combat force. By the evening of December 17, Manteuffel had torn a major gap 10 to 12 miles wide in the American line, and there were smaller gaps as well. Through the holes poured the 2nd Panzer, 116th Panzer, and Panzer Lehr Divisions, as well as the 26th and 560th Volksgrenadier. Only St. Vith and Bastogne stood between Manteuffel and the Meuse River.

Bastogne was a town of 4,000 people in 1944. It had always been a focal point in the German planning in the Ardennes campaign. The entire Battle of the Bulge was essentially a giant battle for roads and road junctions. Gerow's victory at Elsenborn Ridge was a critical turning point in the operation because it solidified the northern shoulder of the bulge and constricted the German advance, denying Dietrich the roads he needed to the north. As a result, 6th Panzer Army was forced to sidestep to the south. Army Group B was trying to sustain the offensives of two panzer armies without an adequate road net, and traffic jams in the rear were mammoth. KG Peiper had been annihilated in large part because of the restricted road system. The Battles of Clerf and St. Vith were all about road junctions. The U.S. 106th Infantry Division had been destroyed because it had failed to prevent Hoffmann-Schoenborn from capturing the major road junctions in its sector. But, as a road junction, the town of Bastogne was more important than any of them. In a region deficient in hard-surfaced roads, no fewer than seven highways converged in Bastogne, including the crucial roads to the Meuse. Even Hitler—a strategic illiterate—came to recognize the importance of Bastogne. He had ordered that centers of resistance be bypassed but specifically stated that the swift capture of Bastogne was critical to the entire operation.

Initially, the Battle of Bastogne was an armored action. Shortly after nightfall on December 18, CCR of the 9th Armored Division was occupying defensive positions at Allenborn, a village about halfway between Clerf and Bastogne. Then, suddenly, the 2nd Panzer Division, led by the dashing Colonel von Lauchert, emerged from the darkness and launched a surprise attack. Spearheaded by his Tigers and Panthers, his men quickly knocked out several Shermans, half-tracks, and armored cars; overran CCR's roadblocks; and inflicted severe casualties on the American infantry. The remnants of CCR quickly fell back to Longvilly, only a few miles from Bastogne. There it joined the 158th Engineer Battalion (which had already laid almost 1,000 antitank mines within three miles of the town) in the Bastogne perimeter.

Fortunately for Middleton, whose VIII Corps' headquarters was in Bastogne, Lauchert turned northwest on a terrible secondary road, passed through the hamlet of Bourcy, and headed for Noville, in an effort to bypass Bastogne to the north. His mission was to capture the crossings on the Meuse. Taking Bastogne was the job of the 26th Volksgrenadier and Panzer Lehr Divisions.

Meanwhile, Bastogne had been reinforced with CCB of the U.S. 10th Armored Division. Middleton ordered its commander, Colonel William L. Roberts, to divide his command into three task forces: one to defend each of the major roads leading into Bastogne. Team O'Hara (500 men and 30 tanks under Lieutenant Colonel James O'Hara) defended Wardin; Team Cherry (Lieutenant Colonel Henry T. Cherry) joined the remnants of CCR/9th Armored at Longvilly; and Team Desobry (Major William R. Desobry) was sent to Noville, on Middleton's northern flank. In the meantime, more reinforcements were on the way (Figure 8.1). On the afternoon of December 17, General Bradley looked at a map in his headquarters in Luxembourg City. It showed 14 German divisions attacking in the Ardennes. "Just where in the hell has this sonuvabitch gotten all this strength?" he muttered. The Americans had also intercepted a directive from Field Marshal von Rundstedt. "Mighty offensive armies face the Allies," it read. "Everything is at stake. More than mortal deeds are required as a holy duty of the Fatherland."[1] That evening, both the U.S. 82nd and 101st Airborne Divisions received marching orders.

The 11,000 men of the 101st Airborne, temporarily under the command of Brigadier General Anthony C. McAuliffe, left Mourmelon-le-Grand, its station 20 miles southeast of Rheims (and nearly 100 miles southwest of Bastogne) in 380 trucks on the morning of December 18. It was initially assigned to the XVIII Airborne Corps (temporarily under the command of Major General James Gavin)[2] and was headed for Werbomont, but, en route, it received orders to join Middleton at Bastogne instead. The only question now was whether it would arrive in time.

It should not have. On the evening of December 18, General von Luettwitz received an intercepted radio message, informing him that two American airborne divisions were heading for Bastogne. The veteran panzer general was not worried.[3] He estimated that they could not possibly arrive before noon on December 19. Surely, Lieutenant General Fritz Bayerlein, the commander of the elite Panzer Lehr, could capture the town by then.

Bayerlein's abilities as a commander are, in my view, highly overestimated by British and American historians.[4] Immediately after the war, Bayerlein cooperated with Western historians and befriended B. H. Liddell Hart, arguably the most distinguished military historian of his day, and helped Hart edit *The Rommel Papers*. Not surprisingly, Hart was sympathetic to Bayerlein, who was able to pass himself off as a highly capable commander and General Staff officer. Subsequent Western historians have generally followed the lead set by Hart. This view was certainly not universally held in the German Army at the time, however; indeed, it seems to be a minority opinion. Major General Gerhard Franz, the chief of staff of the Afrika Korps in late 1942 when Bayerlein briefly served as acting commander, had nothing good to say about him,[5] and Manteuffel also had serious reservations about him. Bayerlein and Rommel had a falling out in early 1943, and the Desert Fox threatened to sack him. When Rommel was given command of an army group later that year, he made no effort to have Bayerlein transferred to his staff, which was a common practice in the Wehrmacht at that time. Conversely, Rommel had several other of his "Africans" assigned to his new headquarters. When Bayerlein was the German chief of staff of the 1st Italian Panzer Army in Tunisia in 1943, he practically commanded the German units in that campaign until he was wounded and evacuated. He failed to make any attempt to cooperate with the army's commander, Italian General Giovanni Messe, who clearly demonstrated in Tunisia that his tactical instincts were superior to Bayerlein's. Bayerlein is hardly ever mentioned in the divisional history of the Panzer Lehr,[6] which is odd in a book of this nature, although other commanders are praised. The late Friedrich von Stauffenberg, an expert on the panzer branch, also felt that he has been vastly overrated by Anglo-American historians.[7] Another prolific historian, Brigadier General S. L. A. Marshall, also held a poor opinion of him, noting that he was highly critical of the mistakes of other commanders, but, when his own mistakes were pointed out, he only laughed. Certainly Bayerlein's performance during the Battle of the Bulge was quite poor, and, on one critical day, he was more interested in seducing a captured American nurse than in the activities of his division.[8]

Bayerlein's initial mistake was to ask Belgian civilians if the roads to the small towns of Oberwampach and Niederwampach were good. They replied that they were. They were lying. He started down the road (the general himself was in the lead tank) and got a few thousand meters before the dirt roads turned into mud. He nevertheless pressed on and reached Niederwampach—six miles from Bastogne—before 8 P.M. on December 18. An hour later he reached Mageret and was on the main road to Bastogne. Here, he paused and asked another Belgian civilian for information. The civilian, who was an Allied sympathizer (like most Belgian civilians), replied that an American armored force of 50 Shermans, 25 self-propelled guns, and dozens of other armored vehicles had passed through Mageret, heading east. He also said it was being commanded by an American major general. Bayerlein swallowed this cock-and-bull story. Convinced that Mageret was defended by a divisional-size force, Bayerlein confined himself to cutting the Longvilly-Bastogne road, deploying his panzers east of Mageret, and laying mines. Actually, Mageret was defended by very weak forces. Bastogne was his for the taking, but Bayerlein let the opportunity pass. Figure 8.1 shows the Battle of Bastogne.

During the night of December 18–19, Colonel Lauchert of the 2nd Panzer Division (with help from the "Greyhounds" of Major General von Waldenburg's 116th Panzer Division) encircled Task Force Booth (Lieutenant Colonel Robert M. Booth) of CCR, 9th Armored Division. On December 19, TF Booth tried to break out but ran into an ambush near Hardigny instead. It lost all of its tanks and 600 men killed or captured.

Figure 8.1
Bastogne, December 19, 1944

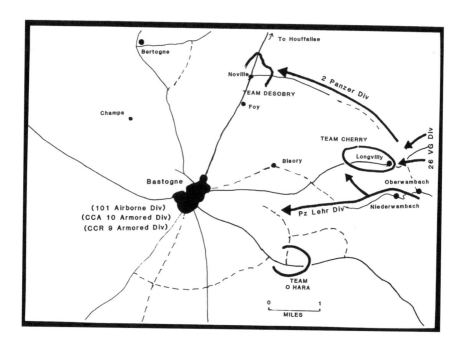

Also that night, Colonel Julian J. Ewell's 501st Parachute Infantry Regiment, the vanguard of the 101st Airborne Division, arrived in Bastogne, several hours before Luettwitz thought possible. At 6 A.M. on December 19, Ewell attacked a reconnaissance force of the Panzer Lehr, which had advanced to within about two miles of Bastogne. He pushed through Mageret but was checked before Hill 510, the main German line of defense. This aggressive attack made Bayerlein even more cautious. Instead of clearing the Longville road to the north, as he had originally planned, the Panzer Lehr leader now decided to divide his command. Leaving strong forces on Hill 510 and along the Mageret-Neffe road, he turned southwest with the bulk of his division, to probe the American defenses, instead of launching a concerted attack. Another day was lost as he struggled to skirt the town to the south over nearly impassable secondary roads. General von Luettwitz was very aggravated by this delay. "If Bayerlein can't read a map, then he should have let one of his staff officers do it!" he snapped to his chief of staff, Colonel Albrecht Kleinschmidt.[9] He was probably even more annoyed when he learned that the next day, December 20, Bayerlein's

902nd Panzer Grenadier Regiment—still struggling forward on the hideous roads—ran into an ambush and suffered severe losses against Team O'Hara, the paratroopers, and the American artillery.

Other German commanders were more aggressive than Bayerlein on December 19, such as Major General von Waldenburg—whose 116th Panzer Division captured Houffalize, an important town and road junction north of Bastogne—and Colonel Heinz Kokott, the promising commander of the 26th Volksgrenadier Division, who approached Bastogne from the south.[10] Along with a detachment from the 2nd Panzer and elements of the Panzer Lehr that Bayerlein had left behind, he destroyed Team Cherry, which was jammed in column formation along the road between Margeret and Longvilly. Twenty-three Sherman tanks, 15 self-propelled guns, and 55 jeeps and trucks were captured intact, and dozens of other vehicles were destroyed. German raiding parties also reached the town of Mande-St. Etienne (due *west* of Bastogne), scattered the quartermaster and ordnance companies of the 10th Armored Division, and captured the bulk of the divisional medical company.

Meanwhile, the 2nd Panzer Division, which had been considerably delayed because of the poor condition of the miserable secondary road from Allenborn to Bourcy and Noville, finally reached Noville (north of Bastogne) and ran into Team Desobry about 7:30 A.M. By this time, however, the U.S. 506th Parachute Infantry Regiment had arrived in the village of Foy, a few miles to the south. Hearing the sound of the battle, Lieutenant Colonel James L. LaPrade, the commander of the 1st Battalion, rushed to Major Desobry's aid, along with a platoon from the 705th Tank Destroyer Battalion. The first German attack was turned back. Convinced that he was facing a formidable force, and with his route west effectively blocked by the force at Noville, Lauchert awaited the arrival of his main body, which was badly strung out on the dirt roads.

Then General Luettwitz arrived. The hard-charging corps commander (who had commanded the 2nd Panzer until September 1944) was convinced that Noville was lightly held, so he ordered another attack with tank support, which he proceeded to direct himself.

Luettwitz was wrong. Noville was not only strongly held—it was defended by fresh, brave, and determined troops. By the time the battle ended a day and a half later, 32 panzers and a number of Shermans were destroyed, and Noville was in German hands. However, the battle had imposed a serious delay on the 2nd Panzer Division. Colonel LaPrade was among the dead. He was reportedly killed when a grenadier spotted an American tank recovery vehicle and fired at it with his *panzerfaust*. He missed the vehicle but hit LaPrade, Desobry, and several other Americans. Desobry later woke up in an ambulance, which was heading for Germany. He spent the rest of the war in POW hospitals or camps.

During the night of December 19–20, Baron von Luettwitz considered what to do the next day. Should he attack Bastogne with all three of his available divisions (2nd Panzer from the north, 26th Volksgrenadier from the east, and Panzer Lehr from the southeast)? He was initially inclined to send the 2nd Panzer west without delay, but Bayerlein and Lauchert finally persuaded him to strike with all three divisions. Manteuffel, however, ordered him to carry out his original instructions (i.e., to stick with Hitler's plan). Young Colonel Lauchert did not want to accept this decision as final. On December 20, in the ruined streets of Noville, he said to Luettwitz: "I propose to drive south in pursuit of the enemy and capture Bastogne."

Mindful of his orders from Manteuffel, Luettwitz snapped: "Forget Bastogne and head for the Meuse."[11]

But this Lauchert could not do. He pushed forward rapidly and seized the Ourthe River bridge at Ortheuville intact, but then his division ran out of gas! All that lay between him and the Meuse was the U.S. 51st Engineer Battalion, which was hardly a match for even an understrength panzer division, but there was nothing Lauchert could do about it.

Meanwhile, the U.S. 84th Infantry Division (Brigadier General Alexander R. Bolling) was moving briskly down from the north to the town of Marche, on the northern flank of the 2nd Panzer Division, while the British XXX Corps began to arrive on the west bank of the Meuse with the 53rd Welch Infantry Division (Major General R. K. Ross), the 2nd Armoured Brigade, and the 2nd Household Cavalry Regiment. Just in case the Germans succeeded in forcing the Meuse, Monty posted the 43rd Wessex Infantry Division at Hasselt, between Ortheuville and Antwerp. All of this was done before Lauchert could refuel his panzers.

Because of the stiffening resistance to the north and east of Bastogne, Luettwitz decided to slipstep to the south and attack the town from that direction. By now, however, the garrison of Bastogne was quite strong and included the 101st Airborne Division, the CCB of the 10th Armored, the 705th Tank Destroyer Battalion, and seven battalions of artillery. The attack failed.

That night, Luettwitz completed the encirclement of the town. Two days before, General Middleton had removed his headquarters to Neufchateau, 18 miles southwest of Bastogne. McAuliffe was on his own.

December 21 was a day of relative quiet, as the Germans and Americans consolidated and improved their positions. Manteuffel, meanwhile, decided that Bastogne should be contained and bypassed. He reinforced Kokott's 26th VG Division with the 901st Panzer Grenadier Regiment from Panzer Lehr and ordered Bayerlein to bypass the town to the south and drive for St. Hubert, 15 miles to the west.

Luettwitz decided to try to take by bluff what he had been unable to take by force and, in the process, amused the enemy, annoyed his peers and superiors, and earned a dubious place for himself in military history for all time. On December 22, he sent General McAuliffe an ultimatum, which read:

To the U.S.A. Commander of the encircled town of Bastogne:

The fortunes of war is changing. This time the U.S.A. forces in and near Bastogne have been encircled by strong German armored units. More German armored units have crossed the river Ourthe near Ourtheville, have taken Marche and reached St. Hubert . . .

There is only one possibility to save the encircled U.S.A. troops from total annihilation: that is the honorable surrender of the encircled town. In order to think it over a term of two hours will be granted beginning with the presentation of this note.

If this proposal should be rejected, one German artillery corps and six heavy A.A. battalions are ready to annihilate the U.S.A. troops in and near Bastogne. The order for firing will be given immediately after this two hour term.

All the serious civilian losses caused by this artillery fire would not correspond with the well-known American humanity.

—The German Commander.

The German messengers reached the forward American positions at 11:30 A.M., and the message was soon presented to General McAuliffe.

McAuliffe sent back his classic monosyllabic retort: "Nuts!"

The German plenipotentiaries—Major Wagner from the Staff, XXXXVII Panzer Corps and Lieutenant Willi Henke from the operations section of the Panzer Lehr Division—were thoroughly confused. The major did not speak English, but Lieutenant Henke did. He asked if "nuts" was a positive or negative reply. They were told by the commander of the U.S. glider regiment, Colonel Harper, that it was decidedly negative. The two Germans were then led back to their escort at the outpost. Once there, Colonel Harper told them, "If you don't understand what 'Nuts' means, in plain English it's the same as 'Go to Hell,' and I'll tell you something else: if you continue your attack, we'll kill every Goddamn German who tries to break into this city."

"We will kill many Americans!" Henke retorted and saluted sharply. "This is war!"

"On your way, Bud," Harper snapped, and then added: "And good luck to you."[12]

Later, Colonel Harper wondered why he added those last five words.

This episode almost cost Luettwitz his career. When Hasso von Manteuffel was informed of Luettwitz's unauthorized action, he was furious. When the emissaries brought back McAuliffe's reply, he was even more outraged. According to postwar interviews, this was the nearly unanimous reaction of all the German commanders when they heard about the incident. The bluff had been called. Luettwitz could not even get his own XXXXVII Panzer Corps artillery to Bastogne over the muddy and cratered roads, much less six heavy anti-aircraft battalions, which he did not have in the first place. In fact, after six days, his three divisions still did not have all of their artillery up.

Manteuffel informed Army Group B Headquarters about the situation at Bastogne and called upon Model to send him as much artillery as he could spare. Failing that, he asked for Luftwaffe air raids. Model was, of course, unable to send any artillery (after all, he was stuck with the same road network as Manteuffel and Luettwitz), but the air force did manage to mount a series of small strikes against the town over the next four days. As was frequently the case with the German Luftwaffe at this stage of the war, they were ineffective.

The unfortunate commander of the XXXXVII Panzer was not allowed to forget about his rash act, either. Manteuffel, who had lost faith in him, spent as much time as he could breathing down Luettwitz's neck. When he was forced to absent himself from XXXXVII Panzer Corps Headquarters, Manteuffel delegated Major General Carl Gustav Wagener, his chief of staff, to oversee the operations of his disgraced corps commander. Indeed, because he felt the way he did, it is difficult to explain why Manteuffel did not remove Luettwitz from command, unless it was because he considered Bayerlein, the senior divisional commander, even less trustworthy than Luettwitz.[13]

Kokott made one more effort to take the town on December 22, but failed. For the rest of the day, Colonel Kokott confined himself to probes and local attacks.

Luettwitz, meanwhile, visited the 2nd Panzer Division south of Marche. He was in a bad mood and delivered a fierce tongue-lashing to the battalion commander who was directing the spearhead and then relieved him of his command. It did little good, however; elements of the 2nd Panzer attacked the U.S. 84th Infantry Division at Marche but were beaten back. Lauchert, in the meantime, bypassed Marche to the south and managed to push a few miles further west, but he was again hamstrung because of a lack of fuel. While Lauchert waited for the fuel trucks to catch up, elements of the U.S. 84th Infantry Division set up blocking positions in several towns and villages west of the 2nd Panzer.

Far to the rear, Field Marshal von Rundstedt ordered Model to attack from the Marche vicinity, wheel to the north, push the Americans against the Meuse and destroy them. Rundstedt thus returned to the "small solution." Model, however, was unable to comply, because the 116th Panzer Division had less than a day's fuel consumption left and about two dozens of its Panthers were already stranded to the rear—out of fuel! The 2nd SS and the 9th SS were in even worse shape. There would be no small solution.

Undeterred, Rundstedt decided to reinforce Manteuffel's success and not Dietrich's failure. He managed to get Hitler and OKW to release the 9th and 167th Volksgrenadier Divisions, commanded by Colonel Werner Kolb and Lieutenant General Hans-Kurt Hoecker, respectively. He promptly assigned them to the 5th Panzer Army to reinforce the attack.

On December 23, the weather finally broke. A high-pressure system caused temperatures to plummet and the skies to clear. More than 3,100 Allied airplanes flew sorties that day, mostly by fighter-bombers, and plastered Kokott's lines with high explosives, napalm, fragmentation bombs, and machine gun bullets.[14] At the same time, 1,200 Allied bombers pounded the German railroads west of the Rhine, effectively paralyzing much of the German supply system, which was already in chaos. Meanwhile, more than 200 aircraft dropped 144 tons of supplies to the garrison of Bastogne. Morale inside the fortress was very high. Even so, Kokott attacked again, this time against the southeast side of the five-mile American perimeter. Initially all went well. The 901st Panzer Grenadier of the Panzer Lehr Division, supported by several tanks, broke through the thin American lines and captured Hill 500, cracking Bastogne's outer defenses. They reached the village of Marvie, where the gliderborne troops checked them in fierce house-to-house fighting that lasted until after midnight.

On Christmas Eve, the Germans regrouped. They had been promised the veteran 15th Panzer Grenadier Division (Colonel Hans-Joachim Deckert), which had two panzer grenadier regiments and 72 tanks and assault guns, but only Colonel Wolfgang Maucke's 115th Panzer Grenadier Regiment actually arrived on time, because of the Jabos and fuel shortages. Manteuffel now had all or parts of seven German divisions surrounding Bastogne. He reinforced Kokott with the 115th Panzer Grenadier. Kokott planned to strike the perimeter from the west, southeast, and northwest simultaneously. Colonel Maucke's regiment, reinforced with the 26th Reconnaissance Battalion of the 26th VG Division, would form the main attack from the west. Once it broke through the American lines, it would divide into two groups, the southernmost of which would drive to Hemroulle and into Bastogne. Simultaneously, two miles to the north, the 77th Grenadier Regiment of Kokott's own division was also to break through the American lines. It would link up with the 115th Panzer Grenadier's left-hand column, cutting off large elements of the U.S. 502nd Parachute Infantry and 327th Glider Regiments. Other elements of the 26th Volksgrenadier Division were to launch a strong diversionary attack from the southeast (see Figure 8.2).

The attack began in the predawn darkness of Christmas Day. At first, the Germans made good progress, and some units had penetrated the American line by 4 A.M. The 115th Panzer Grenadier jumped off at 5:30 A.M. and quickly overran two companies of the glider regiment. Maucke then sent a strong tank column toward Bastogne, with infantry

Figure 8.2
The Siege of Bastogne

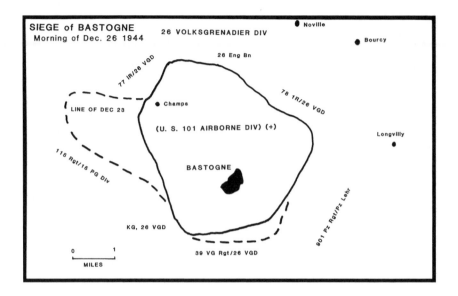

riding aboard the tanks. He was unable to push to the north, to join the 77th Grenadier Regiment, however, because the Americans who had been bypassed or overrun were now coming out of their foxholes and attacking him in the rear. The panzer column then simply seemed to disappear. All contact was lost, and Maucke never heard from it again.

It had not disappeared. It had run into an ambush and had been wiped out by a battalion from the 502nd Parachute Infantry Regiment and a company from the 705th Tank Destroyer Battalion. They attacked the tanks and their supporting infantry with a hail of fire from bazookas, small arms, machine guns, artillery, and tank destroyers. Every single *soldat* was killed or captured. Their 18 panzers were all lost.

After December 25, Manteuffel reported that the forces besieging Bastogne could no longer launch large-scale attacks because they had suffered too many casualties.

THE BATTLE ON THE SOUTHERN FLANK

December 22 was a critical day in the Battle of the Bulge. That day, George S. Patton, who had been attacking toward the east when the offensive began, proved to be as good as his word: despite Eisenhower's skepticism, he turned three divisions 90 degrees and began advancing to the north, in the direction of Bastogne.

The defense of the southern flank was entrusted to Erich Brandenberger, a general of panzer troops who did not have a single panzer. He had entered the service as a *Fahnenjunker* in the 6th Bavarian Field Artillery Regiment in 1911 and was commissioned in 1913. He fought in World War I, served in the Reichsheer, and was chief of staff of Frontier Guard Command Eifel (the German Ardennes) when World War II began. This headquarters was redesignated XXIII Corps on September 1, 1939. Brandenberger (who was promoted to major general on August 1, 1940) held this post until February 20, 1941, when he was named commander of the 8th Panzer Division. He led it in the conquest of Yugoslavia (April 1941) and on the northern sector of the Eastern Front, where he spearheaded the advance of the 4th Panzer Group on Leningrad. He continued to lead the 8th Panzer during the Siege of Leningrad (1941–42) and in the bitter battles on the northern part of the Russian Front. Promoted to lieutenant general on August 1, 1942, he was named acting commander of the LIX Corps (on the northern flank of Army Group Center) in January 1943. Later he commanded XVII Corps in the battles between the Mius and the Dnieper (August 1–November 21, 1943) and XXIX Corps in the retreat to the Dnieper, in the battles of Krivoy Rog and Uman, and in the retreats across the Dnestr and the Bug (November 21, 1943–June 30, 1944). After General Eberbach was captured, Brandenberger was appointed commander of the 7th Army on August 28, 1944.

Unlike General Patton, Brandenberger was a tank leader totally lacking in flamboyance, and he had about as much charisma as a sack of fertilizer. He did not inspire the same emotions as Patton, but, like the famous American general, he rarely made a mistake. He was solid, dependable, colorless, and extremely competent. After three years commanding panzer divisions and corps on the Eastern Front, he adjusted to the demands of the Western Front with incredible speed. He saw at a glance the problems inherit in the *Watch am Rhein*, especially in his own sector. He knew that he would face a counteroffensive from Patton and much more quickly than Hitler thought possible. He therefore demanded a panzer division. Hitler refused. Brandenberger demanded again and continued to do so as forcefully as he dared until Hitler became curt and somewhat threatening in his rejections. Hitler did concede somewhat and promised the general 50 newly manufactured StuG assault guns and the 11th Assault Gun Brigade. The 11th Assault Gun actually arrived, but only about a dozen of the StuGs were on hand on the eve of the invasion. Brandenberger gave them to Colonel Ludwig Heilmann's 5th Parachute Division. The 7th Army had no tanks and fewer than 60 limited traverse assault guns when the offensive began. The typical American infantry division had at least that many. Brandenberger's protests about his inadequate bridging columns also fell on deaf ears.

In the eyes of its general, 7th Army's process on December 16 was not satisfactory (see Chapter III). On December 17, the army continued to struggle forward. A bridge over the Our River at Roth could not be completed on that day, so Brandenberger had elements of the 11th Assault Gun Brigade ferried across the river at Vianden. Meanwhile, the 5th Parachute Division attacked Hoscheid. It lost as least 100 of its 15,000 men killed before it took the town. By nightfall, elements of the division had pushed almost to the Wiltz River crossing at Kautenbach. Colonel Erich Schmidt's 352nd Volksgrenadier Division also experienced some limited successes, pushing the U.S. 109th Infantry Regiment back through the villages of Longsdorf and Bastendorf. On the far southern flank, the experienced and well-led 212th Volksgrenadier Division infiltrated through American lines, pushed into the streets of Echternach, and overcame all resistance except for one infantry company, which fell back into a hat factory and defied all attempts to overwhelm it. The 212th was also able to surround but not defeat a fairly large U.S. battle group at Berdorf, which took refuge in the Parc Hotel. These Americans would hold out for five days, despite the heavy odds against them. Meanwhile, the 212th Volksgrenadier Division surrounded other American detachments at Osweiler and Dickweiler. Throughout the southern sector, small elements of Major General Raymond O. Barton's U.S. 4th Infantry Division were surrounded by the 5th Parachute, 352nd Volksgrenadier, 212th Volksgrenadier, and 276th Volksgrenadier Divisions. They did, however, significantly disrupt the German timetable, and already Patton was sending reinforcements to the hard-pressed Barton. Brandenberger's spearheads were less than 20 miles from Luxembourg City, the home of Bradley's 12th Army Group Headquarters, so Patton reinforced the sector with the CCA and CCR of Major General William H. Morris's 10th Armored Division. This move also fit in well with Eisenhower's concept of operations. Ike felt that the shoulders of the offensive (Elsenborn Ridge in the north and a line near Luxembourg City in the south) must be held before the offensive could be defeated.

On the other side of the line, Model, Rundstedt, and Hitler were also concerned about 7th Army's lack of progress. The dictator ordered that the Fuehrer Grenadier Brigade and 11th Panzer Division be sent forward to reinforce Brandenberger. The grenadier brigade, which was part of OKW reserve, started almost immediately, but would not reach the front for days, because of poor roads (made worse by freezing rain) and gasoline shortages. The 11th Panzer Division, however, belonged to Army Group G. Its commander, General of Panzer Troops Hermann Balck, demurred, stating that a lack of fuel and the damaged railroad lines made the transfer impossible. The truth, however, is that he did not want to lose this depleted but valuable division. OKW and OB West should have sent Brandenberger the division before the offensive began. Had they done so, things might have worked out much differently, but it was too late now.

Brandenberger continued to push the Americans slowly backward on December 18. By December 19, the Americans were rallying. Tanks from the U.S. 10th Armored Division counterattacked and recaptured Berdorf and the high ground overlooking Muellerthal. Shortly thereafter, a German staff car drove down the Berdorf-Muellerthal road and was shot to pieces by the Americans. Inside, they found the body of Major General Kurt Moehring, the former commander of the 276th Volksgrenadier Division, who had been relieved of his command earlier that morning by General Brandenberger.[15] He had been replaced by Colonel Hugo Dempwolff and was on his way back to 7th Army Headquarters when he was killed.[16]

As early as December 19, Brandenberger was positive that Patton would counterattack much sooner than higher headquarters had anticipated. (This was largely because of lax American radio security, a characteristic that, unfortunately, was worse in Vietnam than was the case in World War II and is still a bad American habit to this day.) U.S. Major General Manton S. Eddy's XII Corps was already coming up to reinforce the 4th Infantry and 10th Armored Divisions. Brandenberger accordingly went over to the defensive on his southern flank. Meanwhile, however, on his northern wing, the 5th Parachute and 26th Volksgrenadier Divisions attacked the town of Wiltz, from the south and north, respectively. They nearly bagged the headquarters of the U.S. 28th Infantry Division and did capture six Sherman tanks and 520 prisoners. Simultaneously, after three days of fighting, the 352nd Volksgrenadier Division finally took Bettendorf and pushed into Diekirch, which was the scene of bitter house-to-house fighting. The gallant divisional commander, Colonel Erich-Otto Schmidt, was seriously wounded while personally leading an attack.[17]

The next day, December 20, American resistance against Brandenberger's right wing weakened considerably. The reconnaissance battalion of the 5th Parachute Division pushed west and cut the Bastogne-Arlon road, and by nightfall had captured the town of Martelange, on the main highway south of Bastogne. The 352nd Volksgrenadier Division, meanwhile, finally overwhelmed the American defenders of Diekirch and pushed west, where they were only stopped by a blown bridge at Ettelbruck. Even the half-trained 276th Volksgrenadier Division—which was performing better under the command of Colonel Dempwolff—advanced six miles and (to everyone's surprise) threw the U.S. 10th Armored Division out of Waldbillig. At Echternach, meanwhile, elements of the 212th Volksgrenadier Division, personally led by Lieutenant General Franz Senfuss, the division commander, forced the survivors in the hat factory at Echternach to surrender. Only 116 Americans were taken prisoner. Even then General Senfuss was forced to employ a detachment of self-propelled guns.[18]

December 20 was the high water mark for the 7th Army. General Brandenberger, however, knew that Patton was about to launch his counterattack. He therefore spent most of the next day, December 21, consolidating his positions. The LXXXV Corps took charge of the defensive sector between the Alzette River and the Bastogne-Arlon highway. Only the 352nd Volksgrenadier Division made a significant advance, taking several villages, including Niederfeulen. Ominously, however, the drive of the 276th Volksgrenadier Division was checked near Savelborn; the division was then attacked at Waldbillig by the U.S. 10th Armored Division and CCA of the 9th Armored Division. Remarkably enough, it held its position, although it did lose 100 men captured in the process.

Brandenberger did his best to create a hard defensive shoulder covering the left flank of the 5th Panzer Army and the forces besieging Bastogne, and his accomplishments are certainly noteworthy, given his very modest resources. He knew, however, that it would be extremely difficult at best to check Patton's much stronger U.S. 3rd Army south of Bastogne. He again called for reinforcements. OKW had already ordered the Fuehrer Grenadier Brigade (with 92 armored vehicles) to reinforcement 7th Army, but it had been ordered forward too late and was still struggling to reach the front. Now OKW ordered forward the 79th Volksgrenadier Division. But Patton was moving much faster than the German High Command.

In a windy snowstorm, General Patton attacked early on the morning of December 22 with three divisions abreast: the 26th and 80th Infantry Divisions and the 4th Armored Division, all under the command of Major General John Millikin's U.S. III Corps. He accomplished a remarkable feat without disturbing the blocking force on the southern shoulder of the salient (the 4th Infantry Division [with the 109th Infantry Regiment of Cota's division attached] and 10th Armored Division [minus CCB]). At the same time, the 35th Infantry and 6th Armored Divisions were withdrawing from the Saar front and would soon be ready to join the drive to the north. Patton felt sure of success.

Opposing Patton's attacks from the German right to left (west to east) were the 5th Parachute Division (with the 11th Assault Gun Brigade attached) and elements of the understrength 352nd, 276th, and 212th Volksgrenadier Divisions: a very weak blocking force, considering the legions Patton was about to hurl against it. The 5th Parachute barred the most direct route to Bastogne, south of the town.

The 5th Parachute Division was led by Colonel Ludwig ("King Ludwig") Heilmann. Born in Wuerzbury in 1903, he had joined the Reichsheer in 1921, but in that era of slow promotions had not received his commission until 1934. He was a company commander in the 21st Infantry Regiment when the war began. After fighting in Poland and France, he volunteered for the paratroopers in 1940. After completing jump school, he was named commander of the III/3rd Parachute Regiment, which he led in the battle of Crete, "the graveyard of the German parachute corps." He served on the Russian Front in 1941 and 1942 and distinguished himself in the Battle of the Vyborgskara Bridgehead. He was rewarded by being given command of the 3rd Parachute Regiment (FRJ 3).

Although King Ludwig's courage was legendary, so was his stubbornness and arrogance. In Sicily, his commander, an army general, ordered him to retreat. He replied, "Wherever German paratroopers are, there will be no retreat."[19] As a result, his regiment was cut off south of Primosole Bridge by the British 4th Armoured Brigade on July 14, 1943, and, at one point, was 10 miles behind Allied lines. Fortunately for him, the British were not aware that they had trapped FJR 3. Heilmann and his regiment trekked cross-country, through swamps and olive groves, and reached German lines on July 17. They had been forced to abandon all of their vehicles and heavy weapons in the process. Their commander, however, had learned a valuable lesson: sometimes German paratroopers *do* retreat.

King Ludwig continued to lead the 3rd Parachute Regiment in the Italian campaign, where it earned enduring fame in the defense of Monte Cassino. Afterward, he was given command of the 5th Parachute Division. It was he who would bear the main burden of checking Patton's attack.

Although Heilmann had his division as ready as was possible, and Brandenburger had reinforced him with an assault gun brigade, the 5th Parachute still had a frontage of 24 miles—four times longer than it could be expected to hold against a determined foe, according to the German tactical field manuals.

The U.S. III Corps counteroffensive began along a 30-mile line extending from Neufchateau on the west to the Alzette River on the east. The 80th Infantry on the right attacked from the Mersch vicinity to retake Ettelbruck and the Sure River line; in the center, the 26th Infantry advanced in the direction of Wiltz; and the 4th Armored on the left advanced from Arlon directly on Bastogne.

The 3rd Army's counteroffensive began at 6 A.M. and made considerable progress initially, in spite of blown bridges and damaged roads. By the end of the day, the Americans had gained an average of about seven miles all along the III Corps front. CCB of the U.S. 4th Armored, on Millikin's far left flank, attacked a battalion-size kampfgruppe from the 5th Parachute Division, which had only bazookas, light mortars, and small arms with which to fight. The 4th Armored covered 12 miles by noon on December 22, and was only a dozen miles from Bastogne. Here, however, it was halted by a small but determined German engineer detachment. It blew up the bridge which crossed a small but important stream and checked the combat command in front of the village of Bondorf (Bigonville) for the rest of the day. On CCB's right, CCA neared the Sure River at Martelange during the afternoon, when a company from the tough 15th Parachute Regiment of the 5th Parachute Division blew up the bridge and defied every attempt to drive it out. At Martelange, a single determined company held an entire combat command until 3 a.m. the following morning. It would take CCA another entire day to bridge and cross the river.

Perhaps to instill greater determination into King Ludwig Heilmann, the Luftwaffe promoted him to major general on December 22. This promotion was late because Hermann Goering did not like him—probably because of his outspoken arrogance. But now that the Fuehrer's eyes were on the 5th Parachute Division, he was determined to do anything he could to make the air force look good—even if it meant promoting Heilmann.[20]

The 5th Parachute Division's battle group at Bondorf put up fierce resistance until late afternoon, when it ran out of ammunition. The next day, they were surrounded. They planned to break out that night, but the Americans did not give them the chance. They attacked in strength and captured some 300 men.

One of the captured paratroopers was Josef Schroder of Frankfurt/Main, who spoke English. He was taken into custody by an American lieutenant, who asked Schroder to translate for him. He took the Frankfurter to a German woman, who wanted milk for her baby. Schroder and a guard went to a barn, where Schroder milked a cow. The milk was given to the woman, who fixed Schroder a sandwich. The guard allowed him to eat it. Schroder then began his POW period, which lasted almost two years.[21]

During the night of December 22, much of the elite Fuehrer Grenadier Brigade (from OKW Reserve) finally arrived on the battlefield. Brandenberger committed it to his right flank (southwest of Bastogne, between the 5th Parachute and 352nd Volksgrenadier Divisions) and significantly slowed the advances of the 26th and 80th Infantry Divisions. By nightfall on December 26, the two American divisions had still not reached the Sure, although the Fuehrer Grenadier Brigade had suffered severe casualties and its commander, Colonel Hans-Joachim Kahler, had been seriously wounded.[22] To the west, near Ettelbruck (southwest of Diekirch), the 352nd Volksgrenadier Division was involved in heavy fighting with the advancing U.S. 80th Infantry Division (Major General Horace L. McBride), but generally it held its positions, if only barely.

Meanwhile, the advanced elements of the U.S. 5th Infantry Division reinforced the nearly exhausted U.S. 4th Infantry Division south of Echternach, on the southern shoulder of the American front.

CCB of the 4th Armored finally took Burnon in the early morning hours of December 23, but it met increasingly stiff resistance. It pushed forward two miles, to the tiny hamlet of Chaumont, where it was met by a company from the 14th Parachute Regiment. Armed with Panzerfausts and a few 88mm anti-aircraft guns, the paratroopers fought tenaciously, despite overwhelming odds. The little garrison continued to hold out, even after Chaumont was leveled by swarms of fighter-bombers. For once the Luftwaffe reacted, committing fighters that previously belonged to General of Fighters Adolf Galland's "Great Strike" reserve and, in lulls between the ground attacks, the troops witnessed some spectacular dogfights. It was early afternoon before the American tankers could push the Germans out of Chaumont. Heilmann, meanwhile, brought up the 11th Assault Gun Brigade, which Brandenberger had attached to the 5th Parachute Division. It had 27 StuGs when the battle began and still had most of them. It launched an immediate counterattack, supported by elements of the 14th Parachute, before the Americans could consolidate their positions, and threw CCB out of the hamlet. One U.S. armored infantry company lost more than 60 men; 11 burning Shermans were also left behind. The battle raged all day long on December 24; at nightfall, the Germans still clung to their positions.

Meanwhile, on December 23, the tanks of CCA struck from Martelange and pushed through the village of Warnach, which they thought was unoccupied. After the Shermans had departed, the German paratroopers came out of their hiding places and ambushed the American infantry, which was riding in soft-skinned vehicles. The tanks had to be recalled, but still Warnach could not be taken. CCA finally launched a coordinated counterattack on the village from three sides. Still the battle continued. Using the same tactics the Russians had used in Stalingrad, the paratroopers infiltrated back into houses that previously had been cleared and fired into the backs of the American infantry. Warnach was not secured until noon on Christmas Eve. In the meantime, on the morning of December 23, the U.S. 4th Armored Division committed CCR, on the right of CCA, against a German battalion dug in at Bigonville. Here, also, the resistance was fierce. CCR did not clear the town until 11 A.M. on December 24. "The Germans fought stubbornly and surrendered only when they had no more ammunition," one American officer recalled.[23] All of this bought Colonel Kokott time to launch his Christmas Day attack. Despite the weakness of his army, General Brandenberger certainly succeeded in giving Manteuffel a fighting chance to take Bastogne before Patton arrived.

By now, General Patton had committed or was in the process of committing the U.S. 4th Armored, 26th Infantry, 80th Infantry, 5th Infantry, 11th Armored, 87th Infantry, and 17th Airborne Divisions to the battle. The green 11th Armored and 17th Airborne suffered some unnecessary casualties because of their inexperience. Patton—who was, like Bradley, unhappy that Eisenhower had placed the U.S. 1st Army under Montgomery's command—noted in his diary that there were some incidents of his men shooting German POWs, but he hoped he could keep these war crimes secret. He did.

On Christmas Eve, December 24, the U.S. 5th Infantry Division advanced northward, but ran headlong into the 212th Volksgrenadier Division, which was attacking to the south. Neither division gained much ground. In the center of the 7th Army's line, however, the situation was deteriorating, as the U.S. 80th Infantry Division advanced rapidly and encircled most of the 915th Grenadier Regiment near Grosbous, while the rest of the 352nd Volksgrenadier Division fell back toward Ettelbruck. Continuing its speedy advance, the 80th captured Ettelbruck and forced Brandenberger to try to recapture it via counterattack. He was compelled to commit his only reserves: elements of the Fuehrer Grenadier Brigade and those parts of the 79th Volksgrenadier Division that had arrived in the combat zone. The attacks were without success, but at least the German center was restored.

On the all-important German right flank, which barred Patton's route to Bastogne, the U.S. 4th Armored Division made limited gains in heavy fighting and, in places, actually lost ground. It also lost 10 Shermans to German counterattacks. General Patton was very unhappy. He ordered the U.S. 35th Infantry Division from Metz to the Ardennes.

Meanwhile, American fighter-bombers continued to pound the German defenders and wreaked havoc on their supply columns. On the evening of December 24, King Ludwig Heilmann reported: "At night, one could see from Bastogne back to the West Wall, a single torchlight procession of burning vehicles."[24]

During the night of December 24–25, both CCA and CCB of the U.S. 4th Armored Division were reinforced with infantry battalions from the U.S. 80th Infantry Division. More radically, General Millikin—with an angry Patton breathing down his neck—swung CCR far to the west, behind CCB and CCA, and brought it up on the far left flank of the corps, in an effort to renew his stalled advance. The maneuver worked.

Colonel Wendell Blanchard's Combat Command Reserve consisted of the 53rd Armored Infantry Battalion (Lieutenant Colonel George Jaques) and the 37th Tank Battalion, which was commanded by Lieutenant Colonel Creighton W. Abrams, who later commanded the American forces in Vietnam and was chief of staff of the U.S. Army at the time of his death. CCR also had two battalions of artillery.

Blanchard began his advance on Christmas Day. His first obstacle was the town of Remonville, about five miles southwest of Bastogne. How he knew it was heavily defended is still a mystery; the U.S. Official History speculates that he had a "sixth sense" about it.[25] Regardless, he ordered four battalions of artillery (including two borrowed from CCB) to level the town. Blanchard was right: Remonville was defended by the III Battalion, 14th Parachute Regiment. When CCR finally launched its attack late that afternoon, the III was stunned and did not put up the kind of resistance that its sister battalions had. When the town was cleared at dusk, the Americans had taken more than 320 prisoners. More important, Brandenberger's main line of resistance had been breached. They were only four miles from the Bastogne perimeter when darkness fell. Colonel Heilmann, the commander of the 5th Parachute Division, signaled that an enemy breakthrough was "imminent."[26]

Elsewhere, the U.S. 26th Division attacked the Fuehrer Grenadier Brigade and pushed into Eschdorf, which was still a disputed town as night fell. At the same time, the U.S. 80th Infantry Division kept up the pressure and pushed back the 352nd Volksgrenadier, only more slowly now than before.

Elsewhere, 7th Army experienced other defeats. On the southern shoulder of the bulge, the U.S. 5th Infantry Division captured Waldbillig. Seeing the handwriting on the wall, General Sensfuss began a staged withdrawal from his positions south of the Sauer.

The weather on Christmas Day 1944 was clear and cold. It brought out Allied airplanes in swarms. That day, Army Group B was attacked by 1,700 fighter bombers and 820 medium and heavy bombers. The Luftwaffe responded with 600 sorties. It would launch even fewer in the days ahead.

CCR of the U.S. 4th Armored Division headed for Remichampagne on December 26. The weather was cold, the ground was frozen, and the tanks advanced rapidly. Well supported by P-47s, they quickly took Remichampagne, cleared the woods beyond, and overran Clochimont. Only Assenois now stood between them and Bastogne. This town was defended by elements of the 5th Parachute and 26th Volksgrenadier Divisions. When CCR entered the town, the German infantry emerged from cellars and basements, and a wild infantry battle ensued. The 37th Tank Battalion (Colonel Abrams) joined the battle, but it was nearly midnight before the town was cleared. In the meantime, five tanks and a half-track from the 37th Tank Battalion broke through to the north and headed for Bastogne. A gap developed between the first three Shermans and the other three vehicles. After the first group of Shermans passed, some daring Germans scattered some mines across the road. The half-track was blown up and the two remaining Shermans halted. Meanwhile, the other three tanks pushed forward and reached the Bastogne perimeter at 4:50 P.M. They were greeted by General McAuliffe. "Gee, I am mighty glad to see you," he exclaimed.

The three Shermans were immediately put on the American perimeter as a vital supply convoy followed them into the town. As other elements of the U.S. 4th Armored Division joined the breakthrough, about 400 more Germans surrendered. Colonel Abrams arrived and shook hands with General McAuliffe shortly after 5 P.M.

Bastogne had been relieved, but the battle was not yet over.

CHAPTER 9

The High Water Mark

THE ADVANCE OF THE II SS PANZER CORPS

By December 19, Courtney Hodges's 1st U.S. Army had 208,000 men and hundreds of tanks and guns moving south, into the Ardennes.[1] On the northern wing of the 5th Panzer Army, LVIII Panzer Corps had made fairly good progress, but was now being slowed by the U.S. 3rd Armored Division. In the meantime, Dietrich's 6th Army tried to expand its road net by pushing Gerow's U.S. V Corps off Elsenborn Ridge. They were butting their heads against a stone wall. The Germans advanced through the deep draws leading to the ridge in an effort to dislodge the deeply entrenched U.S. 99th Infantry Division. They were met by a huge concentration of artillery fire. The American artillery battalions fired 10,000 rounds on December 21 alone. When the Germans retreated, they left behind 47 tanks and tank destroyers.

Meanwhile, the veteran U.S. 9th Infantry Division reinforced Elsenborn Ridge.

On December 21 and 22, the 12th SS Panzer Division "Hitler Youth" rejoined the struggle for the ridge. It lost 44 tanks and an estimated 1,200 men in attacks against the U.S. 1st Infantry Division near the village of Butgenbach while, to the south, Otto Skorzeny's 150th Panzer Brigade made one last effort to take Malmedy on the 21st. It was unsuccessful. Skorzeny had 3,500 men and was facing the U.S. 30th Infantry Division, which had four infantry battalions, supported by artillery, tank destroyer, and combat engineer battalions, and was well dug in.

The next day, December 22, Skorzeny attacked again. This time he was supported by elements of the 1st SS Panzer Division. Unfortunately for him, an SS soldier captured shortly before had revealed the plan of attack to the Americans. The SS walked into an ambush and were slaughtered.

Several tanks were destroyed and about 500 SS were killed, with probably twice as many wounded. Skorzeny himself heard for the first time about a U.S. "proximity fuse" artillery shell, designed to explode in the air and significantly increase the casualty zone of the American guns. They worked perfectly. One burst above a German truck caused it to explode. Skorzeny was hit in the face and was knocked unconscious. He was taken back to the hospital and his right eye was saved only through the efforts of Dr. Ludwig Stumpfecker, one of Germany's most distinguished surgeons.

Finally—belatedly—Hitler was convinced that the only hope of winning the battle was to follow up Manteuffel's success. With that in mind, he ordered the II SS Panzer Corps (which was trying to follow the route of KG Peiper) to sidestep to the south and to attack through the crossroads of Baraque-de-Fraiture toward Manhay and Grandmenil. The crossroads lay at the junction of the 3rd Armored and 82nd Airborne Divisions. It was neglected by the Americans until December 19, when, on his own initiative, U.S. Major Arthur C. Parker III began organizing an ad hoc defensive force. From then own, the Americans called Baraque-de-Fraiture "Parker's Crossroads."

Major Parker was the acting commander of the U.S. 589th Field Artillery Battalion, which had lost all but three of its 105 mm howitzers. He used the battalion's service troops as infantry and was reinforced by a detachment from the 203rd Anti-Aircraft Battalion (armed with very heavy .50-caliber machine guns and a 37 mm cannon), a platoon from the 87th Reconnaissance Squadron, and a few passing elements of the 7th Armored Division, which were invited to join the battle and promptly did so. They had several Shermans and 76mm tank destroyers with them.

On December 21, a German reconnaissance patrol of 80 men approached Parker's Crossroads and walked into an ambush. They were decimated. Major Parker, however, was seriously wounded by a German mortar round. He was replaced by Major Elliot Goldstein.

Meanwhile, General Gavin, the commander of the 82nd Airborne Division, realized that, if the crossroads was lost, the Germans would be in a position to bypass his paratroopers to the north, in the vicinity of Trois Ponts, as well as the troops pulling back from St. Vith. He sent most of the 2nd Battalion, 325th Glider Regiment, to reinforce the defenders. In the meantime, the U.S. 7th Armored Division committed its 40th Tank Battalion and a platoon of towed 3-inch guns from the 643rd Tank Destroyer Battalion.

The II SS Panzer was initially delayed by a shortage of gasoline, but its vanguard reached Baraque-de-Fraiture on the morning of December 23. In the morning, it confined itself to probing the American positions, but by 4 P.M. the SS were blasting the area with their heavy artillery; then, about 5:30 P.M., a panzer grenadier regiment attacked, supported by two tank companies. After a violent little battle, the crossroads were finally overrun at 7 P.M. One company of the 40th Tank Battalion was completely wiped out. F Company of the 325th Glider lost all but 44 of its 116 men.

Two Americans, cut off by the attack, walked right through German lines. So many Germans were wearing U.S. Army overcoats that no one paid any attention to them. Later they doubled back and made good their escape.

After the capture of Parker's Crossroads, the 2nd SS Panzer Division headed up the highway toward Liege, while the 560th Volksgrenadier Division continued in the same direction, covering its left flank. The 116th Panzer Division also joined them and headed northwest, skirmishing with elements of the U.S. 3rd Armored and 7th Armored Divisions.

Meanwhile, the abandonment of the "fortified goose egg" freed another division, the 7th Armored, for use by the XVIII Airborne Corps. Counting attached units, it had 15,000 men and 100 tanks. These men, however, were exhausted, their equipment was in poor condition, and their morale was low. Ridgway nevertheless committed them to the Manhay sector.

Reacting quickly to the disaster at Parker's Crossroads, General Ridgway sent CCA of the 7th Armored Division and the 517th Regimental Combat Team (RCT) into the gap, to delay the II SS Panzer south of Manhay. (The 517th RCT was built around the 517th Parachute Regiment of the 17th U.S. Airborne Division. It included an extra artillery battalion and an engineer company, and totaled more than 2,000 men.)

The II SS (which included the 2nd and 9th SS Panzer Divisions) hardly moved during the daylight hours of December 24 because of the Jabos. At 9 P.M. that night, however, SS Lieutenant General Heinz Lammerding's 2nd SS Panzer Division attacked toward Manhay with both of his panzer grenadier regiments abreast. As a result of a gap between the U.S. 3rd and 7th Armored Divisions, he was able push through American lines and cut off and kill or capture 100 men. The Americans lost 19 tanks as well, against negligible losses for the SS. Lammerding pressed his advantage and threw back the exhausted and demoralized 7th Armored Division in confusion, cutting off a large battle group (Task Force Hogan) at Marcouray in the process.

To rescue this formation (which was led by U.S. Lieutenant Colonel Samuel M. Hogan), the Americans attached the newly arrived U.S. 75th Infantry Division to General Maurice Rose's U.S. 3rd Armored Division and launched a hasty counterattack against the II SS Panzer Corps. It was a disaster. One regiment lost 900 men. The men of TF Hogan escaped only by abandoning their equipment and breaking into small groups, but only after they had put dirt in their gas tanks and destroyed everything they could. Then late on Christmas Eve Day, the 2nd SS Panzer took Manhay and thus secured a much better road network in the direction of Liege for the 6th Panzer Army.

SS General Bittrich, however, had no intention of taking Liege. He was following Hitler's orders: drive west for the Meuse. First, he planned to take a river crossing over the Ourthe at Hotton. The 9th SS Panzer, however, failed to keep up with the 2nd SS, and Christmas Day was another good day for the fighter-bombers. The 7th Armored Division rallied, counterattacked, and retook Manhay by nightfall on December 26. The advance of the II SS Panzer Corps had stalled.

THE DEATH RIDE OF THE 2ND PANZER DIVISION

As the German tide reached its high water mark, Colonel von Lauchert's 2nd Panzer Division outdistanced every other unit and was at the forefront of the German Army—not a particularly unusual position for the 2nd Panzers.

The division had been formed at Weimar in 1935, the same day the 1st and 3rd Panzer Divisions were activated. These were the first three panzer divisions in history. Its initial commander was Colonel Heinz Guderian, the "father" of the blitzkrieg. During World War II, the 2nd Panzer had proven that it was one of the best divisions in the German Wehrmacht. It had fought in Poland and France, had spent more than two years on the Eastern Front (where it pushed to within sight of the Kremlin), and had distinguished itself in the defense of Normandy, where it had been brilliantly commanded by Baron Heinrich von Luettwitz. Surrounded in the Falaise Pocket, it had shot its way out, led by its wounded general. It had then rebuilt to a strength of 27 PzKw IVs, 58 PzKw V Panthers, and 20 StuG assault guns—a total strength of 105 armored fighting vehicles. Some of its Panthers were equipped with new infrared night-vision devices, which were used here in combat for the first time.[2]

As we have read, the 2nd Panzer (like the entire 5th Panzer Army) was behind schedule from the beginning. It fought a vicious little battle at Noville, in which it smashed Team Desobry and the U.S. 609th Tank Destroyer Battalion, but at a high cost—20 tanks destroyed and 25 damaged. Despite losing more than 40 percent of its armor, the division had bypassed Bastogne to the north, using Route N–4 to Marche, a road that passed northwest of Bastogne and did not go into the town. Led by the 2nd Panzer Reconnaissance Battalion under Captain von Boehm, it pushed on to the Ourthe River and seized a bridgehead at Ortheville on December 20. It had done little on December 21, partially because of a shortage of fuel and partially because of troop exhaustion. On December 22, however, after receiving a small fuel allotment, it started moving again, driving north toward Namur. Lauchert did not have enough fuel to push forward with his entire division, so he sent the 2nd Panzer

Reconnaissance Battalion forward as a spearhead. The 2nd Panzer Reconnaissance (dubbed KG von Boehm after its commander) was augmented with some engineers, a mortar section, some towed and tracked howitzers, and a few Panther tanks. Another fuel column arrived later that day, so Lauchert sent KG von Cochenhausen after von Boehm. This kampfgruppe was based on the 304th Panzer Grenadier Regiment and included the II Battalion of the 3rd Panzer Regiment, the 74th Panzer Artillery Regiment, and two-thirds of the 273rd Panzer Anti-Aircraft Battalion; it was led by Major Ernst von Cochenhausen, one of the most promising young officers in the *Panzerwaffe*. Immobilized by a shortage of fuel, the main body of the 2nd Panzer Division remained in the Ourtheville bridgehead.

Meanwhile, the spearhead under Captain von Boehm continued heading for the Meuse, pressing through a seven-mile gap between the main body of the U.S. 84th Infantry Division at Marche on the north and a battalion of the U.S. 335th Infantry Regiment (also of the 84th) at Rochefort on the south. Soon it put more than 15 miles between itself and the main body of the 2nd Panzer Division. Manteuffel, meanwhile, ordered Bayerlein and the Panzer Lehr Division to capture Rochefort to widen the gap. At the same time, he instructed Waldenburg's 116th Panzer Division to seize Marche for the same reason. Meanwhile, the 2nd Panzer Reconnaissance Battalion pushed to within three miles of the Meuse, capturing several American jeeps and other equipment in the process. There it halted because of a lack of fuel and formed a hedgehog position around a 17th-century church in the farming village of Foy Notre-Dame. Captain von Boehm was growing increasingly concerned about his exposed position and especially about his fuel shortages. At the same time, KG von Cochenhausen formed a hedgehog in the wooded hills between Celles and Conneux. Although he was within two miles of Boehm, he did not attempt to link up with him, probably because he had been skirmishing with the Americans on the right flank and the enemy knew where he was. He apparently was not sure whether they knew where Boehm was.

They probably did not, but they found out on December 23. The British 29th Armoured Brigade was at Dinant and sent probes to the east. One of them, which included five Sherman tanks, came within 500 meters of the panzer reconnaissance battalion and exchanged fire with Boehm's Panthers. They reported that they knocked out three before they retreated.

Ironically, von Boehm had been forced to stop only three miles from Dinant. It was here, four and a half years before, that the 7th Panzer Division had forced its way across the Meuse during the Ardennes Offensive of 1940. It had been led by Major General Erwin Rommel, who was ably assisted by his principle subordinates, Colonels Erich von Unger, Karl Rothenburg, and Georg von Bismarck. Now, those days seemed like a century ago. Rothenburg had been killed during the first days of the

Russian invasion, Unger fell on the road to Moscow, von Bismarck had been incinerated during the Second Battle of El Alamein, and Rommel, the "Desert Fox," had been forced to commit suicide for his part in the July 20, 1944, attempt on Hitler's life. Most of the men on the 7th Panzer, who had so triumphantly beaten the French in 1940, were now dead. The men of the immobilized spearhead did not know it yet, but at least 40 percent of them were about to join them. They had less than 72 hours to live.

On December 23, Bayerlein attacked Rochefort but could not clear it until the following day. At the same time, Waldenburg's division was stopped cold near Marche, the II SS Panzer Corps could not overcome the American defenses around Manhay, and the leading elements of the 2nd Panzer were running into American armored cavalry near Foy Notre-Dame. Luettwitz asked Manteuffel for permission to withdraw the division, but Manteuffel—knowing what Hitler's reaction could be—refused. It was doubtful if it could have done so in any case. December 23 broke clear and cold, and Allied fighter-bombers had a field day. Resupplying the stationary kampfgruppen was out of the question.

The 2nd Panzer Division had by now advanced more than one-third of the distance to Antwerp. It had pushed forward 60 miles in eight days—more than any other German unit in the Battle of the Bulge. It had, however, lost more than half of its armor (it was down to 40 operational tanks and 10 assault guns) and was now stalled. By the end of the day on December 24, the 2nd Panzer Division was feeling a sense of increasing isolation, was virtually out of gas, and its situation appeared to be growing more serious with each passing hour.

In fact, it was more serious than even Lauchert realized. One of the most brilliant of the American commanders, Major General J. Lawton "Lightning Joe" Collins, the commander of the U.S. VII Corps, was moving against his forward kampfgruppen with two full divisions: Major General Ernest N. Harmon's experienced and well-rested U.S. 2nd Armored Division and Major General Fay B. Prickett's fresh U.S. 75th Infantry Division, which was new to combat. The 2nd Armored (along with the 3rd Armored) still retained their 1942 TOE, which allotted it 14,500 men and 232 Sherman tanks. Other U.S. armored divisions were allowed to have only 10,000 men and 186 Shermans. Counting attached units and light Stuart tanks (which were of limited value), Harmon had 400 tanks. On December 23, his division was located at Havelange, only 10 miles north of Lauchert's spearhead. Furthermore, Belgian civilians had already informed Collins that the panzers were out of fuel. Without bothering to obtain permission from Field Marshal Montgomery, Collins ordered the 2nd Armored Division to immediately attack the 2nd Panzer.

Harmon decided to launch a two-prong attack. CCB would attack KG von Cochenhausen, while CCA would strike south, against Humain and then Rochefort, to keep Cochenhausen isolated from the rest of the 2nd Panzer Division. Meanwhile, the British 29th Armoured Brigade would deal with von Boehm.

The attack began at dawn on Christmas Day. Almost immediately, CCA came across 13 German self-propelled guns. They had been abandoned because they were out of fuel.

At 8 A.M. on Christmas morning, Brigadier General I. D. White's CCB struck southwest to Celles, intent on destroying the German tank concentration at the western tip of the bulge. At the same time, CCA drove southeast toward Humain and Rochefort, to block the road and stop any other uninvited German guests from advancing toward the Meuse and perhaps rescuing the vanguards of the 2nd Panzer Division. Later that day, CCA took Humain. The next day, Panzer Lehr counterattacked and retook the town. It could not, however, help Major von Cochenhausen and his trapped *panzertruppen*.

The slaughter lasted three days. As we have seen, the 2nd Panzer was one of the best divisions in the German Wehrmacht. Now, after five years of war, its men fought their most desperate battle, using all of their lethal skill and experience, despite the overwhelming odds. They were pounded by huge artillery concentrations and attacked over and over again by rocket-firing British Typhoons and American fighter-bombers—not to mention American tanks, which actually had fuel. To the east, the main body of the 2nd Panzer Division and the Panzer Lehr Division tried to fight their way through CCA and swarms of Typhoons and Jabos, while the 116th Panzer Division suffered heavy losses in repeated attempts to break through the U.S. 84th Infantry Division. Neither was successful.

Another German hope was dashed on the evening of December 24, when Major General Harald von Elverfeldt, the commander of the veteran 9th Panzer Division, arrived at Lauchert's command post and announced that the bulk of his division would not arrive in time to help KG von Cochenhausen. It was the same old story: no fuel and too many Jabos.

Part of the 9th Panzer Division did arrive on Christmas Day, allowing Lauchert to spend elements of his division toward Celles, but it was too weak to break through CCA and the U.S. 84th Infantry Division.

At the same time, less than two miles northeast of KG von Cochenhausen, British artillery pounded KG von Boehm; then it was pulverized by Lockheed P-38 Lightning fighter airplanes. Finally, Brigadier C. F. C. Harvey's 29th Armoured Brigade and the U.S. 82nd Reconnaissance Battalion struck the 2nd Panzer Reconnaissance Battalion at Foy Notre-Dame. It was overwhelmed on Christmas Day. One hundred forty-eight Germans were taken prisoner; Captain von Boehm was among them.

Figure 9.1
The Celles Sector, December 25–26, 1944

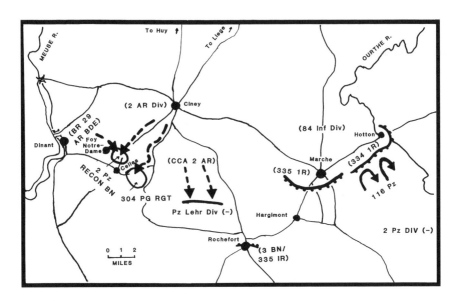

That night, CCB of the U.S. 2nd Armored Division pushed Cochenhausen back and forced him to abandon his towed artillery. Even Hitler recognized that the situation was hopeless. Early the following morning, he authorized Cochenhausen to break out. But it was already too late.

On December 26 and 27, near Celles, KG von Cochenhausen was annihilated. Skillfully led, it fought extremely well but, in the end, succumbed to overwhelming numbers. The 304th Panzer Grenadier Regiment, the II Battalion of the 3rd Panzer Regiment, the 74th Panzer Artillery Regiment, and two-thirds of the 273rd Panzer Anti-Aircraft Battalion were virtually wiped out. About 2,500 German soldiers were killed or wounded and 1,200 more were captured. Some 82 tanks, 81 artillery pieces, and 450 trucks and other motorized vehicles were lost in the carnage. Figure 9.1 shows the Battle of Celles.

Of the two kampfgruppen, only about 600 men, led by the indomitable Major von Cochenhausen, managed to break out of the pocket and eventually succeeded in reaching German lines—on foot. Even this remnant probably would not have escaped had it not been for a heavy snow storm on December 28. Not a single vehicle or tank escaped the American encirclement. Half of the 2nd Panzer Division had been annihilated.

After Celles, all roads led backward for the German Army in the west.

For the panzer troops, getting back was not easy. The 9th Panzer Division was soon involved in heavy fighting, keeping the escape routes open for what was left of the 2nd Panzer, while a regimental-size battle ground of the 116th Panzer (KG Beyer under the command of Colonel Johannes Bayer) was surrounded near Verdenne, just east of Marche, by the U.S. 84th Infantry Division on Christmas Day. The kampfgruppe—which included the division's only armored regiment, the 16th Panzer—broke out during the night of December 26–27, but with heavy losses. The 116th Panzer now joined the list of burned-out German divisions.

To add to the German problems, the weather was good from December 23 to 27, and Allied bombers and fighter-bombers pounded the Ardennes. On Christmas Day, 1,700 fighter-bombers and 820 medium and heavy bombers attacked Army Group B. Some of these aircraft flew more than one sortie. The Luftwaffe responded with 600 sorties. The next day, 3,500 Allied airplanes were committed to the attack. The Luftwaffe answered with 400 aircraft. "The Jabos hung in the air like a swarm of wasps," one grenadier recalled.[3] The situation deteriorated to the point that Field Marshal Model had to issue an order forbidding daylight movement of troops and vehicles.

Elsewhere there was also heavy fighting. South of Diekirch, in the zone of the 7th Army, Patton's forces pushed the 352nd Volksgrenadier Division back across the Sauer on December 26. Its commander, Colonel Erich-Otto Schmidt, was seriously wounded. To avoid capture, some of the grenadiers were actually forced to swim across the river.[4]

Meanwhile, on Christmas Day, Field Marshal von Rundstedt signaled Hitler and, in no uncertain terms, informed him that the offensive had failed. He recommended retreating from the bulge before the Allies severed it from the north and south, trapping most of Army Group B. Hitler, of course, rejected the idea out of hand.

That same night, Manteuffel telephoned Fuehrer Headquarters at Ziegenberg in the Taunus Hills, just behind the Western Front, and told General Jodl that he would attack Bastogne again as ordered, but added that the goal of Antwerp was clearly unreachable. The OKW chief of operations agreed to pass Manteuffel's opinion on to Hitler, but he did not believe that the Fuehrer would agree to alter the objective. On December 26, however, Jodl worked up his courage and told Hitler the truth: "Mein Fuehrer, we must face facts. We cannot force the Meuse!"

The dictator, however, remained obstinate.

Later that night, he was visited by his chief lieutenant, Reichsmarschall Hermann Goering. The two top Nazis soon got into an argument that lasted two hours. Finally, Goering had enough. "The war is lost!" he bluntly declared and suggested that the Third Reich seek a truce. This a furious Hitler refused to allow. He also added pointedly that Goering had better not seek a truce on his own. "If you go against my orders, I will have you shot!" he snapped.[5]

After the defeat of the 2nd Panzer Division and the objections of his top commanders to the continuation of the offensive, however, not even Hitler mentioned Antwerp again. He now focused on Bastogne, which he demanded be taken as an act of revenge.

CHAPTER 10

Clearing the Bulge

With the destruction, the spearheads of the 2nd Panzer Division, Hitler's last great offensive in the west, had failed. The Fuehrer, as usual, refused to recognize this fact; he ordered that Bastogne be captured at all costs. On December 27, the Fuehrer Begleit Brigade arrived in the Bastogne sector, having been delayed by fighter-bombers and fuel shortages. It was ordered to launch an immediate attack—without benefit of reconnaissance. Naturally, the attack failed. (There are cases in history in which attacks succeeded without reconnaissance but not many of them.)

Hitler reacted as he normally did—he changed leadership, although this time he did not fire anybody. He placed Lieutenant General Karl Decker's XXXIX Panzer Corps, which was just up from the Eastern Front, in charge of the siege, and ordered him to take the town, no matter what.[1]

Decker tried. On December 28, in a terrible snow storm, he attacked with the 26th Volksgrenadier Division, the Fuehrer Begleit Brigade, the 115th Panzer Grenadier Regiment (of the 15th Panzer Grenadier Division), and the 901st Panzer Grenadier Regiment from the Panzer Lehr. Patton (who now controlled the VIII Corps) reinforced the garrison with the U.S. 6th Armored Division, CCA of the U.S. 9th Armored Division, and the U.S. 35th Infantry Division (Major General Paul W. Baade). Before the Siege of Bastogne was over, the 9th and 12th SS Panzer and the 340th Volksgrenadier Divisions also joined the fighting. On the other side, Patton committed the 11th Armored and 87th Infantry Divisions to the battle.

The German assault on Bastogne was checked on December 28. Model, meanwhile, was not happy with Decker, who was new to the Western Front, and he had never been as angry at Luettwitz as Manteuffel had been. On December 29, he subordinated Decker to Luettwitz by creating the temporary ad hoc *Armee von Luettwitz*, which controlled both the XXXIX Panzer and XXXXVII Panzer Corps. Armee von Luettwitz's headquarters and that of the XXXXVII Panzer was the same. Luettwitz was thus back in charge of the Siege of Bastogne. His first act was to replace the nearly exhausted 26th Volksgrenadier Division with the Fuehrer Grenadier Brigade on the east side of the Bastogne Corridor. The 26th was allowed only a short breather, however; it would soon be ordered to regroup for another attack.

Unfortunately for Luettwitz, Patton remained in charge on the other side, and he was determined to enlarge the Bastogne Corridor. On December 29, he attacked southwest of the town with Major General Charles S. Kilburn's 11th Armored Division, along with the U.S. 35th Infantry Division. They were met by Heilmann's tough 5th Parachute Division, however, and got nowhere.

On December 30, the newly arrived U.S. 87th Infantry Division joined the 11th Armored in another attack. They ran straight into an attack by the veteran Panzer Lehr and 26th Volksgrenadier west of the town. Because of their depleted numbers and exhausted condition, the two experienced divisions were soon halted by the fresh newcomers. At the same time, the 1st SS Panzer and 167th Volksgrenadier Divisions struck the U.S. 35th and 26th Infantry Divisions, which were supported by elements of the U.S. 4th Armored. They were also beaten back, thanks largely to the efforts of the Jabos. The Allied air forces put 2,600 airplanes into the skies over the Ardennes that day, as opposed to 130 for the Luftwaffe. Nazi Germany lost another 55 tanks that day, plus hundreds of men it could no longer replace. The German divisions in the Bulge were now used-up formations, depleted and exhausted. The 26th Volksgrenadier, for example, now had an effective combat strength of considerably less than 2,000 men, and the Reich no longer had any trained replacements available.

German tank strength was also seriously depleted. The 1st SS Panzer Division had been hastily rebuilt to a strength of 58 tanks and assault guns, but the 116th Panzer Division had only 28 remaining. The 9th Panzer had 75, the 2nd Panzer had 63, and the Panzer Lehr still had 100, having lost only 40 percent of its armor. The Fuehrer Begleit Brigade was down to 51 runners, while the 3rd and 15th Panzer Grenadier Divisions had 41 and 48, respectively. American losses in tanks and tank destroyers had not been light, either, and one combat command was down to 20 runners.[2] The struggle continued.

To this point in the battle, Eisenhower had reinforced the Ardennes sector to a strength of 38 divisions. When the battle began, it had four and a half divisions.

But there was still plenty of fight left in the Germans. When the U.S. 11th Armored Division attacked on December 31, it was met by a hail of lead. By January 3, 1945, it had lost more than 50 tanks and hundreds of men.

Like a gambler who does not know when to quit, Hitler committed the last of Galland's fighter reserve to the battle early on the morning of New

Year's Day, 1945. (Adolf Galland, the general of fighter pilots, had been hoarding these aircraft for months. He intended to use them all in one day to overwhelm the defenses of the American bomber escorts, but Hitler had another use for them.) Flying at treetop level, all available units attacked Allied ground targets and airfields in the Netherlands, Belgium, and Luxembourg. They destroyed or seriously damaged 800 enemy airplanes, but lost 150 themselves, including some of the Air Force's best surviving pilots. With their vast reserves of air power, the Allies could absorb the blow, but Germany could not. "The Luftwaffe received its death blow in the Ardennes," Galland later moaned.[3]

On January 3, 1945, the U.S. 1st Army launched a major offensive from the north, into the bulge. Eisenhower had been impatiently awaiting this offensive for some time and blamed Montgomery for the delays. "Praise God from whom all blessings flow!" he cried when the offensive finally began. (In justice to Montgomery, he had been substituting British for American divisions at the front, so that Hodges would have more U.S. units with which to launch his attack.) But it was not a well-thought-out offensive. General Gerow was highly critical of it (and indirectly of his superior, Hodges) because it was launched too far west and, if successful, would merely flatten out the bulge. An offensive beginning further east and heading south—with the objective of pinching off the bulge—might have trapped most of Army Group B, especially if it were coordinated with an offensive by Patton, driving from south to north. This is exactly what Rundstedt, Model, and Manteuffel feared most. But Montgomery and Hodges were in charge of the northern wing and not Gerow, so the offensive drove from west to east. It was spearheaded by Collins' VII Corps, which controlled the U.S. 2nd and 3rd Armored and 83rd and 84th Infantry Divisions: 100,000 men in all—lavishly supported by artillery and fighter-bombers. Sixth Panzer Army met the onslaught with the 12th and 560th Volksgrenadier Divisions and the 2nd SS Panzer Division: a formidable force—on paper. Actually, the 560th VG had only 2,500 men left, and the 2nd SS had only 6,000. All told, including a handful of miscellaneous GHQ formations, the forces available to oppose Collins numbered fewer than 20,000 men.

Because Army Group B was focused on Bastogne, this offensive took it by surprise. The next day, Hitler ordered Dietrich reinforced, but the American advance was slowed as much by the terrain, the waist-deep snow, the icy roads, fog, and the extremely cold weather as by the Germans, who were nevertheless resisting fiercely. (The winter of 1944–45 was one of the coldest on record.) Soon the U.S. XVIII Airborne Corps joined in the attack, and village after burned-out village fell to the Americans. There were reverses, however. On January 7, 1945, for example, Major General Friedrich Kittel, the commander of the 62nd Volksgrenadier

Division, caught the U.S. 551st Parachute Infantry Battalion in an exposed position and almost wiped it out with a violent counterattack. In general, however, all roads led back to the Reich, as the Americans gained about a mile per day. On January 7, 1945, the critical Baraque-de-Fraiture crossroads (Parker's Crossroads) was lost, and the German generals were acutely concerned that the U.S. 1st and 3rd Armies might soon link up and sever the bulge near its base, trapping much of the 5th Panzer and 6th Panzer Armies. Even Hitler recognized the danger. On January 8, he gave Model a rare authorization to withdraw. The next day, he tacitly admitted defeat by ordering Dietrich's 6th Panzer Army out of the Ardennes. He also issued an order to withdraw the II SS Panzer Corps (including the 1st SS, 2nd SS, 9th SS, and 12th SS Panzer Divisions, plus the two Fuehrer brigades and two Werfer brigades) to the rear of Army Group G for rehabilitation. For them, the Battle of the Bulge was over.

Most of the withdrawing divisions were in very bad condition. The 9th SS Panzer had only six infantry battalions left and they had an average of only 160 men each. Only 30 of its tanks and assault guns had survived the battle. The 12th SS was in even worse shape: it had 26 tanks and assault guns left and only 120 men in its average panzer grenadier battalion.

Hitler was not the only one to recognize that the German armies in the Ardennes had been defeated; George S. Patton realized it too. On January 9, in two feet of snow and in a temperature of minus 6 degrees Fahrenheit, he struck 5th Panzer Army with a massive offensive, employing all eight of his available divisions in the attack: the 26th, 35th, 87th, and 90th Infantry; the 17th and 101st Airborne; and the 4th and 6th Armored. Again German resistance was determined and progress was slow. A gain of two miles a day was considered a good advance. But the German soldiers were now no longer fighting for victory or for a cause they believed in; they were now fighting desperately, just to keep their escape routes open.

This was another unhappy battle for the aggressive Patton. His advance threatened to encircle General of Cavalry Count Edwin von Rothkirch und Trach's LIII Corps southwest of Bastogne, along with the 5th Parachute Division and parts of the 167th Volksgrenadier Division. At the last moment, however, General Bradley ordered him to halt his attack and to pull an armored division out of the line and place it in reserve. The reason for this order was U.S. military intelligence. After missing two German panzer armies in December, they now expected Hitler to pull another rabbit out of his hat and launch another surprise offensive, this one against Luxembourg City, the home of Bradley's army group headquarters. Patton suspected the truth: the Fuehrer was out of rabbits. He convinced Bradley to allow him to resume his offensive the next day, but without the 4th Armored Division.

On January 11, 1945, Patton closed the last escape route of the LIII Corps and captured 1,000 prisoners from the 5th Parachute Division. He would have preferred more but, thanks to the American delay, Rothkirch, Heilmann, and the 5th Parachute would live to fight another day.

Manteuffel and Dietrich extricated their forces as rapidly as they could, but not as rapidly as they would have liked. The lack of fuel, the Jabos, and the constant rearguard actions delayed them considerably. They nevertheless managed to get almost all of their formations out of the trap before Hodges and Patton linked up at Houffalize on January 16.

By this time, the German officers were facing a heretofore almost unheard of problem: troop morale. This problem had occasionally surfaced in green, hastily formed units, non-German units formed by the SS, and in Luftwaffe Field divisions, but now it was affecting the veteran divisions as well. Physical and mental exhaustion set in. To make matters worse, OKW had to reduce their rations. Because most units now needed every man, home leaves were cut, causing further drops in morale. Mail services were now thoroughly disrupted, and the lack of news from home caused much mental anguish. When letters did arrive, the news they contained was usually bad. Leaves to East Prussia and some of the other frontier provinces were no longer allowed—they were now in the combat zone. Those who got leave often wished they had not. They spent much of their time searching for their families and relatives who had been evacuated from bombed-out cities. Many men had the heart-breaking experience of returning home, only to find their neighborhoods had been reduced to fields of ruins, and their homes no longer existed. Others, unable to find their loved ones, spent their furloughs in the local barracks.

"By now," John Eisenhower wrote,

[T]he German troops were tired from long commitments without breaks. Replacements were of low quality and lacked training; forces were poorly supplied, and rations were being cut. The news from the Eastern Front and home had reached them. The American forces were far superior on the ground, and every clear day Allied planes were supreme in the skies. After the high hopes at the beginning of the offensive, failure now stared every soldier in the face.[4]

Not even the SS divisions had fought with their former élan. The 12th SS Panzer Division "Hitler Youth" is a good example. Arguably, no division on either side had fought as well as it did during the Normandy campaign, but it had been smashed during the process. During the hedgerow fighting and the subsequent retreat to the Siegfried Line, it had lost two divisional commanders (one killed, one captured) and, when it was finally sent back to Germany to rebuild, it was commanded by its senior officer: a lieutenant colonel. SS Colonel Hugo Kraas, a former regimental commander in the 1st SS Panzer Division, assumed command of the 12th SS in mid-November and led it until the end of the war, but the replacements he received were mainly former Luftwaffe ground crewmen and excess naval personnel—and all too few of the fanatical young volunteers that had been its trademark a year before. The 12th SS Panzer had lost its eliteness. In the Battle of the Bulge, it lost 9,870 men captured, including 328 officers and 1,698 NCOs.[5] Such a statistic would have been unheard of even six months before then.

On January 12, Stalin unleashed his massive winter offensive in Poland. Soon, the XXXXVI Panzer and XXXXII Corps were smashed; General of Infantry Hermann Recknagel, the commander of the XXXXII, was killed; and the XXIV Panzer and Grossdeutschland Panzer Corps were in danger of being surrounded.[6] Heinrich von Luettwitz's cousin, General of Panzer Troops Smilo von Luettwitz, the commander of the 9th Army, prepared to abandon Warsaw without permission and was relieved of his command.

On January 14, Hitler announced his decision to transfer Dietrich's 6th Panzer Army from the Western Front to the east—he was planning yet another offensive, this one in Hungary. The following day, he gave Rundstedt permission to withdraw the German forces in the Ardennes salient back as far east as Cherain (seven miles northeast of Houffalize). That same day, Hitler shut down his headquarters at Alderhorst and left the Western Front for Berlin, never to return. It was January 22, however, before the 6th Panzer Army could completely extricate itself from the Ardennes; it handed over its few units remaining in the bulge to Manteuffel. The next day, Sunday, January 23, the U.S. 7th Armored Division retook St. Vith. Only three houses in the town were still inhabitable. The Americans continued their slow advance until January 28, when they halted at roughly the same position they held on December 15, 1944. The Battle of the Bulge was over.

During the Ardennes Offensive, the American forces suffered 80,987 casualties, including 10,276 killed, 47,493 wounded, and 23,218 missing.[7] German losses are not known so precisely. German sources place their casualties at more than 76,000 men as a minimum figure,[8] although one source estimated the Germans lost only 68,000 men, including 17,236 killed, 34,439 wounded, and 16,000 missing. No doubt this is too low. The figure accepted by the German High Command of the Armed Forces was 81,834, including 12,652 killed, 38,600 wounded, and 30,582 missing.[9] Most Western sources generally estimate German casualties at 103,000, which is almost certainly a fraction too high. (Overestimation of enemy casualties is natural. The Germans estimated that the Allies lost at least 150,000 men in the Battle of the Bulge and possibly as many as 200,000, along with 2,000 tanks.) In addition, the Germans lost at least 600 tanks and assault guns and may have lost as many as 800. Because of a lack of tank recovery vehicles and fuel, few of the damaged German tanks could be recovered. Panzer Lehr, for example, had to abandon 53 tanks because of a lack of fuel in January 1945 alone. When it reached the West Wall, it had only 16 tanks and assault guns left. It had started the battle with 104.

Losses in other units were similar. On the other side, almost all of the damaged American tanks were eventually recovered, although many could not be repaired. In all, Hitler lost about half of the tanks and assault guns he committed to the offensive and more than one-fifth of his total armored force. The Americans lost 733 tanks and tank destroyers.

Tactically, the American victory in the Ardennes Offensive was not decisive (when the battle ended, both sides were back roughly where they started, with roughly equal losses), but psychologically it was. As General von Manteuffel pointed out, the soldiers in the west would continue to fight on, for a number of reasons, such as the Allied demand for "unconditional surrender," the Morgenthau Plan (which would have destroyed the entire German economic infrastructure and reduced all Germans to the status of peasant farmers), fear of enslavement by Communism, and the threat of reprisals against loved ones at home if they deserted or surrendered before it was absolutely necessary. Loyalty to their comrades in the same squad or platoon was also an intangible—but very real—motivating factor. In addition, Manteuffel adds, the soldier on the Western Front did not want to lag behind the home front in willingness and self-sacrifice; there old and young, men and women, even boys and girls, struggled on to the detriment of their health and often at the cost of their lives, under the terrible conditions imposed on the German people by the merciless bombing terror of the Allies, holding on daily in a way that aroused the admiration and respect of the man at the front and imposed an obligation on him also to give his utmost. Finally, the deliberately misleading encouragement handed out in official publications about new weapons . . . did not fail to have their strengthening effect on the morale of the German people and the German Army. In addition, the confidence of the German soldier in his officers and non-commissioned officers was still unshaken.

With the failure of the Ardennes offensive Germany had exhausted her last reserves, and what strength remained to her was not enough to maintain an effective defence. For a while, the spirit of duty, self-sacrifice, and comradeship made it possible to carry on, but then the will to resist finally collapsed. Helplessly, the man at the front was forced to recognize that the superiority of the enemy on land, in the air and at sea was now so great that there was no longer any chance whatever of putting up a successful resistance.[10]

CHAPTER 11

Epilogue

After the war, **Baron Friedrich von der Heydte** returned to academia, where he had a long and distinguished career as a professor of international law at the Ludwig Maximillian University in Munich. He died on July 7, 1994.

Otto Skorzeny was promoted to full SS colonel in 1945. He fought on the Eastern Front and commanded *Divisionkampfgruppe Skorzeny* on the Oder until March 1945. He was then named commander of *Alpenschutzkorps* (the Alpine Rifle Corps) in the mountains around Salzburg. He hid out in the Alps for a couple of weeks after Hitler's death but was captured by American soldiers on May 15, 1945. He was tried for murder and other war crimes but was acquitted in September 1947. He was nevertheless held in prison until July 1948, when he took matters into his own hands and escaped. Somehow he made his way to Spain, where the dictator Franco was protecting former German soldiers, political leaders, and SS. He went to work as an engineer until a German government arbitration board declared him "denazified." This meant that he could now travel abroad. He resumed his adventures by moving to Argentina, where he worked for dictator Juan Peron and his wife, Evita. He became her chief bodyguard and thwarted at least one assassination attempt. He is rumored to have had an affair with her, but this cannot be confirmed. He also was associated with Odessa, the secret underground SS organization that helped accused war criminals to escape. Skorzeny may have helped Adolf Eichmann to escape and hide. He also worked as a consultant for Egyptian dictator Abdel Nasser. The last five years of his life were difficult because his body was racked by cancer. He died a multimillionaire in Madrid on July 5, 1975. Most remarkably, he died in bed.

Otto-Ernst Remer, the commander of the Fuehrer Begleit Brigade, was promoted to major general on January 31, 1945. That same day, his brigade became a division. He led it until the end of the war. An unrepentant Nazi, he founded a neo-Nazi political party in West Germany after the war but could never garner many votes. He also served a prison term for slandering the conspirators of July 20, 1944. He became disgusted with West Germany and moved to Spain, where he died on October 4, 1997.

Major General **"King Ludwig" Heilmann** was awarded the Knight's Cross with Oak Leaves and Swords for his part in the Battle of the Bulge. He led the 5th Parachute Division during the retreat to the Rhine, but was captured by the Anglo-Americans on March 7, 1945. He was released from prison in 1947 and died in October 1959.

Colonel **Meinrad von Lauchert** led the 2nd Panzer Division in rearguard actions against the American forces in February and March 1945. He was finally promoted to major general on March 1, 1945, but he was sick of the war and disgusted about the fate of the 2nd Panzer. On or about March 20, 1945, the division was pushed against the Rhine River without a crossing point in its zone. Lauchert then ordered the remnants of the division to break into small groups and escape any way they could. Lauchert himself swam across the Rhine with a few members of his staff. He then deserted and walked to his home in Bamberg, the peacetime base of the 35th Panzer Regiment, apparently assuming that the Nazis concluded that he was dead or captured and would not look for him. They did not. After the war, Lauchert lived in a number of locations. He died in the Stuttgart suburb of Moehringen on December 4, 1987, at the age of 82.

Karl Decker, the commander of the XXXIX Panzer Corps, was in despair as the end of the war approached. His Pomeranian homeland had been overrun by the Red Army and, like Field Marshal Model, he faced the prospect of being handed over to the Soviets for trial as a war criminal. Rather than submit to this fate, he shot himself near Gross Brunsrode, Brunswick, on April 21, 1945, at the age of 47.

Field Marshal **Gerd von Rundstedt** continued to command OB West until the U.S. 9th Armored Division captured the Ludendorff Bridge over the Rhine River at Remagen intact on March 7, 1945. Shortly thereafter, Rundstedt was summoned to the Reichschancellery in Berlin, where Hitler awarded him the Swords to his Knight's Cross with Oak Leaves and relieved him of his command. He was replaced by Luftwaffe Field Marshal Albert Kesselring, who surrendered it two months later. At their last meeting, Hitler personally assumed responsibility for the failure of the Ardennes Offensive. Rundstedt himself was captured by American troops at Bad Toelz, Bavaria, on May 1, 1945, the day after Hitler committed suicide. Rundstedt was there recovering from a heart attack. He was sent to "Ashcan," a collection center for high-level war criminals at Spa, Belgium. He was temporarily released so that he could attend the funeral of his only son, Dr. Hans Gerd von Rundstedt, in 1948 and was released from prison in May 1949. He settled in Celle, in the British zone of occupation, and died on February 24, 1953.

Field Marshal **Walter Model** led Army Group B for the rest of the war. With the 5th Panzer and 15th Armies (300,000 men, mostly recently drafted old men and children), he was surrounded in the Ruhr Pocket in April 1945. By now he was drinking heavily at night but was still getting up at 5 A.M. to visit the troops at the front. Major General F. W. von Mellenthin, the chief of staff of the 5th Panzer Army, recalled: "He was visibly seeking a solution to his own inner conflict and clearly perceived that we had lost the war."[1] Hitler, meanwhile, ordered Kesselring to initiate a "scorched earth" policy in the Ruhr, destroying everything the Allies might find useful, including railroads, bridges, power plants, communications facilities, and so on. This Model refused to do, leading to an explosive confrontation between the two field marshals. No one could make Model obey, however, and Hitler did not want to relieve him; so at least the Ruhr was spared that.

It was now public knowledge that the Soviets had charged Walter Model with war crimes in connection with 577,000 deaths in Latvian concentration camps and with the deportation of 175,000 others as slave laborers. Model deliberately exposed himself to American fire several times during the Battle of the Ruhr Pocket, but the GIs could not seem to hit him.

In the pocket, very few of the soldiers wanted to fight for the Third Reich any longer. Surrenders and desertion were common. Rather than capitulate, Model dissolved Army Group B on April 15, 1945. Meanwhile, he received a letter from Major General Matthew Ridgway, the commander of the XVIII Airborne Corps, calling upon him to surrender. He wrote that General Robert E. Lee had chosen honorable capitulation when he was finally surrounded by vastly superior forces, in an effort to help secure a decent future for his defeated people. But Model could not bring himself to do it. His code of honor held that a German field marshal did not surrender. Finally, on the afternoon of April 21, 1945, he said a final goodbye to his staff and shook hands with every man. Then he and his adjutant, Colonel Theodor Pilling, went into a forest near Duisburg, where the field marshal drew his Walther pistol. "Anything is better than falling into Russian hands," he declared. "You will bury me here."[2] He then shot himself in the head.

General von Mellenthin wrote: "Following the collapse of the Wehrmacht, which to Model was synonymous with the crumbling of all his life's desires, aims and ideals, one can scarcely imagine any other end for him than the suicide he chose. It was his way of remaining true to himself."[3]

Colonel Pilling carried out Model's last request and buried him in secret where he fell. Some years later, Model's son asked the colonel to show him the gravesite, which he did. The son (who later became a general in the West German Army) had him reinterred in a military cemetery in the Huertgen forest.

Meanwhile, **Adolf Hitler** was surrounded in Berlin on April 25, 1945. He remarked to his few remaining cronies that if Field Marshal Model could find the courage to take his own life, so could he. At 3:30 P.M. on April 30, with the Red Army only 300 yards away from the Fuehrer Bunker, he did just that.

On February 1, 1945, the 6th Panzer Army was officially redesignated 6th SS Panzer Army. **Sepp Dietrich** led it to its final defeat in Hungary and Austria. He even joked that they called it *Panzerarmee 6* "because we only have six panzers left." He broke with Hitler after the fall of Vienna in early April, surrounded his headquarters with men loyal to him personally, and sent the Fuehrer a dispatch inviting him to kiss Dietrich's backside.

Dietrich surrendered his army to George Patton on May 8, 1945. After stays in several prisons, he (along with Fritz Kraemer, Jochen Peiper, and dozens of others) was put on trial at Dachau for the murder of U.S. soldiers at Malmedy. Because Dietrich was not even in the same country at the time, it is difficult to explain how the U.S. Military Government Court found him guilty and sentenced him to life imprisonment. Among those who pled for leniency on his behalf were Field Marshal von Rundstedt, Heinz Guderian, Lieutenant General Wilhelm Speidel (an anti-Hitler conspirator and Rommel's last chief of staff), and Siegfried Westphal.

Sepp Dietrich was released from U.S. custody on parole on October 22, 1955. His wife, meanwhile, had divorced him. He was soon pursued by the West Germans. The Munich *Landgericht* (Regional Court) found him guilty of being an accomplice to manslaughter in connection with the Blood Purge of the Brownshirts in 1934—and this time he really was guilty. He served seven months at Landsberg before being released in February 1958.

Dietrich spent his last years in poor health at Ludwigsburg, where he died of a heart attack (apparently in his sleep) on April 21, 1966. He had survived Walter Model by exactly 21 years. Seven thousand former SS men and Wehrmacht veterans attended his funeral.

Hasso von Manteuffel led the 5th Panzer Army on the Western Front until February 28, 1945, when he again reported to Fuehrer Headquarters in Berlin. Here, he was awarded the Diamonds to his Knight's Cross with

Oak Leaves and Swords, as well as a check for 200,000 marks. He declined the money. On March 2, he was given command of the 3rd Panzer Army on the Eastern Front. Unable to halt the last Soviet offensive, he adopted a policy of getting as many civilians and soldiers to the west as soon as possible, so that they could avoid being enslaved by Communism. This led to a confrontation with Field Marshal Keitel of OKW, but Manteuffel refused to change his policy. He surrendered to the British at Hagenow on May 3 and was released from prison shortly before Christmas 1946. He went to work for the Oppenheim Bank in Cologne, where he was joined by his wife, who had been living in a refugee camp near Hamburg. Later he went to work for a manufacturing firm, was elected to the town council of Neuss-on-the-Rhine, and was a member of the West German Parliament (the *Bundestag*) from 1953 to 1957. In 1959, he was sentenced to 18 months' imprisonment for having a soldier executed for cowardice in early 1944, but he only served two months. He retired to Diessen on Lake Ammersee, Bavaria, where he died in 1978.

Field Marshal **Wilhelm Keitel** and Colonel General **Albert Jodl** remained in their positions even after Grand Admiral Karl Doenitz replaced the late Adolf Hitler and Joseph Goebbels as chancellor of Germany. (Goebbels held the post for one day before following Hitler in suicide.) Keitel was arrested by the Allies on May 13 and Jodl succeeded him as chief of OKW. He was arrested when the Allies dissolved the Doenitz government on May 23. Both Keitel and Jodl were tried at Nuremberg as major war criminals. Both were found guilty, sentenced to death, and hung on October 16, 1946. Years later, Jodl's second wife, Luise Jodl, managed to get Albert's conviction overturned by a West German court.

Erich Brandenberger commanded the 7th Army until February 20, 1945, when Field Marshal Model relieved him of his command. The two men had a personality conflict and "talked over each other's heads," as the Germans say. Model was a live-wire man of action and "son of the people," whereas Brandenberger was a thoughtful, methodical intellectual. Brandenberger handed command of the army over to General of Infantry Hans Felber on February 22 and left for home. An hour later, Allied bombers flattened the headquarters. Felber was wounded and several officers were killed. Brandenberger, however, was now highly respected throughout the Wehrmacht, and his performance during the Battle of the Bulge had only increased his reputation. On March 25, 1945, he was called out of retirement and was given command of the 19th Army, which was part of Army Group G, on the southern sector of the Western Front. He therefore did not have to deal with Walter Model. He led 19th Army until "final victory" and surrendered to the Anglo-Saxons on May 6, 1945. He remained a prisoner of war until 1948. He retired to Bonn, where he died on June 21, 1955.

Although thoroughly despondent after the Battle of the Bulge, **Baron Heinrich von Luettwitz** continued to lead the decimated XXXXVII Panzer Corps for the rest of its existence. It was surrounded in the Ruhr Industrial Area in April 1945. Realizing that the war was lost, Luettwitz did not try to offer fanatical resistance and, together with Bayerlein (now commander of the LIII Corps) and General of Infantry Erich Abraham (commander of the LXIII Corps), surrendered to the Americans on April 16. Luettwitz was released from prison in 1946 and returned to his home in Neuberg, Bavaria. He had lost his lands in the east but had enough savings to acquire a stable. He began to recultivate his horsemanship and apparently had a happy retirement. He died at Neuburg on October 9, 1969, at the age of 73. His widow, two sons and a daughter survived him.

Fritz Bayerlein continued in command of the Panzer Lehr Division until the end of the Battle of the Bulge, although he was "in a complete daze," according to Friedrich von Stauffenberg.[4] He was relieved of his command on January 25, 1945, but was assigned to the hard-pressed 7th Army as a reserve panzer officer. Here, he was engaged in organizing stragglers into ad hoc formations. On March 6, 1945, however, General of Cavalry Count Edwin von Rothkirch und Trach (1888–1980) accidentally drove into American lines and was captured. As the senior available officer, General Felber gave Bayerlein command of the LIII Corps and ordered him to retake the Ludendorff Bridge at Remagen. He reacted slowly and failed. Field Marshal Model was so dissatisfied with Bayerlein's performance that he transferred all of the LIII Corps's armor to General of Infantry Carl Puechler's LXXIV Corps.

Bayerlein surrendered to the U.S. 7th Armored Division on April 16, 1945. He was released from prison in 1947 and retired to Wuerzburg. Here he contributed to Chester Wilmot's exhaustive *The Struggle for Europe* but refused to assist Milton Shulman in *Defeat in the West*. Stauffenberg suggests that this was because of Bayerlein's deep-seated anti-Semitism.[5] Bayerlein also assisted B. H. Liddell Hart in the writing of *The Other Side of the Hill* and in editing *The Rommel Papers*. He also collaborated with Hans Karl Schmidt (a.k.a. Paul Carell) in the production of *Hitler Moves East*, *Foxes of the Desert*, *Scorched Earth*, and *Sie Kommen*. In influencing these historians, the less-than-candid Bayerlein succeeded in partially rewriting history.

Bayerlein contracted a liver disease while serving in North Africa. It finally killed him. He died in Wuerzburg on January 30, 1970.

Major General **Wilhelm Viebig**, the commander of the 277th Volksgrenadier Division, was released from prison in May 1948. Later that year he became a riding instructor with the British Army of Occupation, a job he held until 1952, when he became a trainer for the riders of the German Olympic Team. He was a stable director in Warendorf after that time. He died in 1982.[6]

Heinz Lammerding, the commander of the 2nd SS Panzer Division, became chief of staff of Army Group Vistula on January 20, 1945. Its commander, Reichsfuehrer-SS Heinrich Himmler, proved to be completely over his head and stepped down "for reasons of health" on March 20, 1945. The new commander, Colonel General Gotthard Heinrici, promptly sacked Lammerding. He retired to Bad Toelz, the site of a former SS training academy, where he died on January 13, 1971.

Wilhelm Mohnke, the commander of the 1st SS Panzer Division, was named commandant of the Reichschancellery in Berlin on February 6, 1945. He assumed command of what was left of the Fuehrer's entourage after Hitler and Eva Braum committed suicide on April 30, 1945. His first order to his men was to shoot Martin Bormann if he created difficulties or refused to submit to Mohnke's authority (which he did not). Although some members of Hitler's inner circle escaped, Mohnke was captured by the Red Army and remained in prison until October 10, 1955. He thus escaped trial for the murder of Canadians in Normandy and also for the Malmedy Massacre tribunal. He was accused of having murdered Jews in Russia but, again, was never tried for it. Protected by friends in the West German government, he ran a successful business and died a wealthy man in Barsbuettel, a suburb of Hamburg, on August 6, 2001.

Guenther Hoffmann-Schoenborn commanded the 18th Volksgrenadier Division until February 5, 1945. Two weeks later, he assumed command of the 5th Panzer Division on the Eastern Front. The division was trapped in the Samland region of East Prussia, cut off from the Reich by all land routes, with its back to the sea. Hoffmann, however, received a serious but lucky wound on April 10. He was evacuated to Denmark by ship on April 15. He apparently made his way home, because he was not taken into Allied custody until December 6, 1945. The Allies decided, however, that they could not convict him of any war crimes, so they released him on March 5, 1948. He moved to Detmold and worked in the private sector of the economy. He died at Bad Kreuznach in the Rhineland on April 4, 1970.

Jochen Peiper was tried for his part in the Malmedy Massacre in 1946. He was convicted and sentenced to death. He was paroled on December 22, 1956, and released from Landsberg prison after 11 years in prison—nearly 5 years of which were in solitary confinement. He was released into a world that he did not recognize. Bitter and disillusioned, he moved to Stuttgart and then to Zuffenhausen, where he went to work as a clerk for the Porsche Motor Company. He rose to company secretary in 1961, but the union objected; they were willing to allow a war criminal to work as a clerk, they declared, but not in an important management position. Porsche revoked the appointment and Peiper (surprisingly) sued the company. He settled for six months' severance pay.

After leaving Porsche, Peiper (who still professed to being a Nazi) worked as a trainer for Volkswagen salesmen in Offenburg, Freiburg, and Stuttgart. From 1969 to 1972, he had a good salary, working for *Auto, Motor and Sport* magazine, whose editor was a personal friend. While there, Peiper bought a secluded second home in Traves, France. He lost his job in 1972, after his friend died.

No longer able to afford his home in Stuttgart, Peiper moved to Traves, where he spent his time translating books for Motor Buch Verlag. His children were now grown (they worked as a lawyer, a professor, and a housewife), so he and his wife lived modestly but in reasonable comfort until the summer of 1976, when local French Communists discovered who he was and threatened his life. He sent his wife away but remained himself. During the night of July 13–14, 1976, the Communists set his house on fire with at least three Molotov cocktails. Peiper fired several shots at them but burned to death in the early morning hours of July 14.

Notes

CHAPTER I: SETTING THE STAGE

1. Dr. Schacht (1877–1970), who later became a Nazi supporter, was Hitler's minister of economics from 1934 to late 1937, and was president of the Reichsbank until January 1939. He split with Hitler in 1939 and ended up in the Dachau concentration camp. He was convicted at Nuremberg as a minor war criminal; he was sentenced to eight years imprisonment in 1946 but was released in 1948.

2. Although a strong Nazi sympathizer, Werner von Blomberg (1878–1946) was never reemployed. He died in prison in Nuremberg. Werner von Fritsch (1880–1939) committed suicide by deliberately exposing himself to Polish machine gun fire during the Siege of Warsaw.

3. Wilhelm Keitel was, in fact, the de facto minister of war. He held this post throughout World War II.

4. Erich von Manstein (1887–1973) was considered by many (including this author) to be the greatest general Germany produced in World War II. A former deputy chief of the General Staff and chief of operations as OKH (1936–38), he served as Rundstedt's chief of staff in the Polish campaign (1939) and originated the plan which led to the fall of France in 1940. During this campaign, he commanded the XXXVIII Corps. Later he led LVI Panzer Corps (1941), 11th Army (1941–42), and Army Groups Don and South (1942–44) on the Eastern Front. He and Field Marshal Ewald von Kleist were sacked by Hitler on March 31, 1944. Neither was ever reemployed.

5. Gerd von Rundstedt (1875–1953) was educated in cadet schools and entered the Imperial Army as a *Faehnrich* (senior officer-cadet) in 1892, when Walter Model and Erwin Rommel were each just one year old. He remained in the service for 53 years, reaching the rank of field marshal on July 19, 1940. During World War II, he commanded Army Group South (1939), OB East (1939), Army Group A (1939–40), OB West (1940–41), Army Group South (1941), and OB West again (March 15, 1942–July 2, 1944, and September 5, 1944–March 9, 1945). He was relieved of his command or forced into retirement by Hitler four times (in 1938, 1941, 1944, and 1945). Held by the British after the war, he was released for reasons of health in

1949. He died at Castle Oppershausen. Rundstedt despised Hitler and his party but nevertheless refused to assist in the attempt to overthrow the regime. He told Field Marshal Rommel: "You are young. You know and love the people. You do it!"

6. Erwin Rommel was born in Heidenheim, Swabia, in 1891. Like Model, he was the son of a school teacher. He entered the service as a *Fahnenjunker* in 1910 and was commissioned in 1912. He earned the *Pour le Merite* during World War I and spent the interwar years as an instructor and in the mountain troops. He wrote *Infantry in the Attack* in the mid-1930s. This book, based on his lectures, became a bestseller. Hitler, one of his readers, named Rommel (commander of the War School at Wiener-Neustadt) commander of his bodyguard during the Polish campaign. Using his influence with Hitler, Rommel managed to get himself named commander of the 7th Panzer Division in early 1940. After distinguishing himself in France (1940), Rommel commanded the legendary Afrika Korps (1941), Panzer Group (later Army) Afrika (1941–42), the 1st Italian German Panzer Army (1942), Army Group Afrika (1943), and Army Group B (1943–44). Seriously wounded by an Allied fighter-bomber on July 17, 1944, he was involved in the plot to assassinate Hitler and was forced to commit suicide on October 14, 1944. He was promoted to field marshal in 1942.

Johannes Blaskowitz was born in East Prussia in 1883. He was educated in cadet schools and entered the army as a *Faehnrich* in the infantry in 1901. During World War II, he commanded 8th Army (1939), 2nd Army (1939), OB East (1939–40), 9th Army (1940), 1st Army in France (1940–44), Army Group G (May 10, 1944–September 21, 1944, and December 24, 1944–January 28, 1945), Army Group H (1945), and OB Niederlande, Fortress Holland (April 7–May 5, 1945). Hitler disliked Blaskowitz, who was never promoted to field marshal as a result. He committed suicide at Nuremberg in early 1948 by breaking away from his guards and throwing himself off of a balcony, crushing his chest.

7. Guenther von Kluge was born in Posen in 1882. He was educated at cadet schools, graduated from Gross Lichterfeld, and entered the service as a lieutenant in the artillery in 1901. He served as a General Staff officer in World War I and was commander of the 2nd Artillery Regiment in 1930. Later he was appointed Artillery Leader III (1931), inspector of signals troops (1933), commander of the 6th Infantry Division (1934), commander of Wehrkreis VI (1935), commander, Army Group 6 (1938), commander of the 4th Army (1939), and commander of Army Group Center on the Eastern Front (from December 19, 1941). Promoted to field marshal on July 19, 1940, he was seriously injured in an automobile accident in Russia in October 1943 and did not return to active duty until July 1944. After the field marshal's suicide, his younger brother Wolfgang, a lieutenant general, was involuntarily retired, as was his son, Hans, a lieutenant colonel of the General Staff.

8. Claus von Stauffenberg had been Ia of the 10th Panzer Division in Tunisia. He was critically wounded in March 1943, losing an eye and an arm.

9. Ludwig Beck had been chief of the General Staff from 1934 to 1938. He resigned in protest of Hitler's aggressive policies, which he believed would lead Germany to disaster. He was the only senior officer to do so.

10. Martin Blumenson, *Breakout and Pursuit*. United States Army in World War II. The European Theater of Operations (Washington, DC: 1961), p. 558.

11. E. G. Kraetschmer, *Die Ritterkreuztraeger der Waffen-SS*. 3rd ed. (Preussisch Oldendorf: 1982).

12. John Keegan, *Six Armies in Normandy* (New York: 1982; reprint, New York: 1983), p. 283.

13. Walter Model Personnel File, U.S. National Archives, Washington, D.C.

14. Ibid.

15. Carlo D'Este, "Model," in *Hitler's Generals*, ed. Correlli Barnett, p. 320 (London: 1989). Pastor Niemoeller spent the entire war in concentration camps.

16. Ibid, p. 321.

17. Like Model, Ernst Busch (1885–1945) was a fervent supporter of the Nazis. Promoted to field marshal for political reasons on February 1, 1943, he replaced Field Marshal von Kluge as commander of Army Group Center on October 12, 1943. He presided over the greatest German military disaster of the war, in June 1944, when Stalin's armies overwhelmed Army Group Center and Germany lost more than 300,000 men. He was relieved of his command by Hitler on June 28, 1944. Briefly given a minor command in northern Germany and Denmark at the end of the war, he died in British captivity.

18. Adolf Strauss was born on September 6, 1879, in Scharmke, Saxony. Educated in cadet schools, he entered the service as a *Faehnrich* (senior officer cadet) in 1898. Commissioned in an infantry regiment the following year, he served in the Reichsheer and was a colonel commanding the 4th Infantry Regiment in 1932. Named inspector of infantry in 1934, he was advanced to Infantry Commander IV (and deputy commander of the 4th Infantry Division at Dresden) in 1935. Two weeks later, he assumed command of the 22nd Infantry Division. In 1938, he became commander of the II Corps, which he led in Poland. Strauss assumed command of the 9th Army on April 30, 1940, and led it during the French campaign. He was promoted to colonel general on July 19, 1940. His failure before Moscow, however, wrecked his career, and he never received another assignment. He died in Luebeck in 1973, at the age of 93.

19. Paul Carell, *Hitler Moves East* (Boston: 1965; reprint, New York: 1966), p. 398.

20. Friedrich Wilhelm von Mellenthin, *German Generals of World War II* (Norman, OK: 1977), p. 149–51.

21. Chester Wilmot, *The Struggle for Europe* (New York: 1981), p. 435.

22. General of Infantry Kurt von der Chevallerie (1891–1945) and General of Infantry Georg von Sodenstern (1889–1955) were both relieved of their commands shortly thereafter, as was their army group commander, Colonel General von Blaskowitz. Neither Chevallerie nor Sodenstern were ever reemployed. Chevallerie was later arrested by the Soviets and was never seen again.

23. See Blumenson, *Breakout and Pursuit*, p. 558. Dietrich von Choltitz was, of course, out of the reach of Nazi "justice." He died in Baden-Baden in 1966. Before being named Wehrmacht Commander of Greater Paris on August 8, 1944, he had commanded the 11th Panzer Division in Russia and the LXXXIV Corps in Normandy.

24. L. E. Ellis, *Victory in the West*, vol. 1, *The Battle of Normandy* (London: 1962), pp. 451–52.

25. Wilmot, p. 434.

26. L. E. Ellis, *Victory in the West*, vol. 2, *The Defeat of Germany* (London: 1968), pp. 48–50.

27. Albert Seaton, *The German Army, 1933–1945* (New York: 1982), p. 238.

28. Ellis, vol. 2, pp. 51–52.

CHAPTER II: PLANNING AND PREPARATIONS

1. Georg Tessin, *Verbaende und Truppen der deutschen Wehrmacht und Waffen SS im Zweiten Weltkrieg, 1939–1945* (Osnabrueck: 1974), vol. 3, pp. 8–9. This unit is sometimes incorrectly referred to as the 6th SS Panzer Army. It did not receive this designation until February 1945.

2. John S. D. Eisenhower, *The Bitter Woods* (New York: 1969), p. 115.

3. Alfred Jodl was born in Wuerzburg, Bavaria, in 1890. He was educated in cadet schools and entered the service as a *Faehnrich* in 1912. He spent most of his career in the artillery. He became chief of operations at OKW on February 4, 1938. He took an assignment as commander of the 44th Artillery Command (Arko 44) in October 1938 but returned to OKW as chief of operations when the war began in 1939. He stood high in Hitler's favor after the Norway campaign (which he planned) and was promoted from major general to general of artillery on July 19, 1940, bypassing the rank of lieutenant general altogether. The chief of operations of the High Command of the Armed Forces throughout the war, he was promoted to colonel general on January 30, 1944, and was hung at Nuremberg on October 16, 1946. His younger brother Ferdinand became a general of mountain troops in 1944.

4. General Buhle (1894–1959) was born in Heilbronn and entered the army as a *Fahnenjunker* in the 124th Infantry Regiment in 1912. He was commissioned second lieutenant the following year, fought in World War I, served in the Reichswehr, and was a colonel and chief of the Organizational Branch of the High Command of the Army when World War II began. A definite Nazi sympathizer, he became chief of the Army Staff at OKW in 1942. He was promoted to major general (1940), lieutenant general (1942), and general of infantry (April 1, 1944). Had he not been severely wounded in the July 20, 1944, attempt on Hitler's life, he might have been named chief of the General Staff of the Army and de facto head on OKH. Ironically, Colonel Claus von Stauffenberg, the leader of the plot, had once been his chief of staff.

Buhle became chief of the Wehrmacht Armaments Office in early 1945. He surrendered to the Western Allies at the end of the war and was released in 1947. He settled in Stuttgart.

5. Ironically, Skorzeny almost lost the job of rescuing Mussolini because of his love of cigarettes. He and General Kurt Student were called to meet with Himmler, who subjected them to a long-winded situation briefing on Italy. Skorzeny ducked out of the meeting to place a telephone call to his commando squad and to sneak a cigarette while he talked. Himmler suddenly walked in and caught him. "These eternal weeds!" he streaked. "Can't you do anything without a cigarette in your mouth? I can see that you're not at all the sort of man we need for this job!" Skorzeny managed to keep his post but eventually died of lung cancer.

6. Otto Skorzeny, *Skorzeny's Special Missions* (London: 1957), pp. 146–50.

7. Gerald Astor, *A Blood-Dimmed Tide* (New York: 1992), p. 63.

8. Skorzeny, pp. 146–50.

9. Colonel General Heinz Guderian (1888–1954), the "father of the blitzkrieg," was acting chief of the General Staff and de facto head of OKH from July 21, 1944, to March 28, 1945. OKH directed operations on the Eastern Front, while OKW supervised all other fronts. Guderian also controlled the powerful panzer inspectorate.

10. Michael Reynolds, *The Devil's Adjutant* (New York: 1995), pp. 22–23.

11. Sepp Dietrich was born in Hawangen, Swabia, on May 28, 1892, the son of a master meatpacker. He dropped out of school at the age of 14 and became an agricultural driver and later an apprentice in the hotel trade. He served in World War I, spending four years on the Western Front, where he was wounded three times and ended up in one of Germany's few tank units. After the war, he served in the Freikorps, joined the Nazi Party and participated in the Beer Hall Putsch. This cost him his job with the Bavarian Provincial Police. In the 1920s he joined the SS, and became Hitler's bodyguard and one of his favorites. He became a member of the Reichstag in 1930 and an SS major general in 1931.

In March 1933, Dietrich organized the Leibstandarte Adolf Hitler (the Adolf Hitler Bodyguard), which grew from 117 men into the 1st SS Panzer Division, with a strength of 21,000 men. Dietrich commanded it for 10 years, fighting in Poland, the Netherlands, France, and Russia. In July 1943, he became commander of the I SS Panzer Corps. Later he was promoted to SS colonel general. He took command of Panzer Group West in June 1944 and remained with it when it was redesignated 5th Panzer Army. He assumed command of the 6th Panzer Army on September 24, 1944.

12. Joachim Peiper, "1 SS Pz Rgt (11–24 Dec 1944)," ETHINT-10 (hereafter cited as "Peiper Interrogation").

13. Walter von Reichenau (1884–1942) was one of Hitler's most capable and most brutal field marshals. He commanded 10th Army in Poland (1939), 6th Army in Belgium, France, and Russia (1940–41), and Army Group South on the Eastern Front (December 1, 1941–January 12, 1942). He suffered a massive heart attack after a six-mile jog and was flown back to Germany. On route, his airplane crashed and he died on January 17, 1942.

14. Reynolds, *Adjutant*, p. 31.

15. Astor, p. 99.

16. It had taken Wilhelm Mohnke almost a year to recover from the loss of his foot. He returned to duty in March 1942, as commander of the 1st SS Panzer Grenadier Replacement Battalion in Berlin. He returned to combat the following July as commander of the 26th SS Panzer Grenadier Regiment of the 12th SS Panzer Division "Hitler Youth." Later, in June 1944, he commanded the regiment in Normandy, where he murdered several Canadian soldiers in cold blood.

17. Peiper Interrogation.

18. Albert Seaton, *The German Army*, p. 239.

19. Siegfried Westphal (1902–82) was born at Leipzig. He entered the service as a 16-year-old cavalry *Fahnenjunker* the day before World War I ended. Commissioned in the 11th Cavalry Regiment in 1922, he spent most of his pre–World War II career in that branch. A general staff officer, he spent virtually the entire war in general staff appointments, serving as Ia of the 58th Infantry Division (1939–40), Ia of the XXVII Corps (1940), and Ia of Panzer Group Afrika

(later Panzer Army Afrika). Severely wounded on May 31, 1942, he did not return to duty until the end of August. He became chief of staff of Rommel's Panzer Army Afrika in October.

From December 1–29, 1942, Westphal commanded the 164th Light Afrika Division. He reported himself sick at the end of the year. After he returned to duty in 1943, he was named chief of staff of OB South (later Southwest), the German command in Italy. He collapsed because of stress, overwork, and exhaustion during the Battle of Rome on June 5, 1944. Rundstedt named him chief of staff of OB West on September 9, 1944. He was promoted rapidly in World War II, from major at the beginning to lieutenant colonel (1941), colonel (1942), major general (1943), lieutenant general (1944), and general of cavalry (1945). He lived in Dortmund and Celle after the war.

20. Milton Shulman, *Defeat in the West* (New York: 1947; revised, New York: 1968), p. 290.

21. William R. Goolrick and Ogden Tanner, and the editors of Time-Life Books, *The Battle of the Bulge* (Alexandria, VA: 1979), p. 53.

22. For the best biography of Hasso von Manteuffel, see Donald Grey Brownlow, *Panzer Baron: The Military Exploits of General Hasso von Manteuffel* (North Quincy, MA: 1975).

23. Franz Kurowski, "Dietrich and Manteuffel," in *Hitler's Generals,* ed. Correlli Barrett, p. 423 (London: 1989).

24. Baron Hans von Funck (1891–1979) spent most of his career in the cavalry before assuming command of the 5th Panzer Regiment in late 1939. He commanded the 3rd Panzer Brigade in France (1940), briefly commanded the 5th Light Division (late 1940–early 1941), and succeeded Erwin Rommel as commander of the 7th Panzer Division on February 15, 1941. He led it until August 1943, spending more than two years on the Eastern Front. Later, he was acting commander of the XXIII Corps in Russia (December 1943–February 1944), before assuming command of the XXXXVII Panzer Corps on March 5, 1944. Despite an excellent performance in Normandy, Hitler (who personally disliked him) sacked him on September 3, 1944. He spent 10 years in Soviet prisons after the war. Baron von Funck was promoted to general of panzer troops on March 1, 1944. Funck's messy divorce in the 1930s played a role in Hitler's decision to force him into involuntary retirement, as did his poor relations with Jodl and his open contempt for Hitler's Italian alliance in early 1941.

25. Percy E. Schramm, "The Preparations for the German Offensive in the Ardennes (Sep to 16 Dec 1944)," Foreign Military Studies MS # A-862. Major Schramm kept the war diary for the operations branch at OKW.

26. Eisenhower, p. 137. Rundstedt generally supported Model's appeals.

27. Danny S. Parker, *The Battle of the Bulge* (Conshohockeu, PA: 1991), p. 23.

28. Fritz Kraemer was born in Stettin, Pomerania, on December 12, 1900, and joined the army just after the end of World War I. He was discharged about 1920 and joined the Prussian police, where he served until 1934, when he reentered the army as a first lieutenant. He attended the War Academy almost immediately, graduated in 1936, and became a company commander in the 55th Infantry Regiment (1936–39). He served on the staff of the 13th Motorized Infantry Division in Poland and France (1939–40) and became its Ia on October 11, 1940, the same day the division became the 13th Panzer Division. He served in this post until August 1,

1943, when he was attached to the SS as an Oberfuehrer. In the meantime, he earned the Knight's Cross and promotions to lieutenant colonel (1942) and colonel (January 1, 1943). He served as Ia of the I SS Panzer Corps under Sepp Dietrich (1943–44). Kraemer permanently transferred to the SS in 1944 and was promoted to Brigadefuehrer und Generalmajor der Waffen-SS on August 1, 1944. He served as acting commander of the 12th SS Panzer Division "Hitlerjugend" from October 24 to November 13, 1944, when he followed Dietrich to the 6th Panzer Army (later 6th SS Panzer Army) as chief of staff. He held this post until the end of the war. He was sentenced to 10 years in the Malmedy Massacre trials but did not serve the entire sentence. He died at Hoexter, West Germany on June 23, 1959. See Mark C. Yeager, *Waffen-SS Commanders* (Atglen, PA: 1997), vol. 1, pp. 326–27, and Franz Thomas, *Die Eichenlaubtraeger* (Osnabrueck: 1997), vol. 1, p. 399.

29. Wilhelm Keitel was born on the family farm, Helmscherode, in Hanover in 1882. All of his life he wanted to be a farmer, but the place was too small for two farms so his father sent him into the army as a *Fahnenjunker* in the 46th Artillery Regiment. He became a General Staff officer, fought in World War I (where he was severely wounded), served in the Reichswehr, and was chief of the Organizational Branch of the Army when Hitler came to power in 1933. He later served as Artillery Commander III and deputy commander of the 3rd Infantry Division (1933–34), commander of the 26th Infantry Division at Bremen (1934–35), and chief of the Armed Forces Office in the War Ministry (1935–38). Hitler named him commander-in-chief of the High Command of the Armed Forces (OKW) on February 2, 1938, precisely because he did not have a strong personality. He nevertheless rose rapidly in rank, from major in 1929 to field marshal on July 19, 1940—seven promotions in 11 years. A "yes man" for the Fuehrer, he was hanged at Nuremberg on October 16, 1946. Throughout his adulthood, he was intellectually dominated by his more ambitious wife. His younger brother Bodewin (1888–1953) became a general of infantry and was head of the powerful Army Personnel Office from 1938 to 1942. As a sign of his displeasure with Wilhelm Keitel, Hitler sacked Bodewin in September 1942. Later, the younger Keitel commanded Wehrkreis XX (March 1943–late 1944).

30. Cole, Hugh M., *The Ardennes: Battle of the Bulge.* United States Army in World War II. European Theater of Operations (Washington, DC: 1965), pp. 66–68; also see Schramm, MS # A-862.

31. Otto von Knobelsdorff was born in Berlin in 1886. Educated in various cadet schools, he joined the army as an infantry *Fahnenjunker* in 1905. After a distinguished career as an infantry and General Staff officer, he was given command of the 102nd Infantry Regiment in 1935. During World War II, he served as chief of staff of the XXXIII Corps Command (1939–40), commander of the 19th Infantry Division (1940), commander of the 19th Panzer Division (late 1940–January 1942), acting commander of the X Corps (1942), acting commander of the II Corps (1942), commander of the XXIV Panzer Corps (1942), commander of the XXXXVIII Panzer Corps (1942–43), and commander of the XXXX Panzer Corps (1944). He distinguished himself on the Eastern Front, earning the Knight's Cross with Oak Leaves and Swords. He was named acting commander of the 1st Army on September 6, 1944. Knobelsdorff, however, proved to be a much better panzer corps commander than commander of an army of predominantly marching infantry.

32. General of Panzer Troops von Knobelsdorff was never reemployed. He died in Hanover in 1966. General of Infantry Hans von Obstfelder was born in Steinbach-Hallenberg, Thuringia, in 1886. An infantry officer since 1906, he had commanded the 28th Infantry Division (1936–40), XXIX Corps (1940–43) on the Eastern Front, and LXXXVI Corps (1943–44) in Normandy and the retreat from France. He led the 1st Army until March 1, 1945, when he assumed command of the 19th Army. Despite his pro-Nazi political convictions, he was relieved of his command by Hitler 25 days later and never reemployed. He retired to Kassel, in the province of Hesse, where he died in 1976.

33. Baron von Elverheldt was born in Hildesheim in 1900. After being educated in various cadet schools, he joined the 1st Guards Regiment of Foot as a *Faehnrich* in the spring of 1918. He fought in World War I, served in the Reichsheer, and was Ia of the 3rd Light (later 8th Panzer) Division during the Polish campaign. Later he served as Ia of the XV Panzer Corps (1940–1941), chief of staff of the LVI Panzer Corps (1941–43), chief of staff of the 9th Army (1943), and chief of staff of the 17th Army (1943). After distinguishing himself on the Russian Front for two and a half years, he was recalled to Germany as part of the instructional staff of a special course for higher-level commanders in early 1944. He was given command of the 9th Panzer Division on September 16, 1944. A captain at the beginning of 1937, he was promoted to major general on September 1, 1944. He was killed during the Battle of Cologne on March 6, 1945. He was so highly thought of at Fuehrer Headquarters that a posthumous promotion to lieutenant general followed.

Siegfried von Waldenburg was born in Gross Leipe (near Breslau, Silesia) in 1898. Also a professional soldier, he entered the army in 1916 and was a major and chief of operations of the 6th Infantry Division when World War II broke out. He was chief of staff of the XIII Corps (1940–41), before being sent to Italy as deputy military attaché and chief of staff to the German General in the Headquarters of the High Command of the Italian Armed Forces (1941–44). He commanded the 26th Panzer Grenadier Regiment in southern Russia and the Ukraine before being given command of the battered 116th Panzer Division on September 14, 1944. He has been promoted to major general on December 1, 1944, the week before his meeting with Hitler.

General von Waldenburg led the 116th Panzer for the rest of the war and died in Hanover in 1973.

34. Hasso von Manteuffel, "Fifth Panzer Army (Ardennes Offensive)," Foreign Military Studies MS B-151 and MS B-151a.

35. Astor, p. 72.

36. Parker, p. 23.

37. Kurt Student was a Prussian, born in Neumark, Brandenburg, on May 12, 1890. He was educated in the Royal Prussian Cadet School at Potsdam and at Gross Lichterfelde Academy, Germany's West Point. He entered the service as a *Faehnrich* in the infantry in 1910, but spent World War I as an aviator. Initially he was a reconnaissance pilot but became a fighter ace on the Eastern Front, where he was severely wounded in 1917. He was selected for the Reichswehr, became a member of the secret General Staff, and was chief of the inspectorate of arms and equipment in the army in the 1920s. After commanding an infantry battalion, he became Director of Technical Training Schools for Germany's air arm, which

became the Luftwaffe. As a colonel in 1935, he was commander of the Test Center for Flying Equipment in Rechlin. Always interested in innovation, he managed to secure an appointment as commander of the 7th Air Division, which was then forming in Muenster. Here he became "father" of the German parachute branch. He served as commander of the 7th Air Division (which became a parachute unit) and inspector of parachute and airborne forces from 1938 to 1940. He was accidentally shot in the head by SS troops during the Battle of Rotterdam (May 1940) and was incapacitated for some time. When he returned to duty, he was named commander of the XI Air Corps, which he commanded in Crete. Later promoted to colonel general in the Luftwaffe, he commanded the 1st Parachute Army (1943–44) and Army Group H (1944–45) on the Western Front. His only child was a fighter pilot who was killed in action in 1944. He surrendered to the British after the war and was tried for war crimes in Crete. He was convicted and sentenced to five years' imprisonment, but the sentence was never confirmed. His happy marriage ended when his wife died. Without the family he so dearly loved, the old airborne pioneer retired at Lemgo and died a lonely old man on July 1, 1978, at the age of 88.

38. Eisenhower, p. 152.

39. Joseph "Beppo" Schmid was born in Bavaria in 1901 and first saw action as a member of General Ritter Franz von Epp's Freikorps in 1919. He transferred to the Luftwaffe around 1935 and rose rapidly in rank, commanding the Hermann Goering Panzer Division in Tunisia (1942–43), where he was flown out of the collapsing pocket on Goering's personal orders. Later he commanded I Fighter Corps (1943–44) and Luftwaffe Command West until April 28, 1945. A prisoner of war until 1948, he then took up residence in Augsburg and worked with the U.S. Air Force's German Historical Monograph Project in Karlsruhe. He died suddenly in 1956.

40. Astor, p. 71.

41. John Toland, *Battle: The Story of the Bulge* (New York: 1958; reprint, New York: 1959), pp. 27–28.

42. Eisenhower, p. 154.

43. Toland, *Story of the Bulge*, p. 28.

44. Astor, p. 72.

45. Eisenhower, p. 153.

46. Ibid.

CHAPTER III: THE OFFENSIVE BEGINS

1. Robert E. Merriam, *The Battle of the Bulge* (New York: 1957), pp. 63–64.

2. Otto Hitzfeld (1898–1990) entered the service as an infantry *Fahnenjunker* in 1915. He was commissioned the following year and was selected for the Reichswehr in 1920. He was adjutant to Erwin Rommel when he was the commander of the War School at Wiener Neustadt (1938–39). During World War II, Hitzfeld commanded the III/158th Infantry Regiment (1939–40), the 593rd Infantry Regiment (1940–41), the 213th Infantry Regiment (1941–43), and the 102nd Infantry Division (1943–44). He was named deputy commander of the LXVII Corps on December 1, 1944. For reasons not made clear by the records, General of Infantry Otto Sponheimer, the commander of the LXVII Corps, was

relieved of his command just before the start of the Ardennes Offensive and Hitzfeld was selected to replace him. General Sponheimer was never reemployed. Hitzfeld, meanwhile, served as corps commander until he was captured by the Americans on April 19, 1945. He was promoted to general of infantry on March 1, 1945, and was acting commander of the 11th Army from April 2–8, 1945. He retired to Heidelburg and died there at the age of 92.

3. Eugen Koenig (1896–1985) entered the service as a war volunteer in 1915 and earned a battlefield commission in the infantry 1917. Discharged in 1920 as a second lieutenant of reserves, he returned to active duty as a first lieutenant of reserves in 1936. He did not attain regular army status until 1942, when he was promoted to lieutenant colonel. During World War II, he served as a regimental adjutant, battalion commander, adjutant of the 246th Infantry Regiment, commander of the 352nd Infantry Regiment, and commander of Division Group 251 (the remnants of the 251st Infantry Division). He attended the four-week Division Commanders' Course in the early summer of 1944 and became commander of the 91st Air Landing Division after its original commander was killed in action on D-Day. Koenig did well and was promoted to major general on September 1, 1944. He was named commander of the 272nd Volksgrenadier Division on December 13, 1944—the very day the American offensive against the division began. An able and effective commander, Koenig was promoted to lieutenant general on March 1, 1945. He surrendered to the Americans on April 18.

Dr. Erwin Kaschner was born in Goerlitz in 1897. He entered the service as a war volunteer, served in the infantry and was awarded a reserve commission in 1917. He served as a platoon leader and orderly officer until July 29, 1918, when he was wounded and captured by the British. He was discharged at the end of 1919, returned to school, and earned a doctorate from the University of Breslau in 1926. He became a warrant officer in the 6th Infantry Regiment in 1927. As Hitler began to secretly expand the army, he applied to have his commission restored and became a captain in 1934. He was a company commander in 1938 and was a major commanding the I/486th when the war broke out. Later he commanded the 486th Infantry Regiment (1941–43) and the 461st Infantry Regiment (1943–44). After attending the month-long Division Commanders' Course, he assumed command of the 326th Volksgrenadier Division, which he led for the rest of the war. He was captured by the Americans on April 28, 1945, two days before Hitler committed suicide. A prisoner of war (POW) until 1947, he settled in Eutin, where he died in late 1973.

4. Friedrich Kittel was born in Lower Franconia in 1896. He joined the army as a war volunteer in 1915 and earned a commission the following year. He became a company commander (a rapid promotion indeed for that time) and was severely wounded in late September 1918. Selected for the Reichswehr, he received an advanced engineering degree from the Berlin-Charlottensburg Technical High School in 1932. A lieutenant colonel on the staff of the Army Weapons Office when World War II broke out, he commanded the 468th Infantry Regiment (1940–42) and then returned to the staff of OKH as a branch chief in the Army Weapons Office. He held this post until September 17, 1944, when he assumed command of the 62nd Volksgrenadier Division. He was injured in a fall six days later and could not return to duty until November 1. Kittel was promoted

to major general on January 1, 1945. On February 1, he returned to the Weapons Office as chief of the Infantry and Artillery Branch and was attached to Army Group South at the end of the war. He surrendered to the Western Allies and was released in 1947. He settled in Ansbach and died there in 1973. His older brother Heinrich (1892–69) was a lieutenant general. As commandant of Metz and commander of the 462nd Volksgrenadier Division, he became a national hero in Nazi Germany for his fierce defense of the Metz fortifications. He was finally wounded and captured by the U.S. 3rd Army on November 11, 1944, after a protracted battle that involved house-to-house fighting. Heinrich joined his brother in Ansbach after the war.

5. Walter Krueger (1892–1973) entered the service as a *Fahnenjunker* in 1910 and was commissioned into the 181st Infantry Regiment the following year. Later, however, he transferred into the cavalry. He fought in World War I, served in the Reichswehr, and became commander of the 10th Cavalry Regiment in 1937. When World War II started, he was named commander of the 171st Infantry Regiment. After the Polish campaign, he decided his future lay with the armored branch, so (as a colonel) he secured for himself an assignment to the staff of the 1st Rifle Brigade. After serving an apprenticeship in mobile operations, he was given command of the 1st Rifle in February 1940. He commanded the 1st Panzer Division in Russia (1941–43) and assumed command of the LVIII Panzer Corps on January 1, 1944. He was promoted to general of panzer troops and led his corps until March 23, 1945, when he was sacked by Hitler. He was nevertheless appointed commander of Wehrkreis IV on April 10.

Rudolf Bader (1898–1983) joined the Imperial Army as a war volunteer when World War I broke out in August 1914. He earned a reserve commission as a lieutenant in the artillery in 1915 and was discharged in 1920. He returned to the service as a captain in 1934, when Hitler began his secret military expansion. A battery commander in 1938, he commanded II/5th Artillery Regiment (1939–40), I/125th Artillery Regiment (1940–42), and 253rd Artillery Regiment (1942–44), and was acting commander of the 134th Infantry Regiment from February to June 1944. He attended the Division Commanders' Course that fall but was not promoted to major general until January 1, 1945. Meanwhile, he led the 560th Volksgrenadier Division from November 10, 1944 to March 1945, when he was appointed Battle Commander of Freiburg, Bavaria. He ended the war as commander of a kampfgruppe in the 719th Infantry Division—a definite demotion. General Bader surrendered to the French and, after being discharged from the POW camps, settled in Freiburg. He died there at the age of 85.

6. Heinz Kokott (1890–1976) joined the army as a *Fahnenjunker* in the 157th Infantry Regiment on October 1, 1918. Six weeks later, World War I ended. He remained in the service and was selected for the Reichswehr but—because of restricted number of officer positions available—he did not receive his commission until 1923. A major and instructor on the staff of the infantry school in 1939, he was given command of the II/337th Infantry Regiment in October. He commanded the 178th Infantry Regiment from late 1941 to May 1942, and the 337th Infantry Regiment from June 1942 to June 1943. Recalled to Germany, Kokott was named commandant of Schule VI for Infantry *Fahnenjunkern*. He commanded the 1135th Grenadier Brigade for about a month before being named commander of the 26th Infantry Division on July 27, 1944. He commanded it until the end of the

war. Heinz Kokott was promoted to lieutenant colonel in 1941, colonel in 1942, and major general on January 1, 1945. He retired to Hamburg.

7. Henning Schoenfeld was born in Stettin in 1894. A *Fahnenjunker* in 1912, he was commissioned in the 7th Ulan Regiment, a cavalry unit, in 1913 and served in that branch until he was discharged in September 1918, apparently because of wounds suffered in World War I. He rejoined the service in 1934 and became commander of the 20th Reconnaissance Battalion (1938–40). A member of the staff of the General of Mobile Troops at OKH from 1940 to 1943, he commanded the 949th Infantry Regiment (1943–44) before assuming command of the 2nd Panzer Division on September 5, 1944. His appointment apparently surprised and displeased the former divisional commander, Baron von Luettwitz, who had just been elevated to the command of the XXXXVII Panzer Corps. Schoenfeld owed his appointment more to his friends at OKH and the Panzer Inspectorate than to any innate qualifications he had to command a tank division. He was promoted to major general on December 1, 1944 and was relieved of his command 15 days later. Never reemployed, he died in Bad Canstatt in 1958.

8. Baptist Kniess was born at Gruenstadt in the Rhineland in 1885. Educated in cadet schools, he entered the service as a *Faehnrich* in the Bavarian 5th Infantry Regiment in 1908. He fought in World War I, served in the Reichsheer, and was a colonel commanding the 63rd Infantry Regiment in 1935. Promoted to major general in 1938, he served briefly as Landwehr Commander of Heilbronn in 1939. When World War II began, he was named commander of the 215th Infantry Division (1939–late 1942). Promoted to lieutenant general in 1940, he was named commander of the LXVI Corps on November 12, 1942, and was promoted to general of infantry 19 days later. He was placed in charge of a special staff in southern France in September 1943 and became commander of the LXXXV Corps on July 10, 1944. As an indication of the secrecy surrounding *Wacht am Rhein*, General Kniess applied for a month's leave from mid-November 1944 to December 16, 1944. He probably never would have made this request had he known of the impending battle—and his superiors certainly would not have approved it had they known. His temporary replacement, Lieutenant General Friedrich-August Schack, was a man known to have been suffering from combat fatigue in September, but obviously the senior German generals felt he could "baby sit" a corps on an inactive sector for a few weeks. Kniess only returned the day the offensive began and Schack was sent on leave.

General Kniess commanded the LXXXV until March 31, 1945, when he was unjustly relieved of his command for failing to halt vastly superior Allied forces. He retired to Munich, where he died in 1956.

Juris Doctor Franz Beyer was born in Bautzen in 1892 and joined the navy as a *Seekadett* (sea cadet) in 1911. He served in the navy in World War I and was discharged as a lieutenant in 1919. He then received a fine legal education and joined the police. He entered the army in 1935 with the relatively high rank of lieutenant colonel. He was made a battalion commander on April 1, 1935—the day he joined the army—despite the fact that his only previous military experience had been in the navy. Bayer nevertheless proved to be a very capable infantry leader. He commanded II/66th Infantry Regiment (1935–39), 131st Infantry Regiment (1939–late 1941), 331st Infantry Division (December 1941–February 1943), and 44th Infantry

Division (March–late December 1943)—mostly on the Russian Front. He was then assigned to Army Group A as a supplementary officer, used to serve as an acting commander to fill temporary vacancies. In this capacity, between February and August 1944, he served as acting commander of XVII, LVII Panzer, V, and XXXXIX Mountain Corps. Transferred to the Western Front, he assumed command of the LXXX Corps on August 7, 1944—his fifth corps in six months. This time, however, it was a permanent appointment, and he led the LXXX until the end of the war. He surrendered on May 8, 1945, and was discharged from the POW camps in 1947. He settled in Bad Wiessee where he died in 1968.

9. Franz Sensfuss (1891–1976) joined the army as a *Fahnenjunker* in the engineers in 1910. Commissioned in early 1912, he fought in World War I, served in the Reichsheer, and was in Fortress Engineer Inspectorate III as a lieutenant colonel in 1938. Promoted to colonel in 1939, he was named commander of Higher Construction Engineer Staff 3 when the war began. This later became the 690th Engineer Regiment. In 1941, he was named Engineer Leader, 11th Army. From December 1941 to December 1943, Sensfuss was Fortress Engineer Commander XVI. At the end of 1943, he attended the Division Commanders' Course and was named commander of the 21st Infantry Division on March 1, 1944. He assumed command of the 212th Volksgrenadier on May 1, 1944, and (except for brief periods of illness or leave) led it for the rest of the war. Sensfuss was promoted to major general on October 1, 1942, and to lieutenant general on August 1, 1944. He held the Knight's Cross with Oak Leaves.

10. Parker, p. 82.

11. Eisenhower, p. 153.

CHAPTER IV: THE BATTLE ON THE NORTHERN FLANK

1. Max Hansen was born in Niebuell, Schleswig, near the Danish border, in 1908. A company commander in 1939 when the war broke out, he was the leader of III/1st SS Panzer Grenadier Regiment in early 1943, when he was awarded the Knight's Cross. Later, he led the 1st SS PG Regiment until the end of the war. Like many of the members of the 1st SS Panzer Division, he fought in Poland (1939), the Netherlands, Belgium, and France (1940), the Balkans (1941), Russia (1941–42), Italy (1943), Russia again (1943–44), Normandy (1944), the retreat to the Siegfried Line (1944), the Ardennes (1944–45), Hungary (1945), and Austria (1945). He was promoted to *SS-Standartenfuehrer* (SS colonel) in Hungary in 1945. He died in the town of his birth on March 7, 1990.

Rudolf Sandig was born in the Eppendorf District of Saxony in 1911. He worked for a time as a craftsman but joined the Leibstandarte before 1933. He was a platoon leader by 1935. He fought in all of the major campaigns of the 1st SS Panzer Division and led the 2nd SS Panzer Grenadier Regiment until the end of the war. He surrendered to the Americans on May 12, 1945, and was released from the POW camps in August 1948. He died on August 11, 1994.

Gustav Knittel was born in Neu-Ulm in 1914. He apparently fought in all of the campaigns of the LAH and led the 1st SS Panzer Reconnaissance Battalion from Normandy to "Final Victory." Arrested by the Americans and tried for involvement in the Malmedy Massacre, he was sentenced to 15 years imprisonment. He was released from Landsberg in 1953 and died in Ulm in 1976. Ernst-Guenther

Kraetschmer, *Die Ritterkreuztraeger der Waffen-SS*, 3rd ed. (Preussisch Oldendorf: 1952), pp. 409, 504, and 677.

2. Joachim Peiper, "1 SS Pz Regt (11–24 Dec 44)," ETHINT 10, 12 July 1949 (hereafter cited as "Peiper Interrogation").

3. Ibid.

4. Charles Whiting, *Massacre at Malmedy* (Briarcliff Manor, NY: 1984), p. 31. Hermann Priess was born near Mecklenburg in 1901 and joined the army as a war volunteer in the 18th Dragoon Regiment in 1919, although World War I was already over. Germany, however, was in the throes of a civil war and Priess first saw action as a member of Freikorps Brandis. He also served in the Baltic States in 1920, where he fought against the Communists. He returned to Germany and was assigned to the 14th Cavalry Regiment at Ludwigslust, but he was not chosen for the Reichsheer and was discharged in 1920. Priess joined the Nazi Party and the SS in 1933 and became an SS lieutenant in 1935. He was an SS captain when the war broke out. He commanded the II Battalion/2nd SS Artillery Regiment in Poland and then transferred to the infamous "Totenkopf" (Death's Head) Division. He commanded II/3rd SS Artillery Regiment in France and the 3rd Artillery Regiment in Operation Barbarossa. In 1943, he was named commander of the SS Panzer Grenadier Division "Totenkopf" (which was later redesignated 3rd SS Panzer Division "Totenkopf"), following the death of Theodor Eicke, who was killed in action in February. Promoted to *SS Gruppenfuehrer und Generalleutnant der Waffen-SS*, he led the Death's Head Division on the Eastern Front until August 1944, when he assumed command of the XIII SS Corps. He was named commander of the I SS Panzer Corps on November 9, 1944. Priess led the corps for the rest of the war. On July 16, 1946, he was sentenced to 20 years imprisonment for the Malmedy Massacre, but was released from prison in October 1954. He died on February 2, 1985. The best book yet written about the senior SS commanders is Mark C. Yerger's *Waffen-SS Commanders*, 2 vols. (Atglen, PA: 1997–99).

5. Reynolds, p. 59.

6. Ibid, p. 72.

7. Ralf Tiemann, *The Leibstandarte* (Osnabrueck: 1998), vol. IV/2, pp. 63–64.

8. Peiper Interrogation, ETHINT 10.

9. "An Interview with Genmaj (W-SS) Fritz Kraemer, 6th Pz Army (1 Nov 1944–4 Jan 1945), 14–15 Aug 1945," ETHINT 21.

10. The destroyed aircraft belonged to the U.S. 2nd Infantry Division. The aircraft belonging to the U.S. 99th Infantry Division took off and headed west just before the Germans arrived.

11. Eisenhower, pp. 221–22.

12. Colonel Wilhelm Viebig was born in 1899 and entered the service as a *Fahnenjunker*. Commissioned *Leutnant* in the artillery in 1917, he fought in World War I, served in the Reichsheer, and was a major commanding the II/23rd Artillery Regiment in 1937. His subsequent career was not particularly distinguished. He was named commander of the 257th Artillery Regiment when World War II broke out but was not promoted to lieutenant colonel until the spring of 1940 and did not become a colonel until 1942. In the meantime, he served on Manstein's artillery staff (something of a demotion), commanded the 23rd Artillery Regiment on the Eastern Front (1941–42), and led the 93rd Panzer Artillery Regiment (1942–44). He assumed command of the 277th Volksgrenadier

Division on August 10, 1944, but was not promoted to major general until January 1, 1945. In early March 1945, Viebig faced an impossible situation. With the German Army in full retreat and in complete disarray, and with his back to the Rhine River, he received a "stand fast" order from Fuehrer Headquarters. Viebig ordered his combat units to continue their retreat across the river, while he "stood fast" in his command post with a handful of men. (He preferred capture by the Western Allies to execution by the Nazis.) He was captured by the Americans on March 7, 1945.

13. Eisenhower, p. 223.

14. Gerhard Engel was born in Guden in 1906. He joined the Reichsheer as a *Fahnenjunker* in 1925 and was commissioned second lieutenant in the Wuerttemberger 5th Infantry Regiment in 1930. He was promoted to captain in 1937 and was appointed Hitler's adjutant on March 10, 1938, after Hitler fired Colonel Friedrich Hossbach for disobeying his orders during the Fritsch crisis. Engel held his post until the fall of 1943. Then he became so inspired by one of Hitler's speeches that he volunteered for frontline duty. He was given command of the 27th Infantry Regiment of the 12th Infantry Division on October 1, 1943. This division was largely destroyed in the Battle of Minsk-Vitebsk on the Eastern Front in the summer of 1944. The divisional commander, Lieutenant General Bamler, was captured on June 27, and Engel (who had been promoted to full colonel on May 1) succeeded him.

Engel managed to escape the destruction of Army Group Center and, when the 12th Infantry Division was rebuilt as a Volksgrenadier unit, he retained command. The rebuilt division was sent to the Western Front, where Engel distinguished himself in the Battle of Aachen. He would be absent twice: in November 1944 and January–February 1945, during which time he was recovering from wounds. He was promoted to major general on November 1, 1944, and was named commander of the newly formed Division Ulrich von Hutten on April 12, 1945. He surrendered this command to the Americans at the end of the war. Released from the POW camps in December 1947, he resided in Dusseldorf and Soecking after the war. He died in 1976.

15. SS Colonel Hugo Kraas was born in Witten/the Ruhr in 1911, the eldest of seven sons. He studied to be a teacher but had to drop out and go to work when his father died. He joined the Brownshirts in 1934 and transferred to the army in 1935. Later that year, he joined the Waffen-SS and began officer training at the SS Junker School at Brunswick. He graduated and was commissioned in 1938, and was assigned to the Leibstandarte. He advanced rapidly and fought in all of the campaigns of the LAH, serving as a platoon leader in the 14th Antitank Company (*Panzerjaegerkompanie*) (1938–39), a platoon leader in the 15th Motorcycle Company (*Kradschuetzenkompanie*) (1939–40), a company commander in the 1st SS Reconnaissance Battalion (1940–41), acting commander of the 1st SS Recon (1941–42), commander of the I/2nd SS Panzer Grenadier Regiment (1942–43), and commander of the 2nd SS Panzer Regiment. He assumed command of the 12th SS Panzer Division on November 15, 1944, and led it for the rest of the war, fighting in the Ardennes, Hungary, and Austria. He surrendered to the Americans and was released from the POW camps in 1948. He was promoted rapidly: 1st lieutenant (1939), captain (1940), major (1942), lieutenant colonel (1943), colonel (1944), Oberfuehrer (January 30, 1945), and major general (Brigadefuehrer) (April 20, 1945).

He died in Schleswig an Herzversagen on February 20, 1980. His younger brother, Boris Kraas, was an SS major and commander of the 3rd SS Tank Destroyer Battalion "Totenkopf." He was mortally wounded in Hungary on February 13, 1945.

16. Parker, p. 100.

17. Heydte's paratroopers were dropped by the 3rd Transport Wing—an old "Stalingrad" unit; however, like most of the Luftwaffe, it had deteriorated considerably since 1942 and many of its inexperienced pilots had never flown in a Ju-52.

18. Cole, p. 262. After the war, a U.S. Military Tribunal at Dachau sentenced 73 former SS men in connection with the massacre: 43 to death, 22 to life imprisonment, and 8 to terms of imprisonment ranging from 10 to 20 years. None of the executions were carried out and many of the sentences were commuted.

CHAPTER V: THE DESTRUCTION OF KG PEIPER

1. Whiting, *Malmedy*, pp. 144–45.
2. Goolrick and Tanner, p. 120.
3. Whiting, *Malmedy*, p. 89.
4. Ibid., p. 163.
5. Reynolds, p. 238.

CHAPTER VI: THE SCHNEE EIFEL

1. The 18th Luftwaffe Field Division consisted of the 35th and 36th Luftwaffe Rifle Regiments (three battalions each); the 18th Luftwaffe Artillery Regiment (three battalions); the Anti-Tank Battalion, 18th Luftwaffe Field Division; the 18th Luftwaffe Engineer Battalion; the Communications Company, 18th Luftwaffe Field Division; the Reconnaissance Platoon, 18th Luftwaffe Field Division; and the Supply Unit, 18th Luftwaffe Field Division. When it was incorporated into the army, the III/18th Luftwaffe Artillery Regiment remained in the air force as the II/52nd Flak Regiment. Georg Tessin, *Verbaende und Truppen der deutschen Wehrmacht und Waffen-SS im Zweiten Weltkrieg, 1939–1945*, 16 vols. (Osnabrueck: 1973–80), vol. 4, pp. 105–6.

2. Guenter Hoffmann-Schoenborn 201 File (Personnel Extract), U.S. National Archives, Washington, D.C. This file was kindly provided to the author by the late Theodor-Friedrich von Stauffenberg in the 1980s.

3. Heinz Guderian, *Panzer Leader* (New York: 1957; reprint, New York: 1967), p. 233.

4. Albert Seaton, *The Russo-German War, 1941–45* (New York: 1960).

5. Wolf Keilig, *Die Generale des Heeres* (Friedberg: 1983), p. 147.

6. Franz Thomas and Guenter Wegmann, *Die Ritterkreuztraeger der deutschen Wehrmacht, 1939–1945*, Teil I: *Sturmartillerie* (Osnabrueck: 1985), pp. 132–33.

7. Dietrich Moll, "18th Volks Grenadier Division (1 Sep 1944–25 Jan 1945)," Foreign Military Study B-688. Unpublished manuscript compiled by the Historical Division, Headquarters, United States Army Europe. Hereafter cited as "Moll MS."

8. Dietrich Moll was born on November 12, 1909, and joined the Reichsheer as a member of the 13th Infantry Regiment in the 1920s. In 1933, he transferred to the 5th Engineer Battalion in Wuerttemberg (1933–38) and was later on Fortress Engineer Staff 6 (1938–39). He was assigned to the Kriegsakademie for General Staff training in 1939 but his course was abbreviated because of the outbreak of the war. He served an apprenticeship on the intelligence staffs of the 231st and 7th Infantry Divisions (1940–41) and was Ic of the 15th Motorized Infantry Division in Russia. Severely wounded on the Eastern Front in October 1941, he did not return to full duty until May 1942, as an officer on the staff of OKW, where he finished his General Staff training. He was promoted to lieutenant colonel on May 1, 1943, and became Ia of the 571st Grenadier Division on September 1, 1944. When the 571st was absorbed by the 18th Volksgrenadier Division, Moll became Ia of the 18th VG—a post which he held until the end of the war. He should not be confused with Lieutenant Colonel Joseph Moll, who served as chief of intelligence of the Afrika Korps (1943) and chief of operations of Army Group C in Italy (1944–45). Christian Zweng, comp. and ed., *Die Dienstlaufbahnen der Offiziere des Generalstabes des deutschen Heeres, 1935–1945* (Osnabrueck: 1998), vol. 2, p. 78.

9. Walter Lucht was born in Berlin in 1882. He entered the service as a *Fahnenjunker* in the summer of 1901 and was commissioned in the artillery the following year. He served in World War I and in the Reichsheer, and retired as an honorary colonel at the end of March 1932. He was recalled to active duty as a supplemental officer in 1937 and was named commander of the 215th Artillery Regiment when the war began. He was promoted to the command of Arko 44 in early 1940 and to Harko 310 (the 310th Higher Artillery Command) on the Eastern Front on January 1, 1942. Although he was considered old for a combat officer, Lucht was named acting commander of the 87th Infantry Division on February 17, 1942, and commander of the 336th Infantry Division on March 1, 1942. He continued to serve on the Eastern Front and was named commander of the critical Kerch Straits sector during the evacuation of the 1st Panzer Army in 1943. He assumed command of the LXVI Corps on November 1, 1943.

10. Lammerding was born in Dortmund on August 27, 1905, the son of an architect. He received an excellent education, earning the Diplom-Ingenieurs degree, and worked in private industry until 1933, when he joined the army's 6th Engineer Battalion for a brief period of active duty. He joined the SA (Brownshirts) in the early 1930s, and became chief of SA engineers in Westphalia in 1934. Later that year, he became adjutant and *Referent* (senior civil servant) of the engineer inspectorate of the Eastern SA. He joined the SS in 1935 as an engineer platoon leader with the rank of 1st lieutenant. By 1937 he was a captain of SS and a company commander, and in October 1939 was transferred to the "Totenkopf" Division as a major. He became chief of operations (Ia) of the division on January 1, 1941. Promoted to SS lieutenant colonel in September 1941, he was named commander of the SS Panzer Grenadier Regiment "Totenkopf" in August 1942. Later he was promoted to SS colonel and assigned to the staff of the II SS Panzer Corps (July 1943). He was named commander of the 2nd SS Panzer Division in December 1943, with a promotion to Oberfuehrer. He was promoted to SS-Brigadefuehrer und Generalmajor der Waffen-SS on November 9, 1944. Lammerding had been wounded during the retreat from France on June 26, 1944, and his replacement, SS Colonel Christian Tychsen, had been killed by soldiers of

the U.S. 2nd Armored Division on June 28. SS Colonel Otto Baum then assumed the post of acting divisional commander. Lammerdring would resume command on October 23. Nikolaus von Preradovich, *Die Generale der Waffen-SS* (Berg am See: 1985), pp. 172–73.

11. Moll MS.

12. Ibid.

13. Ibid.

14. Ibid.

15. Milton Shulman, *Defeat in the West* (London: 1947; reprint, New York: 1968), pp. 279–80.

16. Moll MS.

17. Ibid.

18. Ibid.

19. Ibid.

20. Parker, p. 45.

21. Moll MS.

22. Eisenhower, p. 425.

23. Ibid.

24. Ibid.

CHAPTER VII: ST. VITH

1. Karl Rettlinger was born in Gunzenhausen, Middle Franconia, in 1913. He joined the Leibstandarte in 1933 and remained with it until it surrendered in May 1945.

2. According to another version of this story, General Jones refused to even see Devine. In either case, the colonel was relieved and was evacuated through medical channels to Bastogne that same night, his military career ruined.

3. Both Clarke and Hasbrouck had low opinions of General Jones, who seemed to alternate between optimism and depression. On December 19, Jones got out of the way when he evacuated his headquarters from St. Vith to Vielsalm.

4. Otto-Ernst Remer was born in Neubrandenburg in 1912. He entered the service as a *Fahnenjunker* in 1933 and was commissioned in 1935. He was a first lieutenant commanding a company in the 479th Infantry Regiment when the war began. He later commanded an infantry gun company in the 701st Motorized Regiment (1940–42), I/10th Rifle Regiment (1942), and the IV Battalion of the elite Grossdeutschland Panzer Grenadier Regiment (1942). He was promoted to major on January 1, 1943. After being wounded on the Eastern Front, he was named commander of the Watch Regiment, a Grossdeutschland replacement-training unit stationed in Berlin, on May 1, 1944. He played a major role in suppressing the Stauffenberg conspiracy of July 20, 1944. He seized the headquarters of the Replacement Army, caused the coup to collapse, became a hero of Nazi Germany, and earned Hitler's undying gratitude. The Fuehrer rewarded him with a promotion to colonel, bypassing the rank of lieutenant colonel altogether.

5. Ralph E. Hersko, Jr., "Battle Slowed by Traffic," *World War II* (June 1992), p. 29.

6. Eisenhower, p. 301.

7. Moll MS.

8. Cole, p. 422. These figures include the losses the remnants of the 14th Cavalry Group suffered at St. Vith, but it was so small by then that its casualties were relatively small.

CHAPTER VIII: THE SIEGE OF BASTOGNE

1. Astor, p. 200.

2. Gavin was normally commander of the 82nd Airborne, but the permanent commander of the XVIII Airborne Corps, General Matthew Ridgway, was in England, reviewing Operation Market-Garden. The permanent commander of the 101st Airborne Division, Major General Maxwell Taylor, was in Washington, D.C., lobbying Congress for more paratroopers. Ridgway would return in time to play a major role in the Battle of the Bulge. Taylor would not. Brigadier General Anthony McAuliffe was normally the artillery commander of the 101st.

3. Baron Heinrich von Luettwitz, the son of a Silesian Junker, was born on the family estate in 1896. When World War I began, he ran away from home (at age 17) and enlisted in the army as a private. He nevertheless earned his commission in the infantry before his 18th birthday. Twice wounded, he was selected for the Reichsheer and spent the Weimar era in the cavalry. A noted equestrian, he nevertheless saw that the future lay in the motorized and panzer units, so he arranged to command the I/8th Cavalry Regiment (a motorized unit) (1931–35) and the 3rd Motorized Battalion (1935–37), which was equipped with PzKw I tanks.

In 1936, Luettwitz led the German Olympic Equestrian Team but failed to win the Gold Medal. This put him in a professional "dog house" until Operation Barbarossa, when high casualties among field grade officers resulted in his being named commander of the 59th Panzer Grenadier Regiment on July 2, 1941. Later, Luettwitz led the 20th Rifle Brigade and the 20th Panzer Division, before being assigned to a special staff in Berlin, where his job was to study and evaluate new tank models. He was given command of the 2nd Panzer Division on the Eastern Front on February 1, 1944. It was soon transferred back to France, and Luettwitz led it in the Normandy campaign, where he was wounded for the sixth time in his career. He assumed command of the XXXXVII Panzer Corps after Baron von Funck was dismissed by Hitler on September 5, 1944. Baron von Luettwitz was promoted to general of panzer troops on November 1, 1944.

4. Fritz Bayerlein was born in Wurzburg, Bavaria, on January 14, 1899, the son of a senior police inspector. He entered the army as a *Fahnenjunker* in 1917 and took the field with the 9th Infantry Regiment in May 1918. Remaining in the Reichsheer, he was commissioned second lieutenant in 1922. He commanded the machine gun company of the 21st Infantry Regiment and then the regiment's motorcycle detachments. In May 1932, he took his Wehrkreis examinations and scored high enough to undergo General Staff training. On June 1, 1935, he joined the staff of the 15th Infantry Division at Kassel and by 1936 was division Ia. In 1937, he became commander of the divisional armored car company.

Promoted to major in 1938, Bayerlein was named Ia of XV Motorized Corps and became Ia of the 10th Panzer Division when the war began. In February 1940, he was appointed Ia of Guderian's XIX Panzer Corps, which did so well in the French campaign. This led to Bayerlein's promotion to lieutenant colonel in

October. He remained with Guderian when his headquarters was upgraded to 2nd Panzer Group and fought in the early stages of the Russian campaign; then he was sent to North Africa, where he served as chief of staff of the Afrika Korps (1941–42) and chief of staff of the 1st Italian-German Panzer Army (1942–43). He also served briefly as acting commander of the Afrika Korps (November 5–21, 1942). Promoted to major general on March 1, 1943, he left North Africa on May 2, 1943—just in time to escape the surrender of Army Group Afrika. He was unemployed until October 1943, when he assumed command of the 3rd Panzer Division on the southern sector of the Eastern Front. On January 10, 1944, he was named commander of the Panzer Lehr Division, then forming in France. Bayerlein commanded the division in the Normandy campaign, the Falaise Pocket, the retreat to the Seine, and the retreat to the West Wall. He was promoted to lieutenant general on May 1, 1944.

5. British Interrogation of Major General Gerhard Franz, on file at the Air University Archives, Maxwell Air Force Base, Alabama.

6. Stauffenberg MS; Helmut Ritgen, *Die Geschichte der Panzer-Lehr-Division im Westen, 1944-1945* (Stuttgart: 1979).

7. Stauffenberg MS.

8. Stauffenberg MS.

9. Stauffenberg Papers.

10. Heinz Kokott was born in Gross Strelitz in 1890. He joined the army as a *Fahnenjunker* in the 157th Infantry Regiment in October 1918 but almost certainly did not see action in World War I. He was retained in the Reichsheer and was commissioned second lieutenant in the 7th Infantry Regiment in 1923. At the start of World War II, he was a major and an instructor at the Infantry School. He was named commander of the II/196th Infantry Regiment in October 1939. During the Russian winter offensive of 1941–42, he was named commander of the 178th Infantry Regiment on the northern sector of the Russian Front. He had been promoted to lieutenant colonel only two months before. Kokott underwent a short training course in May 1942, followed by another tour as regimental commander—this time the 337th Infantry Regiment on the central sector of the Eastern Front from June 1942 to June 1943. He then returned to Germany as commandant of School VI (for infantry *Fahnenjunkern*). Kokott briefly commanded the 1135th Grenadier Brigade in July 1944 before being named commander of the 26th Volksgrenadier Division in August. He was promoted to colonel on April 1, 1942, and would be promoted to major general on January 1, 1945. Heinz Kokott led the 26th VG Division until the end of the war. He settled in Hamburg and died on May 29, 1976.

11. Stauffenberg MS.

12. Astor, pp. 294–95.

13. Stauffenberg MS.

14. It must be noted that the Allied air forces were not always accurate. Mistaking Malmedy for St. Vith, they bombed it not once, but three times and on three successive days, December 23, 24, and 25. They killed at least 125 civilians and 37 American soldiers.

15. Parker, p. 139. Kurt Moehring was born in Gross Lipschin on January 3, 1900. He was educated in cadet schools and joined the army as a *Fahnenjunker* in 1916 (at age 16). He was commissioned in the infantry in 1917, fought in World

War I, and was discharged in 1921. He was allowed to rejoin the army in 1924 as a second lieutenant in the East Prussian 1st Infantry Regiment. When the war began, he was commander of the III Battalion, 82nd Infantry Regiment (III/82nd Infantry Regiment). After a brief period as acting commander of the 458th Infantry Regiment in January 1942, he assumed command of the 82nd Infantry Regiment in February. On December 6, 1942, he was named commander of the elite Gross Deutschland Infantry Regiment. He next was given command of the 196th Infantry Division (December 1943), before assuming command of the 276th Volksgrenadier Division in the fall of 1944. After he was killed, he was posthumously promoted to lieutenant general.

16. Hugo Dempwolff was born in Suederneuland in 1898 and entered the service as a *Fahnenjunker* in the 92nd Infantry Regiment in 1916. He was commissioned the following year and was selected for the Reichsheer as a second lieutenant in 1919. He was promoted to major in 1937 and became adjutant of the 5th Infantry Division the following year. After the Polish and French campaigns, he became adjutant of the V Military District (1940–42). On August 1, 1942, he assumed command of the 489th Infantry Regiment on the northern sector of the Russian Front. Later (January 1–March 16, 1944) he commanded the 80th Infantry Regiment on the southern sector. Here, he was apparently wounded; in either case, he did not return to active duty until December 1944, as a replacement division commander for 7th Army. He was promoted to major general on March 1, 1945, and led the 276th Volksgrenadier Division until the end of the war. A POW until the spring of 1948, he settled in Hanover and died in December 1984, at the age of 86.

17. Erich-Otto Schmidt was born in Annaberg, Silesia, in 1899. He was educated in various cadet schools and joined the army in 1919, after the end of World War I. He was commissioned in the 10th Infantry Regiment in 1924 and became adjutant of the 52nd Infantry Regiment in the fall of 1938. A major when World War II began, he was promoted to regimental adjutant the same day, but spent most of the first half of the war as an instructor or battalion commander at officer or weapons training schools. He was finally given command of the 679th Infantry Regiment on the Eastern Front on September 1, 1942, and held this command until the end of 1943, when he was named commander of a training staff at the Infantry School at Doeberitz. He was decorated with the Knight's Cross in 1943 and assumed command of the 352nd Volksgrenadier on November 1, 1944. Although he was never reemployed after being wounded, Schmidt was promoted to major general on January 1, 1945. He died in 1959.

Schmidt was temporarily replaced by his senior regimental commander. His permanent replacement, Major General Richard Bazing, arrived on December 23.

18. Parker, p. 144.

19. Hugh Pond, *Sicily* (London: 1962), p. 149.

20. Heilmann's staff was appointed by Goering's people at OKL (the High Command of the Luftwaffe) and reported back to them regularly, often behind Heilmann's back. They were not loyal to their commander, who was not allowed to fire them. In Hermann Goering's Luftwaffe, anything was possible.

21. Parker, p. 198.

22. Hans-Joachim Kahler was born in Moerchingen in 1908 and joined the Reichsheer as a *Fahnenjunker* in 1927. He was commissioned *Leutnant* in the 14th Cavalry Regiment in 1932 and was a squadron commander when the war broke

out. He commanded a company in the 156th Reconnaissance Battalion and in the 1st Motorized Anti-Tank Battalion before being adjutant of the 12th Panzer Division (September 1940–February 1942). He led the 22nd Motorcycle Battalion (March–June 1942), the 34th Motorcycle Battalion (July 1942–March 1943), and became acting commander of the 12th Panzer Grenadier Regiment in April 1943. After its colonel was wounded, Kahler served as acting commander of the 4th Panzer Reconnaissance Battalion (July 18, 1943). On September 1, 1943, he assumed command of the 5th Panzer Grenadier Regiment. He became commander of the elite Panzer Grenadier Brigade "Grossdeutschland" on July 1, 1944. This unit was later redesignated Fuehrer Grenadier Brigade (later Division). Except when he was recovering from wounds, Kahler led this unit for the rest of the war. He was promoted rapidly: major (1942), lieutenant colonel (1943), colonel (1944), and major general (January 30, 1945). Kahler surrendered his command to the British on May 8, 1945. Released from prison in early 1946, General Kahler lived in Hamburg. He died on January 14, 2000 at the age of 91—one of Hitler's last surviving generals.

23. Goolrick and Tanner, p. 172.
24. Parker, p. 187.
25. Cole, *Ardennes*, p. 552.
26. Parker, p. 198.

CHAPTER IX: THE HIGH WATER MARK

1. Eisenhower, p. 350.
2. Kevin R. Austra, "Germany's Bridge Too Far," *World War II* (November 1994), p. 32.
3. Parker, pp. 198–201.
4. For a thumbnail biography of Erich-Otto Schmidt, see Note 17, Chapter VIII.
5. Parker, pp. 206–7.

CHAPTER X: CLEARING THE BULGE

1. Karl Decker was born in Borntin, Pomerania, on November 30, 1897. He joined the army as a *Fahnenjunker* immediately after World War I began and was commissioned in the infantry in 1915. He fought in World War I, served in the Reichsheer, and, as a major, commanded the 38th Motorized Anti-Tank Battalion (1936–40). He was promoted to lieutenant colonel (1939), colonel (1942), major general (1943), lieutenant general (1944), and general of panzer troops (January 1, 1945). He successively commanded the I/3rd Panzer Regiment (1940–41), the 3rd Panzer Regiment (1941–43), 21st Panzer Brigade (1943), 5th Panzer Division (1943–44), and XXXIX Panzer Corps (from October 15, 1944)—all on the Eastern Front.
2. Parker, p. 227.
3. Adolf Galland, *The First and the Last* (New York: 1954; reprint, New York: 1987), p. 249.
4. Eisenhower, p. 425.

5. Craig W. H. Luther, *Blood and Honor: The History of the 12th SS Panzer Division "Hitler Youth," 1943–1945* (San Jose, CA: 1987), pp. 239–40. Kraas (1911–80) ended the war as an SS major general.

6. They were surrounded but formed a "floating pocket" and later succeeded in breaking out, despite the efforts of seven Soviet armies to destroy them.

7. Goolrick and Tanner, p. 188.

8. Juergen E. Foerster, "The Dynamics of Volkegemeinschaft: The Effectiveness of the German Military Establishment in the Second World War" in *Military Effectiveness*, eds. Allan R. Millett and Williamson Murray, vol. 3, *The Second World War* (Boston: 1988), pp. 180–220.

9. Parker, p. 293.

10. Hasso von Manteuffel, "The Battle of the Ardennes 1944–45," in *Decisive Battles of World War II: The German View*, eds. H. A. Jacobsen and J. Rohwer, p. 417 (New York: 1960).

CHAPTER XI: EPILOGUE

1. Frederick Wilhelm von Mellenthin, *German Generals of World War Two* (Norman, OK: 1977), p. 156.

2. David Lippman, "Field Marshal Model," *World War II* (March 1989), p. 16.

3. Mellenthin, *Generals*, p. 158.

4. Stauffenberg MS.

5. Ibid.

6. Information kindly supplied by Gareth Collins, www.forum.axishistory.com. This, in my humble opinion, is the best Axis history forum on the Internet.

Bibliography

Absolon, Rudolf, comp. *Rangliste der Generale der deutschen Luftwaffe nach dem Stand vom 20. April 1945.* Friedberg: 1984.

Astor, Gerald. *A Blood-Dimmed Tide: The Battle of the Bulge by the Men Who Fought It.* New York: 1992.

Austra, Kevin R. "Germany's Bridge Too Far." *World War II.* November 1994.

Barnett, Correlli, ed. *Hitler's Generals.* London: 1989.

Bayerlein, Fritz. "Additional Questions—Ardennes Offensive." Foreign Military Studies MS # 945.

Bender, Roger James, and Hugh P. Taylor. *Uniforms, Organization and History of the Waffen-SS.* Mountain View, CA: 1971.

Berberich, Florian. "Gustav Wilke." In *The D-Day Encyclopedia,* edited by David G. Chandler and James Lawton Collins, Jr. New York: 1993.

Bidwell, S., and D. Graham. *Firepower: British Weapons and Theories of War, 1904–1945.* London: 1982.

Blumenson, Martin. *Breakout and Pursuit.* United States Army in World War II. European Theater of Operations. Washington, DC: 1961.

Blumenson, Martin, and the Editors of Time-Life Books. *Liberation.* Alexandria, VA: 1978.

———. "Recovery of France." In *A Concise History of World War II,* edited by Vincent J. Esposito. New York: 1964.

Blumentritt, Guenther. *Von Rundstedt: The Soldier and the Man.* London: 1952.

Bradley, Omar N. *A Soldier's Story.* New York: 1951.

Brandenberger, Erich. "Seventh Army (1 Sep 1944–25 Jan 1945)." Foreign Military Studies MS # 447.

Breuer, William B. *Hitler's Fortress Cherbourg.* New York: 1984.

———. *Operation Dragoon.* Novato, CA: 1987. Reprint, New York: 1988.

Brown, Anthony C. *Bodyguard of Lies.* New York: 1975.

Brownlow, Donald Grey. *Panzer Baron: The Military Exploits of General Hasso von Manteuffel.* North Quincy, MA: 1975.

Buechs, Herbert. "The Ardennes Offensive (Sep-Dec 44)." ETHINT 34.

———. "The German Ardennes Offensive." Foreign Military Studies MS # D-739.

Carell, Paul. *Hitler Moves East, 1941-1943*. Boston: 1965. Reprint, New York: 1966.

———. *Invasion: They're Coming!* Boston: 1965. Reprint, New York: 1966.

Chandler, David G., and James Lawton Collins, Jr., eds. *The D-Day Encyclopedia*. New York: 1993.

Chant, Christopher, ed. *The Marshall Cavendish Illustrated Encyclopedia of World War II*. 20 vols. New York: 1972.

Chant, Christopher, Richard Humble, William Fowler, and Jenny Shaw. *Hitler's Generals and Their Battles*. New York: 1976.

Choltitz, Dietrich von. *Soldat unter Soldaten*. Konstanz: 1951.

Clark, Alan. *Barbarossa: The Russian-German Conflict, 1941–45*. New York: 1965.

Cole, Hugh M. *The Ardennes: Battle of the Bulge*. United States Army in World War II. European Theater of Operations. Washington, DC: 1965.

Cooper, Matthew. *The German Army, 1933–1945*. Briarcliff Manor, NY: 1978.

D'Este, Carlo. *Decision in Normandy*. London: 1983. Reprint, New York: 1983.

Dietrich, Wolfgang. *Die Verbaende der Luftwaffe, 1935–1945*. Stuttgart: 1976.

Eisenhower, Dwight D. *Crusade in Europe*. New York: 1948.

Eisenhower, John S. D. *The Bitter Woods*. New York: 1969.

Ellis, L. E. *Victory in the West*. Vol. 1, *The Battle of Normandy*. London: 1968.

———. *Victory in the West*. Vol. 2, *The Defeat of Germany*. London: 1968.

English, John A. "R. F. L. Keller." In *The D-Day Encyclopedia*, edited by David G. Chandler and James Lawton Collins, Jr. New York: 1993.

Esposito, Vincent J., ed. *A Concise History of World War II*. New York: 1964.

Foerster, Juergen E. "The Dynamics of Volkegemeinschaft: The Effectiveness of the German Military Establishment in the Second World War." In *Military Effectiveness*, edited by Allan R. Millet and Williamson Murray, vol. 3, *The Second World War*. Boston: 1988.

Foley, Charles. *Commando Extraordinary*. New York: 1989.

Forman, James. *Code Name Valkyrie: Count von Stauffenberg and the Plot to Kill Hitler*. New York: 1975.

Fuerbringer, Herbert. *9.SS-Panzer-Division*. Heimdal: 1984.

Galland, Adolf. *The First and the Last*. New York: 1954. Reprint, New York: 1987.

Gavin, James M. *On to Berlin*. New York: 1978.

Gersdorf, Rudolf von. "The Ardennes Offensive." Foreign Military Studies MS # A-909.

———. "Results of the Ardennes Offensive." Foreign Military Studies MS # A-933.

Goolrick, William K., Ogden Tanner, and the editors of Time-Life Books. *The Battle of the Bulge*. Alexandria, VA: 1979.

Goralski, Robert. *World War II Almanac, 1931–1945*. New York: 1981.

Graber, Gerry S. *Stauffenberg*. New York: 1973.

Greenfield, Kent R., ed. *Command Decisions*. Washington, DC: 1960.

Guderian, Heinz. *Panzer Leader*. New York: 1957. Reprint, New York: 1967.

Guderian, Heinz Guenther. *From Normandy to the Ruhr with the 116th Panzer Division in World War II*. Bedford, PA: 2001.

Harrison, Gordon A. *Cross-Channel Attack*. United States Army in World War II. European Theater of Operations. Washington, DC: 1951.

Hart, B. H. Liddell. *History of the Second World War*. 2 vols. New York: 1972.

———. *The Other Side of the Hill*. London: 1951.

Hastings, Max. *Das Reich*. New York: 1981.

Haupt, Werner. *Das Buch der Panzertruppe, 1916–1945*. Friedberg: 1989.

———. *Rueckzug im Westen, 1944*. Munich: 1978.

Hersko, Ralph E., Jr. "Battle Slowed by Traffic." *World War II*. June 1992.

Hitzfeld, Otto. "Ardennes Offensive." Foreign Military Studies MS # 936.

Hoffman, Peter. *The History of the German Resistance, 1933–1945*. Cambridge, MA: 1977.

Irving, David. *Hitler's War*. New York: 1977.

———. *The Trail of the Fox*. New York: 1977.

Jacobsen, H. A., and J. Rohwer, eds. *Decisive Battles of World War II: The German View*. New York: 1965.

Keegan, John. *Waffen SS: The Asphalt Soldiers*. New York: 1970.

———. *Six Armies in Normandy*. New York: 1982. Reprint, New York: 1983.

Keilig, Wolf. *Die Generale des Heeres*. Friedberg: 1983.

Keitel, Wilhelm. *In the Service of the Reich*. Briarcliff Manor, NY: 1979.

Kraemer, Fritz. "Sixth Panzer Army in the Ardennes Offensive." ETHINT-21, ETHINT-22, and ETHINT-23.

Kraetschmer, E. G. *Die Ritterkreuztraeger der Waffen-SS*. 3rd ed. Preussisch Oldendorf: 1982.

Kriegstagebuch des Oberkommando des Wehrmacht (Fuehrungsstab). 4 vols. Frankfurt-am-Main, 1961.

Kurowski, Franz. "Dietrich and Manteuffel." In *Hitler's Generals*, edited by Correlli Barrett. London: 1989.

———. *Das Tor zur Festung Europa*. Neckargemuend: 1966.

Lippman, David. "Field Marshal Model." *World War II*. March 1989.

Lucas, James, and Matthew Cooper. *Hitler's Elite Leibstandarte SS, 1933–1945*. London: 1975.

Luck, Hans von. *Panzer Commander*. New York: 1989.

Luettwitz, Heinrich von. "Ardennes Offensive." Foreign Military Studies MS # 936.

Luther, Craig W. H. *Blood and Honor: The History of the 12th SS Panzer Division "Hitler Youth," 1943–1945*. San Jose, CA: 1987.

MacDonald, Charles B. *The Siegfried Line Campaign*. United States Army in World War II. European Theater of Operations. Washington, DC: 1963.

Manteuffel, Hasso von. "The Battle of the Ardennes, 1944–45." In *Decisive Battles of World War II: The German View*, edited by H. A. Jacobsen and J. Rohwer. New York: 1960.

———. "Fifth Panzer Army (Ardennes Offensive)." Foreign Military Studies MS # B-151 and B-151a.

———. "Mission of Fifth Panzer Army (11 Sep 1944–Jan 1945)." ETHINT-46.

Mehner, Kurt, ed. *Die Geheimen Tagesberichte der deutschen Wehrmachtfuehrung im Zweiten Weltkrieg, 1939–1945*. 12 vols. Osnabrueck: 1984–90.

Mellenthin, Frederick Wilhelm von. *German Generals of World War Two*. Norman, OK: 1977.

———. *Panzer Battles: A Study in the Employment of Armor in the Second World War*. Norman, OK: 1956. Reprint, New York: 1976.

Merriam, Robert E. *The Battle of the Bulge*. New York: 1957. First published 1947 as *Dark December*.

Messenger, Charles. *Hitler's Gladiator: The Life and Times of Oberstruppenfuehrer und Panzergeneral-Oberst der Waffen-SS Sepp Dietrich*. London: 1988.

———. *The Last Prussian: A Biography of Field Marshal Gerd von Rundstedt, 1875–1953*. London: 1953.

Meyer, Hubert. *The History of the 12. SS-Panzerdivision "Hitlerjugend."* H. Harri Henschler, trans. Winnepeg: 1994.

Millet, Allan R., and Williamson Murray, eds. *Military Effectiveness*. Vol. 3, *The Second World War*. Boston: 1988.

Mitcham, Samuel W., Jr. *Men of the Luftwaffe*. Novato, CA: 1988.

Moll, Otto E. *Die deutschen Generalfeldmarshaelle, 1939–1945*. Rastatt/Baden: 1961.

Montgomery, Bernard Law, The Viscount of Alamein. *Normandy to the Baltic*. London: 1958.

OB West and OKW maps. U.S. National Archives and Bundesarchiv.

Pallud, Jean Paul. *Battle of the Bulge, Then and Now*. London: 1984.

Parker, Danny S. *The Battle of the Bulge*. Conshohocken, PA: 1991.

———, ed. *Hitler's Ardennes Offensive: The German View of the Battle*. London: 1997.

Perrett, Bryan. *Knights of the Black Cross*. New York: 1986.

Poeppel, Martin. *Heaven and Hell: The War Diary of a German Paratrooper*. Louise Willmot, trans. London: 1988.

Pond, Hugh. *Sicily*. London: 1962.

Preradovich, Nikolaus von. *Die Generale der Waffen-SS*. Berg am See: 1985.

Reynolds, Michael. *The Devil's Adjutant*. New York: 1995.

Ritgen, Helmut. *Die Geschichte der Panzer-Lehr-Division im Westen, 1944–1945*. Stuttgart: 1979.

Rommel, Erwin. *The Rommel Papers*, edited by B. H. Liddell Hart. New York: 1953.

Ryan, Cornelius. *A Bridge Too Far*. New York: 1974.

Scheibert, Horst. *Die Traeger des Deutschen Kreuzes in Gold: das Heer*. Friedberg: n.d.

Schramm, Percy E. "The Course of Events of the German Offensive in the Ardennes (16 Dec 1944–14 Jan 1945)." Foreign Military Studies MS # A-858.

———. "Preparations for the German Offensive in the Ardennes (Sep to 16 Dec 1944)." Foreign Military Studies MS # A-862.

Seaton, Albert. *The Fall of Fortress Europe, 1943–1945*. New York: 1981.

———. *The Russo-German War, 1941–45*. New York: 1960.

———. *The German Army, 1933–1945*. New York: 1982.

Skorzeny, Otto. *My Commando Operations*. David Johnson, trans. Atglen, PA: 1995.

———. *Skorzeny's Special Missions*. N.p.: 1997.

Shulman, Milton. *Defeat in the West*. London: 1947. Reprint, New York: 1948.

Snyder, Louis L. *Encyclopedia of the Third Reich*. New York: 1976.

Stacey, C. P. *Official History of the Canadian Army in the Second World War*. Vol. 1, *The Victory Campaign* (The Operations in North-West Europe, 1944–1945). Ottawa: 1960.

Staudinger, Walter. "Artillery Leadership and Artillery Assignment During the Course of the Ardennes Offensive." Foreign Military Studies MS # 759.

Stauffenberg, Friedrich von. "Panzer Commanders of the Western Front." Unpublished manuscript in the possession of the author.

———. "Papers." Unpublished manuscript in the possession of the author.

Stoves, Rolf. *Die Gepanzerten und Motorisierten deutschen Grossverbaende: Divisionen und selbstaendige Brigaden, 1935–1945*. Friedberg: 1986.

Stumpf, Richard. *Die Wehrmacht-Elite: Rang- und Herkunfstsstruktur der deutschen Generale und Admirale, 1933–1945.* Boppard am Rhein: 1982.

Tessin, Georg. *Verbaende und Truppen der deutschen Wehrmacht und Waffen-SS im Zweiten Weltkrieg, 1939–1945.* 16 vols. Osnabrueck: 1973–80.

Thomas, Franz. *Die Eichenlaubtraeger.* Osnabrueck: 1997.

Thomas, Franz, and Guenter Wegmann. *Die Ritterkreuztraeger der deutschen Wehrmacht, 1939–1945.* Teil I, *Sturmartillerie.* Osnabrueck: 1985.

Tieke, Wilhelm. *In the Firestorm of the Last Years of the War: II. SS-Panzerkorps with the 9. and 10. SS-Divisions "Hohenstaufen" and "Frundsberg."* Frederick Steinhardt, trans. Winnepeg: 1999.

Tiemann, Ralf. *Die Leibstandarte.* Osnabrueck: 1998.

Tippelskirch, Kurt von. *Geschichte des Zweiten Weltkrieges.* Bonn: 1951.

Toland, John. *Adolf Hitler.* New York: 1976. Reprint, New York: 1977.

————. *Battle: The Story of the Bulge.* New York: 1958. Reprint, New York: 1959.

United Kingdom C.S.D.I.C. G.G. (Interrogation) Reports. On file at the Historical Research Center, Air University Archives, Maxwell Air Force Base, Montgomery, Alabama.

Viebig, Wilhelm. "277th Infantry Division (13 Aug–8 Sep 1944)." Unpublished manuscript, Washington, DC: Office of the Chief of Military History.

Wagener, Carl. "Fifth Panzer Army, 2 Nov 44–16 Jan 45." Foreign Military Studies MS # B-235.

Weigley, Russell F. *Eisenhower's Lieutenants.* Bloomington, IL: 1981.

Whiting, Charles. *Massacre at Malmedy: The Story of Jochen Peiper's Battle Group, Ardennes, December 1944.* Briarcliff Manor, NY: 1984.

————. *Skorzeny: "The Most Dangerous Man in Europe."* London: 1998.

Wilmot, Chester. *The Struggle for Europe.* New York: 1952.

Wistrich, Robert. *Who's Who in Nazi Germany.* New York: 1982.

Yerger, Mark. *Waffen-SS Commanders.* 2 vols. Atglen, PA: 1997–99.

Zanssen, Leo. "Ardennes, 16 December 1944–25 January 1945." Foreign Military Studies MS # 739.

Ziemke, Earl F. *Stalingrad to Berlin: The German Defeat in the East.* Washington, DC: 1966.

Zimmermann, Bodo. "OB West: Command Relationships." Foreign Military Studies MS # 308. Unpublished manuscript, Washington, DC: Office of the Chief of Military History.

Zweng, Christian, comp. and ed. *Die Dienstlaufbahnen der Offiziere des Generalstabes des deutschen Heeres, 1939–1945.* 2 vols. Osnabrueck: 1998.

Index of Military Units

General Index

Stackpole Military History Series

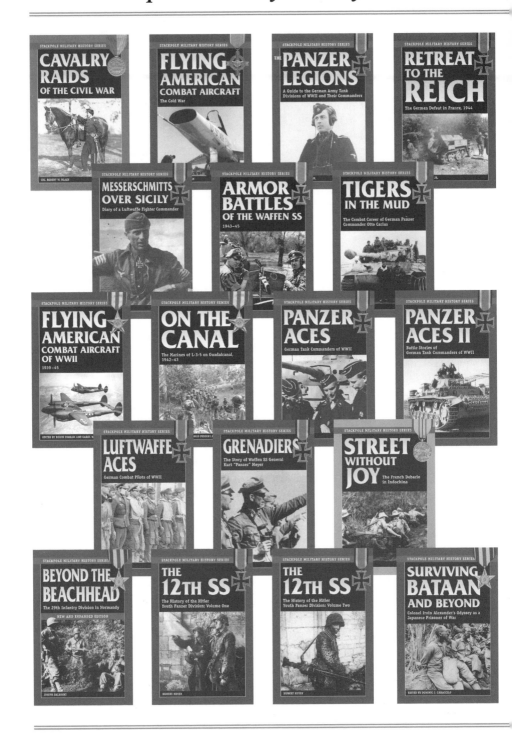

Real battles. Real soldiers. Real stories.

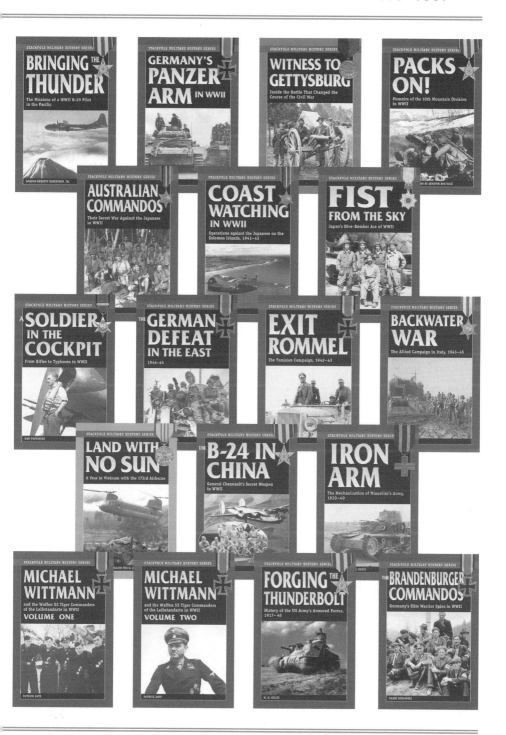

Stackpole Military History Series

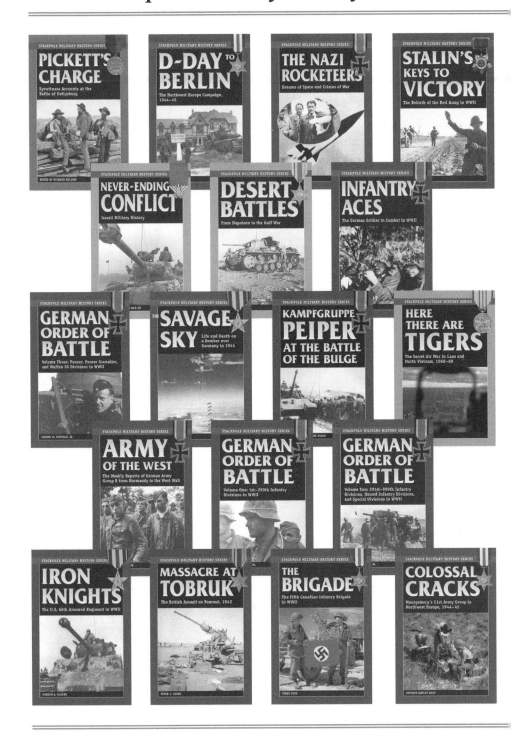

Real battles. Real soldiers. Real stories.

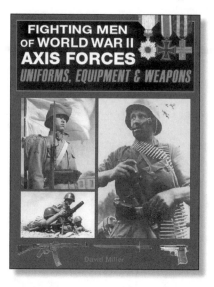